War, Nation and Europe in the
Novels of Storm Jameson

War, Nation and Europe in the Novels of Storm Jameson

Katherine Cooper

BLOOMSBURY ACADEMIC
LONDON • NEW YORK • OXFORD • NEW DELHI • SYDNEY

BLOOMSBURY ACADEMIC
Bloomsbury Publishing Plc
50 Bedford Square, London, WC1B 3DP, UK
1385 Broadway, New York, NY 10018, USA
29 Earlsfort Terrace, DUblin 2, Ireland

BLOOMSBURY, BLOOMSBURY ACADEMIC and the Diana logo are
trademarks of Bloomsbury Publishing Plc

First published in Great Britain 2020
This paperback edition published in 2021

Copyright © Katherine Cooper, 2020

Katherine Cooper has asserted her right under the Copyright, Designs and Patents
Act, 1988, to be identified as Author of this work.

For legal purposes the Acknowledgements on p. viii–ix
constitute an extension of this copyright page.

Cover design: Eleanor Rose
Cover images: Storm Jameson, circa 1936 © Pictorial Press Ltd / Alamy Stock Photo; WW2
Map of Europe © Antiqua Print Gallery / Alamy Stock Photo

All rights reserved. No part of this publication may be reproduced or
transmitted in any form or by any means, electronic or mechanical,
including photocopying, recording, or any information storage or retrieval
system, without prior permission in writing from the publishers.

Bloomsbury Publishing Plc does not have any control over, or responsibility for, any
third-party websites referred to or in this book. All internet addresses given in this
book were correct at the time of going to press. The author and publisher
regret any inconvenience caused if addresses have changed or sites have
ceased to exist, but can accept no responsibility for any such changes.

A catalogue record for this book is available from the British Library.

A catalog record for this book is available from the Library of Congress.

ISBN: HB: 978-1-3500-9443-7
PB: 978-1-3502-4320-0
ePDF: 978-1-3500-9444-4
eBook: 978-1-3500-9445-1

Typeset by Integra Software Services Pvt. Ltd.

To find out more about our authors and books visit www.bloomsbury.com
and sign up for our newsletters.

We have no frontiers, or our frontiers are the edges of the world.
(Jameson, 1935: 330)

Contents

Acknowledgements	viii
Copyright and permissions	x
Introduction	1
1 'The living nerves which bind nation to nation': Britain, France and pacifism in *The Moon Is Making* and *Cousin Honoré*	29
2 'The tide of cruelty': *Europe to Let* and the path to war	51
3 'The memory of sacrifice': Culture, myth and the occupied nation in *Then We Shall Hear Singing*	71
4 'Two sorts of human beings': Culture and myth-making in the German nation in *The Other Side* and *The Black Laurel*	91
5 'The same tricks, the same corruption': Aftermath, resistance and reconciliation in *The Hidden River* and *The Moment of Truth*	111
6 'The same disconcerting shapes': The Cold War, Empire and terrorism in *A Cup of Tea for Mr Thorgill* and *Last Score*	131
Conclusion	153
Notes	157
Bibliography	168
Index	183

Acknowledgements

This book has been the product of almost ten years of work, beginning as a PhD at Newcastle University in 2009 and ending in the spare moments around my postdoctoral work at University of East Anglia. It has gone through several iterations in that time and is hopefully much better for it. With that in mind, I would like to thank all of those who have read, listened, discussed, reviewed and helped to knock it fondly into the shape in which it appears here.

Firstly, I would like to thank the Arts and Humanities Research Council UK for funding this project with a three-year doctoral fellowship, as well as for funding a research trip to the Harry Ransom Center at the University of Texas, which holds so much invaluable archival material. I would also like to thank all at the S.Y. Killingley Trust for helping me financially through the course that equipped me to embark on my PhD study. Thanks also to Clara Herberg and Lucy Brown at Bloomsbury for their faith in the project and their guidance in shaping this book.

A lot of people have been involved in bringing this book to fruition. A huge thank you to my supervisor Dr Stacy Gillis who has stood by this project ever since I bumbled into her office in 2007, wittering about someone called Jameson (she thought I meant Fredric). Fellow supervisors Alison Light and, after her departure, Melanie Bell were indispensable for their advice and shrewd observations. Special thanks to my PhD examiner Professor Gill Plain for her invaluable advice and suggestions in my viva and beyond. Thanks also to colleagues and students at Newcastle University, especially Ruth Connolly, Jennifer Orr, James Procter and the incredible Emma Short, who proofed the whole thing. Twice.

Thanks also to the wonderful postgrad community who created such an invigorating, fun and supportive atmosphere, especially Katherine Farrimond, Siân Harris, Ellen Turner, Viccy Adams, Jodie Phillips Laird, Caroline Rae and Alex Adams. Friends and colleagues at UEA took up the Jameson baton admirably, and special thanks for support and encouragement in the final stages must go to Rachel Potter, Matthew Taunton, Nonia Williams, Sara Helen Binney and Nathan Hamilton.

On a personal note, none of this would have been possible without the kindness and indulgence of friends like Sonia Elks, Les Hutchins, the Elks/Graeber families, Dani Charlton, Louise Howliston, Jenny Kilgour, Katy Ramirez, Jennifer Ferriter, Caroline Normanton and Lucy Weidner. Not to mention the wider academic network in midcentury, war and women's studies for confabs formal and informal over Jameson, modernism, feminism, the future of academia and everything in between, especially Alice Kelly, Cathryn Setz, Becky Bowler, Nadine Muller, Helen Davies and Claire O'Callaghan.

Last but most importantly, I would like to thank David, Elizabeth and Alistair Cooper for bearing with me throughout this process and for never doubting that I would finally do it.

Copyright and permissions

The author and publisher would like to thank the copyright holders for kind permission to reproduce extracts.

Extracts from various titles and unpublished correspondence by Margaret Storm Jameson reprinted by permission of Peters Fraser & Dunlop (www.petersfraserdunlop.com) on behalf of the Estate of Margaret Storm Jameson.

For permission to use material from their collections, The Harry Ransom Humanities Research Centre, University of Texas at Austin (Storm Jameson Collection, PEN Collection) and The Trustees of the Liddell Hart Centre for Military Archives (Basil Liddell Hart Archives, Kings College, London). Thanks also to Hannah Trevarthen for permission to reproduce materials from the English PEN Archive at the Harry Ransom Research Center, University of Texas at Austin.

Despite every effort to trace and contact copyright holders before publication this has not been possible in every case. If contacted, the publisher will be pleased to rectify any errors or omissions at the earliest opportunity.

Introduction

Margaret Storm Jameson wrote in 'The Future of the Novel' (1930) that, within the literary landscape, 'there has always been the main stream and there have always been neglected backwaters and tributary streams, some of which are trickles lost in the sand and others that are broad strong rivers' (1930: 3–4). Jameson could not have predicted her own literary fortunes, nor at this early point in her career have guessed that, despite the critical and commercial success she enjoyed during the mid-twentieth century, she would become herself a trickle lost in the sand. Although she published forty-eight novels, three autobiographies and numerous pieces of journalism across a sixty-year career, Jameson's work has historically been neglected within academia and by general readers. This study seeks to rectify this, not through rigorous expurgation of the meanings and reasons for her neglect, but through a sustained critical engagement with her most significant body of work: her war novels. Examining these novels within their literary and historical context, alongside processes of nation-building and national myth-making, it explores the ways in which Jameson's work describes key processes in the life of the nation at war and in the life of nations at war. I argue that Jameson's work offers not only a useful and sustained engagement with ideas of war, nation and Europe but also a significant departure from perceived literary trends which assert that British writers during this period chose to concentrate their efforts on analysis of Britishness or of British experiences of war. In exploring the ramifications of Jameson's desire to present Europe and European experiences of war, this book posits that consideration of her work offers an important counterbalance to a literary history which has long assumed British writers' preoccupation with ideas of Britain and Britishness during this period.

As the eldest daughter of a merchant seaman from Whitby, a small town on the North Yorkshire coast of the UK, Jameson grew up with a feel for the transnational: Whitby was a busy port with a constant influx of people and goods from across Europe and the wider world, and she and her mother often travelled aboard her father's ship when she was a child, visiting Bordeaux, Dieppe and even Vera Cruz. As Jennifer Birkett asserts in her biography of Jameson, from Whitby 'the view out to sea, to the northern coasts of Europe, promised new ways and different paths to those experienced by many Englishmen and women of her generation and class' (2009: 18). This informed a love of travel which underpinned both her later life and her writing. Through her work as the English President of PEN (Poets, Essayists and Novelists) Club from 1938 to 1944, she travelled widely all over the world, but it was Europe that captured her imagination.[1] Jameson was captivated by European identities and by the cultural cross-pollination which had influenced European culture over the centuries. She viewed Europe as a continent civilized above all other and saw the roots of this civilization deep within its artistic landscape, cultivated by European thinkers from Voltaire to Goethe, Plato to Brecht. Her novels of the Second World War are particularly illuminating from this perspective, presenting the evolution of individual characters, nations and the continent as a whole in the context of a war which Jameson feared may destroy Europe and the intellectual civilization she associated with it.

This book considers Jameson's writing of the Second World War – the most important and influential period of her life in terms of her sense of Europe, her socialism and her anti-fascist views – in order to recuperate her as a pivotal figure of the period. Concentrating on the novels she published between 1937 and 1961, it posits that Jameson's writing is indicative of a different kind of approach in the mid to late 1930s when, for critics such as Jed Esty, 'metropolitan modernism gives way to the *petits recits* of national culture' (2004: 5) and English writers came to concentrate on Britishness and Britain. Jameson, however, chose to look outwards to Europe, in direct contrast to many of her peers, to produce a Europe-wide perspective on the war. She presents a more expansive vision of the war, one which stands in contrast to the established 'Anglocentric turn of the 1930s and 1940s' (Esty, 2004: 5) in which 'modernists were compelled to scrutinise the political and moral claims of insular nationality' (MacKay, 2007: 2). While as Phyllis Lassner and Kristin Bluemel have noted, Jameson was not the only British writer to attempt such an expansive approach to the representation of war, I suggest that she was in many ways the most prolific, publishing at least a novel every year during the Second World War (2018: 27). In this she presents the most sustained engagement with Europe, cataloguing changing views across a number of novels which take in countries from Czechoslovakia to France, Hungary to Cyprus.

However, it is complex to provide an assessment of the viewpoints and perspectives on a writer who has been both ever-present and notably absent from both literary and historical studies of the twentieth century. While Jameson appears to have been central to many elements of literary and intellectual history, through her presidency of English PEN in the war years and her friendships with writers such as Vera Brittain, Walter de la Mare, H.G. Wells, Phyllis Bottome, Noel Streathfeild, J.B. Priestley, E.M. Forster and countless others, her connections to more prominent figures and her role within these networks have often been erased or down-played in critical and historical work. Jameson's name and influence appear fleetingly but often in studies of great modernists, great novelists or great literary figures, to end up, again, lost in the sand. In part this stems from her own resistance to literary groupings and, often, to stylistic identification with any particular school, as I go on to show. As Birkett notes, it often seems that her work is more at home among the European novelists she admired, such as Balzac, Stendhal or Goethe, than among her British contemporaries. I want to draw attention to the importance of her representations of Europe as a whole and of individual European nations and their particular experiences, from the rise of the Nazi threat in Germany, through the occupation of Czechoslovakia to the difficulties of rebuilding the European continent. Bringing these representations into dialogue with their wider historical context, as well as with theories of nation and war, this book hopes to offer new ways of reading Jameson and of thinking about the relevance of her work to contemporary debates and issues. Through this, it hopes to offer a first step towards re-establishing her influence and her place within the wider literary history of the midcentury.

'[T]he invisible aunt of English letters': Marginalization, modernism and gender

Jameson was both popular and critically well-received from the 1920s and into the mid-1950s. She sold tens of thousands of books across Europe, picking up sales in Portugal, Italy, France, America, Egypt and South Africa, and her novel *The Hidden River* (1955) was made into a successful play opening on Broadway and going on to London, Paris and Vienna.[2] Both reviews and the dustjackets of her novels during this time attest to her critical acclaim over a long time period, praising her as a 'promising' young novelist destined for great things (*Manchester Guardian*, sleeve of *The Pitiful Wife*, first edition, 1924) and later as a 'writer of unquestioned literary ability' (*The Times*, 2 October 1958). Alongside this critical acclaim she was widely read, as fellow writer Ethel Mannin attests: 'I heard two Harrod's waitresses talking about you. "I like her books". They argued about whether it was James-son or Jam-es-son!' (18 May 1936). Jameson was also extremely well connected in literary circles at this time: not only was she, during the 1920s, the European representative for Alfred J. Knopf's publishing house, bringing her into contact with a number of writers in Britain and across the continent, but she also struck up friendships through her work with the PEN Club.

However, by the 1960s, Jameson's success was beginning to wane and she began to feel popular and critical tides turning against her. Her reaction was both defensive and disappointed, as the words of the critics now reflected the feelings of doubt and inadequacy which she had felt towards her own work for decades – she writes in 1962 to her literary agent and close friend A.D. Peters that 'I've forgotten what it was like to get good notices. It must have been wonderful' (21 January 1962). During this later stage of her life, she lambasted the newer literary modes and younger critics. She was particularly concerned about the critical reception of her husband, Guy Chapman, autobiography, *A Passionate Prodigality* (1975), which she finished following his death in 1972, writing that 'I have been so afraid that a book which is civilised and thoughtful, and direct and honest [...] will be overlooked in the literary climate of today' (Letter to Francis Henry King, 20 February 1975). Tellingly, she was comfortable in her feelings about the superiority of Guy's work in a way that she never was about her own and was able to attack more confidently the new critics who she believed were unable to perceive its value. Until the end of her life, she continued to lack confidence in her own literary output.

In many ways, Jameson's placelessness within the literary canon reflects her own lifelong sense of placelessness: as an exile from the North living in Southern England for economic and professional reasons; as a member of the Northern merchant middle class often a little adrift among the intellectual elites of London; as a novelist who looked to Europe in a society often infatuated with Englishness and nationalism. This sense of placelessness stemmed from an early age when Jameson's mother took her out of the local school to send her a short distance to Scarborough to a more prestigious establishment, one that eventually would afford her the opportunity to win a place at Leeds University. Jameson's success at Leeds – where she gained a First in English Literature – of course yielded another move, this time to take up a place at King's College London, where she composed a thesis on modern European drama. From this point, Jameson's fortunes as a writer were tied to London and to its intellectual environment, its opportunities for employment in publishing or advertising, and the possibilities it offered for professional networking. This estrangement from Whitby was characterized by a great ambivalence – as Jennifer Birkett describes, for Jameson Whitby was both 'the home of nostalgic desire and the place [she] most need[ed] to escape from' (Birkett, 2009: 29). Jameson was torn throughout her life between a desperate desire to return to the simplicity and rootedness of Whitby and troubled by its parochialism and anti-intellectualism. Like many forced to leave home to pursue economic or intellectual advancement, she enjoyed elements of her old and her new surroundings but was rarely truly at home in either.

This early independence put a great deal of pressure on Jameson's written work to provide some sort of stable income. Her parents were not sufficiently well-off to be able to support her in London and she had to take a series of jobs simply to survive. By the 1920s, with a son to support and an absent husband, she was publishing a book a year simply to pay her rent. She lived throughout her life in a state of constant fear of financial collapse, even after her second marriage to the historian Guy Chapman. She also refused to settle, spending prolonged periods on the continent and living in small hotels, usually in order to avoid the domestic work she felt would stifle her writing. As a result, Jameson did not value her own work. She always felt that she wrote too quickly and for the wrong reasons and that, as a result, her work had little historical value or literary merit. She wrote to her literary agent, A.D. Peters, that one of her books was 'as like a novel as I am like the Queen [...] I won't tell you what I think of it' (3 January 1957), to her friend Vera Brittain that she wished to 'sink without a trace' (Jameson quoted in Clay, 2006: 6), and destroyed a great number of her own letters and writings in order to avoid critical attention after her death.[3] Jameson's displeasure with her literary output can be linked to her own feelings of placelessness within the literary scene itself, one which became in many ways a self-fulfilling prophecy.

It was this placelessness within London's metropolis, her lack of confidence in her work and her tendency to be prolific for financial rather than stylistic reasons which underpinned Jameson's distancing from other literary groupings. Just as writers such as Katherine Mansfield were looked down upon by Bloomsbury because of their colonial roots, Jameson's Northernness, her lack of confidence in her work and her hostility towards the metropolitan elites that characterized the Bloomsbury world made her a prickly and often unwanted inclusion both socially and stylistically within many of London's literary circles. Jameson satirizes what she sees as the cliquey and self-satisfied nature of the influential literary groups of the early twentieth century through characters such as the society hostess and sponsor of the arts Evelyn Lamb, in novels such as *None Turn Back* and *Before the Crossing*. Lamb is depicted as fickle and shallow, using a coterie of artists and writers to bolster her own feelings of intellectual superiority: 'I enjoy what is difficult, abstract, witty' (1947b: 101).[4] However, in the early years of her work, even Jameson's publishers sought to include her within the umbrella of the more experimental and fashionable modern writers. The inside cover of the dustjacket of *A Pitiful Wife* has a mysterious but 'distinguished' French critic declaring Jameson 'above anything else, modern' and the back cover declares her 'ultra-modern', emphasizing her publishers' desire to associate her firmly with other modern novelists (Jameson, 1924). Although not associating her with Bloomsbury itself, her publishers' repeated references to her as 'modern' and to her critical work can be seen as a move to market Jameson as a highbrow, literary and, indeed, modern writer. It is noteworthy, then, that in spite of all of these attempts to link her work to a movement or idea, Jameson herself shunned such obvious literary associations both in her work and in her social life.

Although modernism is a retrospective grouping, its association with what Malcolm Bradbury and James Macfarlane refer to as 'introversion [...], internal self-scepticism' (1976: 96) was in many ways at odds with Jameson's desire to look outwards and to engage with wider the social problems which underpinned the individual's relationship with the world. In 1930, she writes in a draft for 'The Future of the Novel' that 'the important thing was to tell what happened, to explain this event or that person, not to make experiments in style' (1930: 7), adding that if Virginia Woolf were 'less concerned with what she writes than with how she writes it', she may have 'produced great novels and not charming ones' (1930: 7–8). Jennifer Birkett and Chiara Briganti, in the Introduction to their edited collection, *Margaret Storm Jameson: Writing in Dialogue* (2007), suggest that Jameson's relationship to modernist stylistics was much more nuanced, arguing that Jameson 'manufactured her own version of stylised realism, both in tune with her times and in advance of them, in which the innovative forms of 1930s social documentary, fiction and film were married to the different modernities of Stendhal, the Symbolistes, Eliot and Auden' (2007: 1). The stylistics of her writing are informed by a number of different writers and contexts but, in many ways, this very hybridity alongside her passion to depict social and political truths seems at odds with certain modernist tendencies, making her a difficult inclusion within early studies which sought to document a more canonical or high modernism.

As a result Jameson's name was often left out of studies of early- and mid-twentieth-century literature and, more especially, its articulation within the academy. Kristin Bluemel and Phylliss Lassner assert that, for scholars working particularly on the neglected women writers of the early twentieth century, this critical focus on modernism can be limiting and problematic because it 'diminishes the integrity of our research and limits its impact upon the larger field of literary, historical, and cultural studies' (Lassner and Bluemel, 2018: 22). With more recent and more expansive critical responses to Modernism, or modernisms, Jameson might be an easier inclusion, as scholars seek to expand the boundaries of modernist literature in terms of high and low literary culture (Jaillant, 2014), gender (Kime Scott, 1990; 2007; Dowson, 2002), geography (Doyle, 2011; Berman, 2012; Kalliney, 2015), stylistics and even time (Miller, 1999). Bluemel's edited collection *Intermodernism* (2009), for example, takes Jameson as one of its key figures, suggesting new ways of reading the work of those writing between the Depression and the Second World War as 'intermodernist' in ways which seek to open up modernism's temporal and generic parameters. Bluemel's introduction suggests that the parameters of existing study cannot 'do justice to the web of sometimes subtle, sometimes obvious associations between the writers, institutions and cultural forms of the middle years of the twentieth century' (2009: 2). Indeed, the first essay of the volume is Elizabeth Maslen's essay on Jameson. Whether she might legitimately be understood as modernist is beyond the scope of this study, but the inability to easily fit her within the literary groupings which came to define the period in which she was writing might explain her long-standing absence from many accounts of twentieth-century literary history and also from the canon and university syllabi informed by them.

Even before her death in 1986, other attempts were already being made to recuperate the literary reputations of both Jameson and her female peers, such as Sylvia Townsend Warner, Antonia White and Winifred Holtby. In 1973, the Virago publishing house was formed, its mission to republish in paperback form the work of neglected female writers of the twentieth century. Virago presented Jameson, as it did many of her contemporaries, as a woman writer of the middlebrow, and its publications tended to focus on her novels of the 1920s and 1930s which feature largely female protagonists and issues such as romance, relationships and the domestic.[5] This republication of Jameson's work can be read in the context of its importance as a feminist enterprise. It coincided with the publication of Nicola Beauman's definitive study, *A Very Great Profession: The Woman's Novel 1914–1939* (1983), also published by Virago, which focused on what Beauman describes as 'women's novels' (1983: 3), and referred to some of Jameson's own journalism and critical work, as well as to her early novels. Beauman's discussions of these 'women's novels' were a crucial precursor to the establishment of the middlebrow as a field of critical study. It was a thriving genre during the early and mid-twentieth century, one which was devoured by armies of middle-class female readers, who enjoyed, as Beauman describes, '"the drama of the undramatic", the steadfast dailiness of a life that brings its own reward, the intensity of emotions and, above all, the importance of human relationships' (1983: 5). A good many of Jameson's novels from this period and beyond – from the romance of *The Pitiful Wife* through the complex female lives explored in *Women against Men* (1933), and even to the examination of motherhood and professional success in *A Month Soon Goes* (1962) – can certainly be described as middlebrow, dealing with, as Nicola Humble describes, features of 'the romance and the country house novel, through to domestic and family narratives' (2004: 4). Although these by no means represent the full scope of Jameson's literary output, they do represent some of her best-known and most popular work.

The wartime novels on which this book focuses also address issues of female experience, empowerment and even resistance. They depict the importance of women and of purportedly female spaces, such as the home, as the centres of certain kinds of wartime experience, particularly during occupation. In many of these novels, women are the passive victims of war, at the mercy of a sequence of events which results in the loss of their sons, husbands and lovers and the invasion and occupation of the places for which they are responsible. However, beyond these caring and domestic roles and the perceived passivity of loss and victimhood, Jameson's women also embrace spheres beyond the home, working in government offices and playing small but key roles in resistance movements. Women like Hana Čarek in *Europe to Let* (1940) and Sarah Leng in *Last Score, or the Private Life of Sir Richard Ormston* (1961) work in the male-dominated world of politics, government and the media, promoting the causes they believe in, from the freedom of Czechoslovakia to anti-colonialism. These women move beyond the echelons of the middlebrow, allowing Jameson's work to take in more ideas and more perspectives on war. This movement is in itself feminist and yet can be seen to remove Jameson's work from the sphere of the middlebrow itself, as a feminist enterprise.

Jameson complicates the automatic association of her own work – as a female writer – with the female sphere of the domestic and the home (front) by giving as much weight to male experience, of battle, warfare and politics. She also sought to avoid any immediate association with the female by using her middle name

'Storm' on her books, rather than 'Margaret', and wrote three of her novels under the male pseudonyms William Lamb and James Hill to avoid the charge that a female novelist should not be tackling such topics as nation and war.[6] She often adopted a male voice or perspective in her war narratives, developing as close a relationship with prolific male protagonists such as David Renn, who also appears in the *Mirror in Darkness* trilogy, as well as in *Before the Crossing* (1947) and *The Black Laurel* (1947), as with their female equivalents. As Diana Wallace asserts, fiction has always allowed women writers to 'adopt male narratives and protagonists, and to write about the "male" world of public and political affairs' in this way (2004: 7).[7] Renn, as a recurring character, shares much of the background and preoccupations of the more outwardly autobiographical Mary Hervey Russell, but Renn's gender allows Jameson access to experiences which a woman like Hervey could not have had, even in the outwardly more permissive society of wartime Britain. In *Company Parade*, Renn is a former First World War soldier, allowing Jameson to weave into her story a narrative about his sense of placelessness and loss and his experience on the battlefield, while in *Before the Crossing* Renn is a secret policeman tasked with the interrogation and exposure of a fascist cell in London, and in *The Black Laurel* he works with the British in occupied Berlin in 1945. The presence of these male perspectives in the novels allows Jameson to present a more comprehensive examination of the war from both a female and a male perspective, but it also, in the eyes of contemporary critics at least, can be seen to use male characters to give authority to works that tackled themes such as war.

As Jenny Hartley points out, this marks out a troublesome aspect of Jameson's work, and of her war novels in particular. Hartley argues that 'Jameson's personification of the writer was emphatically male – only in men's clothing could the image of the writer carry sufficient gravitas' (1997: 10). Hartley maintains that this choice enforces rather than challenging the tendency within war writing to privilege the male voice and the male perspective as inherently more authoritative. As I argue elsewhere, Hartley's view is a little simplistic – Jameson does depict a good deal of female wartime experience, in novels such as *Then We Shall Hear Singing* (1942) and *The Moment of Truth* (1949). Furthermore, there is no reason to expect that, as a woman writer, Jameson should censor her own imagination nor limit the scope of her texts if this impedes her expression of certain ideas or processes. I would argue that Jameson's decision to depict this male perspective of war is less of a conscious choice pertaining to gender than a realist desire to present what Georg Lukács would refer as the 'social totality' of war and the private and political processes which underpinned it (Lukács, 1970: 38). Certainly, this would be more in keeping with the tendency towards the realism of Balzac or Stendhal which Birkett discusses in her biography.

Hartley's book *Millions Like Us* (1997) forms part of a number of studies which appeared in the 1990s and which sought to make a feminist intervention within the field of war studies and war literature in particular. Scholars such as Alison Light (1991), Mary Joannou (1995), Gill Plain (1996), Janet Montefiore (1996), and Phyllis Lassner (1998) sought to reclaim women's writing of both the First and Second World Wars and the interwar period. Building on the 1987 study by Margaret Higonnet, *Behind the Lines: Gender and the Two World Wars*, these works sought to reassess women's writing from a feminist perspective, often foregrounding and privileging women's experiences of war or political activism. Although Jameson is frequently mentioned within all of these studies, she continues to represent a difficult inclusion within many of them, this time as a result of the issue which Hartley raises: her tendency to cross-write and to problematize the feminist praxis of these projects through a tendency to privilege male experience. Nonetheless, these efforts, alongside later works exploring the burgeoning field of mid-century studies, have begun to shed increasing critical light on Jameson as both a literary and a political figure leading to a renewed critical interest in her works and life.

As such, scholarly interest in Jameson is growing, and rightly so. Two sizable biographies have appeared in recent years by Jennifer Birkett (2009) and Elizabeth Maslen (2014) both of which seek to use Jameson's life and experiences to discuss the evolution of her novels and her writings throughout her career. Both biographies make the case for Jameson as a key figure in the literary and institutional landscapes of the mid-century – detailing her associations with key figures such as Wells, Forster and Vera Brittain, placing centrally her work as President of English PEN Club and situating her within key historical and political contexts. They also weave incisive readings of her fiction throughout their accounts of her life. In 2007 Jennifer Birkett and Chiara Briganti brought together a number of key scholars of women's writing and women's war writing in *Margaret Storm Jameson: Writing in Dialogue* (2007), which showcased a range of critical responses to her work. Since those crucial early forays into Jameson's life and works increasing numbers of scholars have sought to reclaim and re-include her as a writer of the 1940s (Plain, 2014), a Cold War writer (Piette, 2012) and a key figure within interwar feminist networks (Clay, 2006). Nonetheless, I would suggest that Jameson's work continues to be a contentious or troublesome inclusion within middlebrow studies, women's writing, feminist writing, modernism and even war writing because of its hybridity, its transgressive qualities and its somewhat ambivalent attitudes to gender. It remains, like its author, somewhat difficult to place.

'No man has a right to turn aside': War, politics and PEN

Perhaps as a result of this and of her own ambivalent attitude to her place, socially, geographically and professionally, ideas around belonging, nationhood and exile mark out key areas of interest within her war novels. Jameson's war writing represents both a point of interest and a point of incongruity in her oeuvre, spanning decades of her career. For Jameson, during the 1930s and 1940s, in particular, writing about war was a moral obligation.[8] As she describes in 1949, great writers are those 'whose courage is equal to their honesty; who are prepared to risk themselves, their strength, their reputation, perhaps even their sanity, to penetrate the darkness closing around us' (1949: 2). Aspiring to be a great writer, or at least a socially responsible one, Jameson felt she must engage with this 'darkness', interrogating all of its social and political aspects, as well as the far-reaching implications of war. These war novels, from *Cousin Honoré* and *Europe to Let* in 1940 to *Last Score* in 1961, represent her attempts to rationalize her anxieties and her hopes regarding the Second World War. They depict the costs of war for both the individual and the nation, raising questions about civilization, nationhood and the future of Europe as she understood it. They also draw on Jameson's own experiences with PEN, her travels in Europe in the interwar period and the Second World War, and her personal political convictions about European civilization and culture.

For Jameson, the First World War was the definitive experience of her generation, one that, as a novelist, she had to confront and articulate. From the beginnings of her writing career in *The Pot Boils* (1919), repeated experiences of European war cast a shadow over her work (and her life), occupying a central place in her novels, her journalism and her day-to-day experiences for decades. Her novels of the 1920s and early 1930s represent either an escape from war by way of the historical novel, such as *The Triumph of Time* trilogy,[9] or mournful depictions of young men and their wives tormented and divided by the First World War, as in *Farewell to Youth* (1928) or *The Pitiful Wife*. Here, Jameson is much in line with her female contemporaries and there are clear parallels between her examination of the costs of the First World War particularly for women and novels such as West's *Return of the Soldier* (1916),

May Sinclair's *The Tree of Heaven* (1917) or Woolf's *Mrs Dalloway* (1925). By the 1930s, her novels are indicative of an overlap between representations of what she called 'Class 1914' (1933: 102), still struggling with the scars of the First World War, such as the traumatized veteran Phillip in *Company Parade*, and her anxieties about the war to come, as in the fascist dystopia *In The Second Year* (1936). Her nonfiction work of the interwar period is similarly dominated by her feelings and attitudes to war: her first autobiography, *No Time Like the Present* (1933), is characterized by her experiences of the loss of friends and family in the First World War and rails against the possibilities of another war, while both the edited collection *A Challenge to Death* (1933) and the essays in *Civil Journey* (1939) chronicle her changing attitudes to the coming conflict, her movement from pacifism to acceptance and even support of the war.[10] These prewar texts chart her changing feelings and experiences as she moved from the shadow cast by the First World War at the beginning of the 1920s towards the increasing inevitability of the Second World War at the end of the 1930s. As Chapter 1 describes, the movement between novels such as *The Moon Is Making* (1937) set in Whitby and *Cousin Honoré* (1940) and *Europe to Let* (1940) set in Europe shows Jameson putting aside a nostalgic conservatism embedded in the past and moving to look outwards to the continent, to the next war and to the future.

Through this look outwards and forwards, Jameson's novels from 1940 onwards can be seen as a significant shift in her politics and in her outlook, albeit one informed by her previous convictions about Europe. Her novels of the Second World War represent – in every sense – a realist approach to total war. They explore every facet of the war, weaving a bewildering number of characters and perspectives through a complex mesh of real and imagined circumstances across Europe, from the occupation of Czechoslovakia in *Then We Shall Hear Singing* to the fate of German Jews in *The Black Laurel*. It is this look outwards, as I have suggested, which marked her out from many of her English contemporaries who, like Margery Allingham, Virginia Woolf, Elizabeth Bowen, Betty Miller or Elizabeth Taylor, tended to concentrate their work in Britain or London. Even after 1945, both wars remained crucial points of reference within her work, continuing to affect both politics and nation-building in the Europe of her novels, as in France in *The Hidden River* and in European colonies across the world as in *Last Score*. Although later in her career she did tackle spies and analyse the new threat of Communism and the Cold War in *The Moment of Truth, The Green Man* (1952) and *A Cup of Tea for Mr Thorgill* (1957), and even the meaning and value of literature and literary celebrity in *The*

Road from the Monument (1962) and *A Month Soon Goes*, Jameson remained deeply invested in the Second World War and its aftermath.

The Second World War does not share the literary associations of its predecessor (Plain, 2013: 233), but there is a good deal of contemporaneous writing about this war, by both men and women, many of whom draw out similar themes to Jameson, from social justice to the clash of civilizations, the culture war to ideas of justice and expediency: Leonard Woolf writes in 1939 of the demise of civilization as the Nazi threat to Europe grew, Betty Miller explores the gender politics at work in a small rural community dominated by a local barracks in *On the Side of Angels* (1945), while Elizabeth Bowen juxtaposes the fear and the romance of the London blitz in *The Heat of the Day* (1949). Numerous other writers from Rose Macaulay to Margery Allingham and Robert Graves to W.H. Auden depict both world wars in their poetry and fiction, discuss war in their journalism and agonize over it in their personal lives, just as Jameson did. Jameson's contribution and what distinguishes her work among these accounts are the ways in which her novels range across a number of elements of war, from the political to the domestic, from Czechoslovakia to Germany, and from male experience to female experience. Furthermore, her experiences during this period, as the mother of a son of military age, as someone wholly committed to Europe as an intellectual, social and political project, and most crucially as the English President of the PEN Club, also added to her expansive depiction of war.

This political commitment can be charted throughout her novels, which often act as intellectual exercises in which she weighs the strengths and weaknesses of a political approach or situation. The novels of the late 1930s document Jameson's change of heart from a founding member, alongside Vera Brittain, of the PPU (Peace Pledge Union) in 1936, to a fervent supporter of a war against Nazism in Europe in 1939. She discusses this change of heart in her letters to Colonel Basil Liddell Hart, then a key figure in the military establishment and an influential military historian and strategist, with whom she struck up a strong friendship.[11] She wrote to him in 1941 that 'in 1939 the choice for us was not between a wise postponement (we had not the spiritual or moral basis for that) and war, but between submission and war. It was better that we chose, rather blindly, war' (3 April 1941). This correspondence continued throughout the war, documenting her realization that the choice in 1939 was only between 'submission and war' (6 April 1940) and going on to discuss every element and political decision throughout the conflict, from her assertion that 'I am more frightened of after the war than of anything' (6 April 1940) to her hope that 'when the war ends in exhaustion […] we are given the beginnings of a new society' (3 April 1941). In light of the detailed discussions in these letters, the novels can be understood to represent a battleground in themselves, both for Jameson's changing ideas and for her desires to convince and persuade others of the right course of action.

Her dedication to the polemical qualities of her novels stems from Jameson's conviction about what it means to be a writer. When she addressed the PEN *Coming of Age* Conference in 1942 (celebrating twenty-one years of PEN), she quoted Fyodor Dostoyevsky on the subject, arguing that 'Dostoyevsky has something useful to say here – "man has no right to turn aside and take no notice of what is happening in the world around him"' (Jameson, 'Speech to the PEN Coming of Age Conference', 1942). For Jameson, every writer has a duty to represent the great question of their generation, because 'every age asks its artists, its thinkers, a question' (1950, 1). In the 1930s and 1940s this question was, she believed, 'fascism or democracy? Slavery or freedom? Tyranny or liberal humanism?' (1950: 2). She remained a socialist throughout this early stage of her writing career, writing in her autobiography in the late 1960s that 'in the thirties, millions of half-fed hopeless men, eating their hearts out, gave off a moral stench which became suffocating' (1984a: 293). For Jameson, this 'moral stench' must be unflinchingly depicted by the novelist, because 'a care for justice, a detestation of cruelty, are no more than one expects of an honest writer' (1939: 13). A number of writers were of a similar mind in the 1930s, inspired by the growing popularity of film and newsreels, social realism and the documentary movement, which encouraged both writers and film-makers to present balanced depictions of social problems, prompting accounts such as George Orwell's *The Road to Wigan Pier* (1937) and the launch of journals such as *FACT*. Jameson herself contributed to *FACT*'s fourth issue, *Writing and Revolt*, an essay called 'Documents', which Janet Montefiore describes as 'a passionate defence of documentary realism as the significant form of socialist writing' (1996: 99). This essay calls for writers to create a socialist literature which is 'a detailed and accurate presentment, not presentation, of this moment and this society' (1937: 15). At this time Jameson wishes writers to harness the apparent dispassion of the camera lens or the modern recording device to present without prejudice every element of society in order to raise awareness of the true inequalities of everyday life, because only truth can be a persuasive advocate for change.

This pursuit of realism and of authority can also be seen in Jameson's representations of war. In part this is a response to the emphasis in war writing on authority and experience as basic qualifying factors for any writer offering a perspective on war. Many scholars have noted that 'the woman writer who trespassed into the territory of war fiction transgresses many taboos' (Higonnet et al, 1987: 206) and 'society censors those who write outside of what is considered to be their gender-specific experience: women should not write about the front as a lived experience' (Cooke and Woollacott, 1993: xii). A woman, like Jameson, writing about war, raises questions not only of the gendered spaces and boundaries which I discussed earlier, but also of authenticity and authority. Kate McLoughlin dedicates an entire chapter in her book on the literary representation of war to the importance of authority for the war writer, explaining that, when examining the reception and longevity of war writing, 'it quickly becomes apparent that the chances of success are greatest if the account in question is *salient* and, crucially, *credible*' (2011: 22; original emphasis). Jameson may have lacked the experience and indeed, the gender, to make her account credible as McLoughlin describes, yet she believed that the representation of soldiers, battles and ministerial offices was crucial to her narrative and, as her notes for these novels reveal, went to great lengths to ensure their accuracy. In March 1946 while writing *The Black Laurel*, set in Allied-occupied Berlin in 1945, Jameson made fastidious notes and collected newspaper articles about the black market activity and control of civilians that she wished to discuss in the novel, as well as questioning those with direct experience of the events she wished to portray.[12] She meticulously researched those elements which were outside her experience in order to ensure that her writing was not only salient but, crucially, a credible representation of war. This pursuit of an 'honest' portrayal of war was informed not only by her pursuit of this socialist writing but also her desire to appear authoritative.

Certainly the greatest influence on these representations of war and her attitudes to writing itself came through her involvement with English and International PEN. Joining PEN in 1922, a year after the organization was founded, she became English President in 1938 and remained so until 1944, playing a pivotal role in supporting writers in occupied Europe and galvanizing both public and political opinion in their interests.[13] As Rachel Potter describes, the PEN Charter as ratified at the 1927 Congress in Brussels states that 'literature, national though it may be in origin, knows no frontiers' (Potter, 2013a: 157). This is, as I go on to suggest, entirely in keeping with Jameson's sense of herself as both English and European but also to her understanding of national literatures as being simultaneously part of an overarching transnational dialogue. Her role as English President of PEN brought her into contact with writers across Europe and America and saw her establish close friendships in countries such as Germany,

Austria and Czechoslovakia. Alongside her colleague and friend Hermon Ould, who became the English and International Secretary of PEN, she rallied PEN members into a campaigning force, organizing petitions and statements, raising money for refugee writers and using her contacts and influence to acquire British and American visas for refugees fleeing occupied Europe. In 1940, she wrote on behalf of English PEN 'To the Conscience of the World', in which she apologized for the appeasement policy of Prime Minister Neville Chamberlain. She asked PEN members to tell their countrymen that the British and their Allies were now fighting for the shared belief 'that every man, of any race or religion, […] that men should respect each other and their minds should be free' ('To the Conscience of the World', 24 May 1940). In Jameson's hands, PEN became not only a social entity but a political force, aiming to influence government policy and public attitudes at home and abroad.[14]

'You can't kill a nation': Nation, myth and resistance

Jameson's desire to represent war accurately, underpinned by the internationalist principles of PEN, her socialist convictions and her evolving political attitudes, led her to engage with nations far beyond Britain. In this endeavour, she enacts an analysis of the national experiences and of national myth-making in nations like Czechoslovakia, Germany, France and Austria. She writes in her essay 'The Novel Today – 1949' that a great novel 'takes us to another country' (1950: 39), going on to state that 'we reach there an understanding of the heart and its ecstasies and its wickedness, a Pisgah-view of man's place in the universe, that we could never have reached by our own smaller audacity and own weaker sight' (1950: 39–40). Many of Jameson's novels 'take us to another country' in a very literal sense, and there reveal not only more about war but also about the nation itself, its constituent parts and its relationship to others. Jameson's sense of these changing modes of self-definition and national myth-making during wartime details national responses to threats of invasion, occupation to defeat. In documenting these processes, these novels come to interrogate the nation under threat, in *Cousin Honoré*, *Europe to Let* and *The Moon Is Making*, the occupied nation in *Then We Shall Hear Singing: A Fantasy in C Major*, *The Other Side* (1946) and *The Black Laurel*, and finally, the postwar nation in *The Hidden River*, *The Moment of Truth*, *Last Score* and *A Cup of Tea for Mr Thorgill*. As theorists of nation Anthony D. Smith and John Hutchinson note, 'The central difficulty in the study of nations and of nationalism has been the problem of finding adequate and agreed definitions of the key concepts, nation and nationalism' (1994: 4). Here, I read nation not as a static territorial, ethnic, or cultural concept, but, as Walker Connor defines it, as an identification with the nation in the minds of its citizens and foreigners, often channelled through these ideas, as what constitutes a nation is 'subjective and consists of the self-identification of people with a group – its past, its present and most importantly its destiny' (1994: 4). This is how nation is articulated in Jameson's work, as an imagined identification taking place both within and outside the nation itself.

Jameson was not, however, a proponent of nationalism, writing in 'City to Let – Berlin 1932' that 'I look up at the shabby flags and think that the greatest day in history will be when they burn the lot' (1939: 51). Rather, she was an interested observer of the interactions between the individual, the nation and the wider world. In her novels, Jameson is committed to exploring the elements of difference between nations, as well as those values and practices held in common. In the 1930s, she visited a number of countries as war threatened to engulf Europe: Austria and Hungary in 1932, Prague and Bratislava in 1938, and Paris in 1939, and in doing so she came to identify far beyond England, and the small Yorkshire community in which she grew up. Following this experience, the survival of these countries and their unique and shared elements became paramount for Jameson. For Jane Mackay and Pat Thane, the ability to identify beyond the nation is highly gendered because national identity is historically located within the masculine, and for centuries 'women were perceived to possess trans-national qualities [...] women indeed had no fixed nationality' (1986: 191). The nation was predicated upon the male citizen who could fight, pay taxes and be democratically involved in its political processes. In this sense, perhaps, it is this distance from the imagined (male) citizen which allowed Jameson to cross national boundaries in this way, particularly in her fiction, allowing her to identify and to empathize with different nations at different stages throughout the war.

Although nations are most often linked with the struggles for independence and territory in the twentieth century, these concepts were by no means new. They emerged in the eighteenth and nineteenth centuries with what Smith and Hutchinson have described as the early ideological stage of nation-building. This was 'permeated by neo-classicism, the conscious return of letters, politics, and the arts to classical antiquity and, above all, to the patriotism and solidarity of Sparta, Athens, and Republican Rome, the models and exemplars of the public, and often heroic virtues' (1994: 5). Hutchinson and Smith trace these qualities back to the European intellectuals often referred to as the 'founding fathers' of the modern nation: German philosopher Johann Gottlieb Fichte, French writer Jean-Jacques Rousseau, Italian nationalist Giuseppe Mazzini and the Greek scholar Admontios Korais (1994: 5). This early neoclassical conception of the nation resembles Jameson's own understanding of it, and she makes frequent references to elements of a great European intellectual tradition, one which included writers such as Rousseau and Fichte, and this was central, not only to her ideas about the cultural and national identities of individual nations, but also to the function of Europe itself. Most importantly, like these thinkers, she equated nation and nationality not with the totalitarian regimes of modern Europe, but with mutually informing scholarly traditions and traditional ways of life which she believed defined the European nations of the past and which, she hoped, would shape the European nations of the future.

French intellectual Ernest Renan observed in his definitive essay 'What Is a Nation?' (1882) that 'a nation is a soul, a spiritual heritage' (1994: 17), and this idea of nation as an emotional attachment, one with a basis in the past and which is linked to family and heredity, is very significant in terms of Jameson's work. It manifests throughout these novels as a strong emotional attachment to a landscape, a set of shared values or, most frequently, a cultural product or tradition. Despite her belief in a shared European culture, Jameson also depicts nations as created and defined through their own individual cultural traditions, such as food, music, art and even furniture, in short, through a national culture. The importance that Jameson accorded to culture and history as generators of nation is integral to her novels of wartime, as culture creates a 'rallying point' for these nations (Birkett, 2009: 234). In *The Black Laurel*, through her depiction of the plundering of Poland's libraries and museums by Nazi troops (1947a: 91), she draws attention to the importance of this national culture for building and maintaining the nation through the occupiers' compulsion to destroy it. As the German art historian Gustave Leist comments, with their removal, 'the past of this absurd people was being effaced, nothing of it, when the armies withdrew, would be left here' (1947a: 95). This incident, alongside numerous other examples in her work, from the love and care of furniture in occupied homes in *Then We Shall Hear Singing* to the references to German and French literature in *The Other Side*, points to the defining role taken by cultural products in Jameson's representations of wartime nations.

Cultural artefacts also underpin the national myths at work in these wartime nations and the ways in which they are constructed and maintained. As critics such as Benedict Anderson and Eric Hobsbawm have observed, nations are, to an enormous extent, inventions of certain periods in history. Anderson's definitive study of the subject describes nation as 'an imagined political community' (1983: 6). In the same year, Hobsbawm writes that this construction of the nation, and the myth-making associated with it, was necessary because of widespread enfranchisement within European nations during the nineteenth century – he posits that, as populations moved from subjects (of monarchy) to citizens, these 'invented traditions' galvanized populations towards certain national ideals or political ideologies (1983: 269). This early work on the inherent constructedness of nation redefined the ways in which historians, sociologists and anthropologists understood nationality and modern nations and these processes of national construction and reconstruction can be traced throughout Jameson's work, most evidently in her representations of Czechoslovakia in *Europe to Let* and in *Then We Shall Hear Singing*. During the 1930s, in particular, Czechoslovakia feared Nazi invasion and sought to draw attention to certain myths of the Czech nation, such as its longevity, its innate Europeanness and its democracy, in the hope of securing protection from stronger Western nations. Jameson, in part, reproduces these myths in her work. Her echoing of these myths can be seen as an explicit reproduction of Czech propaganda, which often coincided with Jameson's own views and hopes for Europe but can also be seen as a conscious interjection into the myth-making processes of this nation. As such, Jameson's novels engage with these myths of nation in a way that both supports and perpetuates them, as well as subverting and drawing attention to them as nation-building apparatus.

In fact, the novel is often seen as a key instrument in the manufacture of national myths. This idea of the invention of nations also maintains they are the products of certain processes of production, such as printing, which established linguistic uniformity and which, for Anderson, created these feelings of community and of shared stories and experiences (shared through a unifying language). These processes allow for these national myths and myth-making processes to be used not only by politicians and individual citizens, but also by writers. For postcolonial scholars such as Homi Bhabha, literature itself is part of national myth-making, particularly for the newly independent postcolonial nation. He argues that it is from 'traditions of political thought and literary language that the nation emerges as a powerful historical idea' (1990: 1). Similarly for Antony D. Smith, 'the creation of a canonical literature represents another popular strategy: Shakespeare, Milton and Wordsworth; Racine, Moliere and Balzac, Pushkin, Tolstoy and Lermonter' (1999: 166). In this case certain nations can be seen to use the literature of the past in order to secure the identity and legitimacy of the nation in the future, as the so-called Czech Awakeners, writers and historians of the late eighteenth century, such as F.M. Pelcl and Josef Dubrovský, did.[15]

These literary representations have, as Bhabha goes on to argue, meant that written articulations of nation are marked by 'a temporality of culture and social consciousness more in tune with the partial, over-determined process by which textual meaning is produced through the articulation of difference in language; more in keeping with the problem of closure which plays enigmatically in the discourse of the sign' (1990: 2). For Bhabha, the nation can always be seen in a constant process of evolution, and so identifications with it, both externally and internally, are in a perpetual state of flux. Smith notes that these cultural and particularly literary artefacts 'have created an image of the nation for compatriots and outsiders alike and in doing so have forged the nation itself. Signifier and signified have fused. Image and reality have become identical; ultimately, the nation has no existence outside its imagery and its representations' (1994: 166). Here, the 'imagined community' of the nation exists fluidly in a constant state of re-identification through cultural artefacts and textual narration. Texts then can become more recognizable expressions of the nation than its real-life qualities, rewriting its history, its politics and even its geography to fit certain literary or political perspectives.

The idea of nation and national identity as arising from or being strengthened by ideological conflict – such as this struggle between two cultures, in close proximity – is particularly prominent in postcolonial theory, yet it is clearly relevant in other nation-forming practices, such as revolution and war.[16] Indeed, Paul Betts and Greg Eghigian observe that, in wartime, 'such a massive mobilisation on behalf of nation requires a sense of belonging that by no means came naturally [...] individuals historically have had to learn how to feel, act and be nationalist' (2003: 17). This is an important process in which the wartime nation is repeatedly brought into being through a constant process of evolution and re-identification on the part of its citizens. These processes are integral to the maintenance of national myths because 'only out of struggle is nation, always prone to decay, regenerated' (Hutchinson, 1994: 129). Jameson's novels do much to illuminate these processes of decay, regeneration and reconstruction of the nation during wartime, most notably, in their representation of Germany in novels such as *Cousin Honoré*, *The Other Side* and *The Black Laurel*. Even in the late 1930s, when she attacked Germany in *Cousin Honoré* or *Europe to Let*, Jameson writes of being 'conscious all the time of an older Germany surviving strongly under the new, caring intensely for music, for friendship, and completely indifferent to lesser values' (1939: 51). It is to this Germany which she returns in her later novels when Allied victory seemed likely, depicting in *The Other Side* a deeply cultured nation, at odds with her earlier portrayals but in keeping with her desire to recuperate and reconstruct Germany. These portrayals reflect the impact of war on national consciousness, and in particular, the changes in processes of regeneration and reconstruction of nations and national myths before, during and after conflict. Due to her own sense of placelessness and her own lifelong struggle with belonging and with her relationship to the British nation, Jameson is, I suggest, highly-sensitive to these processes and acutely aware of their tendencies and limitations. As she searches for her place in Britain and in Europe, she comes to identify and re-identify with different European nations throughout the war, articulating her own sense of national decay and regeneration through her novels.

'A new faith': Civilization, culture and Europe

Beyond these national musings, Jameson's novels of the Second World War comment not only upon the national structures of the time but the supranational structures surrounding them, notably Europe itself. For her, it was Europe and the civilization it symbolized which was at risk from war, and it was this fear which underpinned her fictional and non-fictional writing at this time. She posited alongside this her hope for a better future and for a more united, just, and democratic Europe after the war, writing in 1934 that the artist must preach to all men 'a new faith' (1939: 178), and calling for writers to rebuild Europe in the image of a 'wider, finer, grander, and more dignified democracy' (1939: 176). This European element in Jameson's work has been discussed at length in both Maslen's and Birkett's biographies, and Birkett is correct to point out that Jameson's life and writing owe much to her sense of a 'triple cultural heritage: the regional, the national and the European' (2009: 6). However, I would argue that the ideas underpinning Jameson's highly-charged representations of Europe merit greater critical scrutiny: Jameson's conceptions of Europe are mired in her own intellectual and political background and predicated on a certain somewhat elitist and even imperialist conception of Europe's strengths and weaknesses. They are also underlain with her socialist convictions and the associations she makes between what Orwell hoped would become the united socialist states of Europe and the future of Western civilization as she conceived of it.[17]

The idea of Europe is as much a contested and constructed concept as the nations that form its constituent parts. For Pim Den Boer, 'the term "Europe" has a long history, but the idea of Europe is a recent phenomenon' (1993: 13). In fact, the evolution of the idea of Europe as we currently conceive it, although it can be traced back to the early modern period, arose concurrently with conceptions of the modern nation itself. As Gerard Delanty explains, 'The idea of Europe became closely linked to the emergence of a Western European polity of nation-states and gradually came to take the character of a normative idea' but was 'rarely seen as an alternative to the nation-state' (1995: 65). Although following the French Revolution the increase in nationalist movements throughout the continent should have led to a decline in the idea of Europe, it was largely agreed that 'these reborn nations should become part of the brotherhood of European peoples' (Den Boer, 1993: 74).[18] The fate of Europe as an idea has always been tied to that of the nation itself, with the two concepts acting not only in unison but also perhaps as another point of conflict or difference through which each community comes to define and redefine itself.

It was following the First World War that the drive towards a united Europe took on a new urgency as older nations sought security among a wider European community, and newer nations, such as Czechoslovakia, sought to harness their newly discovered independence to a more secure and established supranational structure, as I describe in Chapter 3. As Wilfried Loth points out, during the Second World War many Europeans had discovered that 'the Nazi empire could be overthrown only by a combination of efforts; and resistance to an extreme form of nationalism had caused many of them to rediscover the tradition of shared European values' (1985: 2). Europe itself – like its constituent national parts – was forced to repeatedly redefine itself through conflict and continued evolution. A great many resistance movements, from Hungary to France, came to identify as a key aim of their struggle the desire to form an independent nation-state, which would stand within a wider European community of nations. Even as the Second World War came to symbolize the battle to save Europe, many politicians and intellectuals looked to the idea of Europe to galvanize the public during the fight and to provide an attainable image of future security. Europe was simultaneously both the symptom of its own demise and the symbol of its salvation. Jameson's novels are filled with just such ambivalences, looking alternatively to Europe as saviour and symbol of civilization and as the architect of its own downfall.

Jameson's faith in the idea of Europe stems not only from Renaissance ideas of a Europe which drew upon Roman and Greek civilizations, but also from her own studies and experiences of the continent. She wrote in 1941 that 'European civilisation [is] an order in which certain words, law, truth, humanity, have known a significance which has been pressed into them by generations of patient effort' (1941: 21). This defines the terms in which Jameson viewed and valued this European civilization: Jameson's fears for Europe's future characterize her writing of the 1930s and of the Second World War itself, convincing her at the end of the decade that war in Europe was necessary because 'the spiritual heritage of Europe is being destroyed' (1941: 18). Each of the nations she describes in her fiction fits into this European civilization, marked out as an essential part of it. Their struggles with occupation, with defeat and with victory are each understood in terms not only of their national but their European responsibilities and identity: France, Czechoslovakia, Hungary, Germany and Britain embody Europe's civilized values, as Jameson understands them. However, these values were based upon Renaissance associations of Europe with ideas of freedom and equality, justice and cooperation, now resurgent in the face of the political upheavals of the Second World War. Furthermore, this Europe seems, like Anderson's imagined national communities, to 'loom out of an immemorial past' (1991: 12), a past constructed in the present to serve certain political purposes. In Jameson's case, tracing Europe back to this idealized realm of cooperation and justice (as opposed to imperialism and bloodshed) advocates for its survival, justifying the war itself.

For Jameson, it was European literature that provided this idealized version of Europe, just as it did for the European nations themselves. As Elizabeth Maslen explains:

> Jameson had always been drawn to the literature of Europe: before World War One she redirected her MA to explore the largely uncharted territory of European drama; she took part in the translation of de Maupassant's short stories in the early twenties, and she read continental works voraciously, with a particular but not exclusive love of French Literature. (2014: 24)

Europe, in Jameson's mind, was always culturally defined, epitomized by a European community of letters. It was Erasmus in the fifteenth century who first identified Europe with the idea of a 'Respublica Litteraria', and this idea was expounded upon by other scholars such as Voltaire, who also wrote of 'a republic of letters established in Europe' in which knowledge and culture were shared across borders (Voltaire [1756] 1963: 375). Echoing Voltaire's words, Jameson wrote that one of Europe's great strengths as a continent was that ideas could 'cross and re-cross without being held up at frontiers' (1950: 37), and her work mirrors that of Voltaire in thinking about this European community of letters. Her work with PEN, across the frontiers of Europe both during the Second World War and into the Cold War period, is testament to this conviction.

Jameson's novels can also be seen as persuasive tools to promote and sustain the idea of a European community of letters, constituting her own contributions to it. They circulated her ideas across the continent selling in their thousands in Italy, Portugal and France, according to her correspondence with her agent A.D. Peters, placing her within a tradition of European writers, writers whom she had always admired, such as Malraux, Heine, Goethe and Voltaire.[19] In her critical work she subscribes, in particular, to Voltaire's idea that it was through the arts and sciences that Europe continued to rise from the ashes of a myriad of crises and conflicts. He wrote in 1756 that 'the details and devices of politics sink into oblivion; but sound laws, institutions and achievements in the sciences and the arts remain forever' (1963: 375). Jameson hoped that the Second World War would be no exception to this rule, writing that perhaps 'the genius of Europe, its old traditions, its old habit of growth and discovery, its young energy, will lift us out of the shadows' (1950: 35), and strove to do her part in ensuring this. Within Jameson's novels, there are numerous references to this shared European culture. In her war novels, this shared culture defends and maintains Europe itself, representing hope and solidarity in the face of violence and oppression, as it does in *Europe to Let* when Shakespeare is performed in Prague in 1938 (146) or in *The Other Side*, as the book of poetry by Pierre Ronsard is saved from the fire by the youngest member of the family. Appreciation of the cultural output of other nations was a defining characteristic of being a good European in Jameson's eyes. These cultural qualities, the value of ideas which 'cross and re-cross without being held up at frontiers' (1950: 37), were an integral part of her vision of Europe.

Many of her contemporaries shared this view, connecting their convictions about the future of a united Europe with a sense of literature as representing a key point in Europe's shared culture. As Rachel Potter observes, 'The ideas of literature as "common currency" and the "patrimony of humanity at large" were elegant universal claims that chimed with the utopian spirit of international cooperation in the interwar period' (2013: 73). Potter is speaking here of English and International PEN, and Jameson's work with this organization certainly informed and was informed by her sense of herself as a European writer and her hopes and ambitions for a united Europe in the future. Other PEN members and influential voices within the British literary community were of a similar mind. H.G. Wells, himself President of English PEN between 1933 and 1936, had written as early as 1921 that 'Europe has to stop thinking in terms of the people of France, the people of England, the people of Germany, the French, the British, the Germans and so forth. Europe has to think at least of the people of Europe' (328), and his work with the League of Nations during this period reflects this stance. While Wells' later work such as *The Fate of Homo Sapiens* (1939) or *The Rights of Man* (1940) saw him take a more international than European approach to these problems, his convictions remained the same: that national borders must be dissolved or at least subsumed within a great and more united entity to ensure future human security, prosperity and even survival. Fellow PEN member E.M. Forster echoed similar ideas in *The Twilight of Reason* (1940:3), in which he ties Europe's fate as a civilization to the survival of a free and uninhibited literature. Jameson's faith in the European project in her novels of the Second World War clearly reflects more widely held beliefs among her social and intellectual circle.

However, this sense of Europe as a civilization, or as uniquely civilized, is one which occupies a precarious position in the work of many of these writers. Its unqualified use belies a certain imperialist superiority, which we see elsewhere in Jameson's oeuvre. Richard Overy writes that 'in reality the definition of civilisation, and the description of those who could qualify as civilised, was shaped by the social position and moral assumptions of those who chose to write about it' (2009: 22). Civilization is, like nation, a subjective construct, one prone to change depending on certain historical and personal factors: Jameson's ideas about civilization were based on elements of her upbringing in middle-class Whitby, but most crucially on her experiences at Leeds and the intellectual encounters she had with European literature there and during the writing of her Masters dissertation at King's. Fernand Braudel writes that the original definition of civilization meant 'broadly the opposite of barbarism [...] on the one side were civilized peoples: on the other primitive savages or barbarians' (1994: 4). In order to reinforce this idea of Europe as uniquely civilized, it is consistently juxtaposed in the novels with ideas of savagery, barbarism and the uncivilized. These terms are imbued with the prejudices of Europe imperialism and claims to racial superiority, yet Jameson's preoccupation is not racial but rather the cultural barbarism of Nazism. This is in keeping with Forster's configuration of civilization and with Europe and European letters as both its expression and its protector in works such as *Nordic Twilight*. Jameson's sense of this European civilization is not unproblematic then but is heavily influenced by literature and by the literary circles in which she moved.

There was a feeling among commentators and academics throughout the 1930s that Europe was in decline and that what passed for progress was instead degeneration. This was a common idea in both scholarship and popular literature, one which gained ground as war looked more likely towards the end of that decade. Overy's book, *The Morbid Age: Britain between the Wars* (2009), charts the 'networks of anxiety' (7) operating in British intellectual circles at this time. He describes how the evolution of these fears about the demise of European society had been growing in intellectual and popular discourses for some time by 1939. The threat to Europe was expanded in Jameson's writing, as in that of others at the time, to encapsulate not only the continent itself, but a unique and long-established way of life. By the beginning of the 1940s, even politicians described the coming war in the same terms, as a struggle for European civilization: Brittain describes hearing Winston Churchill give a speech to the House of Commons on 18 June 1940, in which he told the country that 'the Battle of Britain is about to begin. Upon this battle depends the survival of Christian civilisation' (quoted in Brittain, 53), while she, a committed pacifist, embraced a similar rhetoric, writing that the 'civilisation of half a dozen countries is going up in flames' (*England's Hour*, 37). This link between civilization and Europe, and the threat to both, was a device through which to galvanize Britain and Europe both for and against the coming war.

This juxtaposition of civilization with barbarism is part of a Classical tradition and Jameson and her contemporaries understood it in these terms. As T.S. Eliot wrote in 1957, 'We are all, so far as we inherit the civilisation of Europe, still citizens of the Roman Empire' ('Virgil and the Christian World', 4). As I describe in Chapter 2, the sense of this battle for civilization and its classical roots becomes tied to anxieties about modernity and progress, which question Europe's claim to be civilized at all. Jameson's attachment to civilization, both as a mode of description for Europe or a European way of life and as a topic of discussion in her novels and essays, is subject to significant change throughout this period. Her recourse to words like 'civilization', 'civilized' or 'reason' to describe European thought or society alters drastically during the war itself, chronologically and even from book to essay to polemic. In the 1930s, her uncritical use of the word 'civilization' and her pitting of it against words like 'barbarism' or 'barbarians' reflects, I suggest, a certain faith in Europe and its concepts. These words and formulations are significantly less present in her postwar works, such as *The Black Laurel* (1947) or *Before the Crossing* (1947), in which she seems to search for signs of this civilization, for justification for any pretence to being civilized in light of the events of the Holocaust, or for the ongoing injustices being carried out in the name of Europe. In *Last Score, or the Private Life of Sir Richard Ormston* (1961), arguably Jameson's only postcolonial novel – the word seems obsolete, particularly with reference to an increasingly irrelevant and dishonourable Europe. Her association of the civilized with the European reflects throughout the strength of her faith in Europe itself, a faith which has all but disappeared by the Cold War period.

The period following the Second World War is, as Lyndsey Stonebridge explains in *Justice after Nuremburg* (2011), 'we are often told, the dawn of a new era of human rights: a conclusion to the worst that could have happened that would give the world a new moral and political beginning' (2011: 2) and Jameson's later novels come to examine the viability of this world, as she sees it unfolding. However, as Samuel Moyn has pointed out it was only really in the 1970s that the discourse and vocabulary of human rights really began to penetrate public and intellectual discussion (2010: 3). Jameson's books, while they deal with the problems of postwar justice, or retribution and reconciliation as I describe in Chapters 5 and 6, do not deal so specifically with human rights as we now understand them, because these concepts are often not available within public or even intellectual discourse until long after they have been enshrined in international law. As Allan Hepburn describes, 'The novel, which plots dilemmas and corrects injustices, is particularly suited to the representation of citizenship and rights claims' (2016: 5), and certainly the relations between the citizen and the state, and the place of the citizen within international systems of justice are central to all of Jameson's war novels. However, Jameson's characters exist in many ways at the inception of this process and their creator remains mired within a pre-human rights discourse, underpinned by her ongoing disappointment at the failure of prewar humanist ideals. Perhaps Jameson's inability to adapt to or really to embrace the postwar world in these later novels stems in part from her inability to come to terms with a world in which these basic rights and privileges would have to be provided for in international legislature because no government or political system could be relied upon to bestow them upon their citizens. Without her faith in Europe and in the traditions of democracy and intellectualism with which she associates it, Jameson's postwar novels cling to the experiences of the past while looking in horror at the inconsistencies and inadequacies of the postwar future.

Having established the four key elements underpinning this study – marginalization, war, nation and Europe – this book comes to examine

Jameson's work across six chapters, moving chronologically through her work from 1937 to 1961. It serves to illustrate the evolution not only in Jameson's own thought and writing but also in the nations she chose to depict, chronicling her representations alongside each nation's history and changing circumstances. I move beyond examining Jameson's marginalization, to recuperate her literary reputation by investigating the value of her work as an exploration of the reconfigurations of nation, national identity and European identity taking place during immediately before, during and after the Second World War. Jameson's tendency during this period to look outwards to Europe is not only unusual and significant in light of contemporary literary discourses which were more usually preoccupied with ideas around Englishness and isolationism, but demonstrates important elements about the author's own preoccupations and those of a wider Europe. Her engagement with European nation-building during this period is not only indicative of her concerns about Europe and about Britain itself, but also points to wider cultural concerns about the future of European civilization and the demise of European political and intellectual culture. This critical study seeks to make a positive intervention into the discourses surrounding the marginalization of women writers and argues for the pivotal role that Jameson played as a literary and political figure during this period, through placing her at the central point of an oft-overlooked literary vanguard, one which strove to look outwards, beyond the confines of national identity, to evaluate the world from a range of perspectives.

1

'The living nerves which bind nation to nation': Britain, France and pacifism in *The Moon Is Making* and *Cousin Honoré*

As the 1930s drew to a close, Jameson, like many of her contemporaries, struggled to come to terms with the likelihood of another world war in her lifetime. Having lived through the hardships and personal losses of the First World War – Jameson lost her brother Harold, a pilot, in 1917 – many joined the growing pacifist movement through organizations like the Peace Pledge Union. Like many of her literary contemporaries, Jameson came to use her fiction, as well as her journalism and essays, in an attempt to articulate the causes of this coming second conflict, as well as to reconcile her own fears over its potential consequences on both a personal and a national level. However, unlike her contemporaries, it was during this decade that Jameson began to anticipate the consequences of war not only for herself, her family and her country, but also for wider Europe. Where her earlier novels of the 1920s and early 1930s foreground a familiar Britain, based in London or in Whitby, by the end of that decade she had moved to a wider consideration of Germany, France, Austria, and even Czechoslovakia. This movement looks forward to her war novels of the 1940s, which roam freely across the continent, taking in the wartime experiences of both ally and enemy. The beginnings of this look outwards can be traced through her novels of the 1930s, beginning with *The Moon Is Making* (1937), before moving on to the rendering of France in *Cousin Honoré* (1940). It can be linked to Jameson's changing political opinions, as she moved from an isolationist pacifism rooted in her fears for her family to a pro-war stance linked firmly to her hopes and fears for the wider European continent. This change in outlook is reflected in several key tropes of these novels – her romanticization of the landscapes of both Britain and France, her use of the pastoral to explore conservative ideas about gender and nationhood, and the amalgamation of these two ideas to suggest a sense of cohesion between the territories of the Continent – human and non-human – and the territories of Britain. This creates a sense of a shared threat from a war and a modernity which could destroy not only traditional ways of life but also more pervasive cultural ideologies and ideas.

In *The Moon Is Making*, this threat is to Britain and to British life, stemming not only from the chaos on the Continent but also from the challenge to traditional rural life from growing urbanization and modernity itself. Alison Light suggests that this conflict between nostalgia and modernity was 'the dominant move between the wars, one which could be conservative in effect and yet was often modern in form; a conservatism itself in revolt against the past, trying to make room for the present' (1991: 11). Whilst Jameson identified as a socialist throughout her life, as Jennifer Birkett describes (Birkett, 2006: 85), some of the tropes with which she engages during this interwar period might most often be described as conservative in this sense. I would suggest that Jameson's is an emotional conservatism and one which very much seems at pains to 'make room for the present' within a physical and political landscape threatened, not only by war, but by the forces of the modern, capital-driven society. This conservatism stems also from Jameson's own nostalgic longings for her hometown following her relocation to London. As Elizabeth Maslen describes, Jameson was 'a self-imposed exile from her own community, her roots in a past that was rapidly vanishing' (Maslen, 2014: 181). As I have described, Jameson struggled throughout her life with feelings of ambivalence about her decision to leave Whitby. Within these novels of urban and rural life, Jameson's conflicted feelings about the freedom and independence accorded her by her life in modern London play out against her longing for the simpler existence she might have enjoyed had she stayed at home. As such her depiction in *The Moon Is Making* of an isolated English town emphasizes tradition, the unique nature of the British countryside and longevity of age-old customs. In places, it represents these as unassailable elements of Britishness, evoking a safety and comfort in enduring ways of life, while in others it challenges the shortcomings and short-sightedness of these rural idylls.

As Light expounds, many interwar female writers display a latent or explicit conservatism in their writing of this period, detectable in the more outwardly conservative voices of Ivy Compton Burnett or Agatha Christie which she discusses, but also bringing out seams of conservatism within more progressive voices such as Margery Allingham, Virginia Woolf and even Jameson herself: in Margery Allingham's *The Oaken Heart* (1941), the ways in which an English village and its wartime sacrifices and hardships might become a metaphor for the nation or in Virginia Woolf's *Between the Acts* (1941) she tackles similar issues of tradition and community in wartime. If, as Light asserts, conservativism might involve 'a commitment to family life, to the idea of nationhood, to the notion of necessary authority' (1991:18) then these are characteristics which Jameson vocally rejects in her polemical writings and in her autobiography but which can be detected in many of her interwar novels, presented sometimes critically, sometimes uncritically. These are ideas which she explores, guided by the push-pull of her feelings for Whitby – the pull of the past but the promise of a newer bolder future, the safety of home and the possibilities of the unfamiliar. *The Moon Is Making* reflects these wider trends in interwar writing, whilst displaying clearly the interplay within Jameson's work between her socialist convictions and her somewhat nostalgic longings towards certain more conservative forms of British rural life.

During this period, Jameson's conservatism is not confined to British life and British traditions. By the late 1940s, she was also beginning to look to France as a bastion of rural tradition and of a shared European life. In *Cousin Honoré* the eponymous protagonist's concerns are not only epitomized in the threat stemming from Nazi Germany but also characterized by anxieties about the impact of both of modernity and of socialism on his wealth and his standing. Jameson deploys this sense of the regional – informed by her own sense of herself as a Yorkshire woman – to illustrate the shared values and shared anxieties of rural-dwellers in both Britain and France. Emphasizing Honoré's love of the land and his sense of himself, not as Frenchman but as an Alsatian, she creates a character recognizable across both countries, through his stoic conservatism, his embodiment of tradition and his reverence for the Alsatian landscape (and the personal wealth it symbolizes) over and above national concerns. The characters in both of these novels then come to represent not only the weaknesses of these traditional ways of life – their obsession with hierarchy, their casual misogyny and their greed – but also the strengths of the regional. Both novels demonstrate that the homogenized nation is not the battleground in this coming conflict but that what each citizen defends in wartime is his/her small corner of the nation and the traditions and idiosyncrasies which drive the rhythms of his own life. This is the same, Jameson seems to suggest, in France as in Britain, wherein the regional communities often hold more in common than the great national centres.

Jameson's movement between these two novels is at once spatial and temporal. She is held between her nostalgic look backwards towards the rural past of two nations, two regions – one familiar and homely, another familiar and yet enticingly other – and her desire to move forwards into a future about which she feels ambivalent at best, trepidatious at worst. As Paul Saint-Amour expounds in his exploration of an extended interwar period ruled by a Cold-War-esque dread of what he refers to as the conditional 'tense future' and the known, anxious present, this is not perhaps unusual in a writer trapped within these difficult years. As Saint-Amour expounds, 'what I have called the anticipatory syndrome of the interwar period should be understood as a set of psychic and cultural responses to the First World War and its apparent legacy' (Saint-Amour 2015: 14). Jameson is at once pulled by the nostalgic safety of an idealized and conservative vision of the past and a drive towards future progress, which, whilst it holds for her some hope for a united Europe built around a liberal socialist vision, is tied to a fear of the kind of progress, political and material, which has brought the world to the brink of war. Her ability to make the imaginative move to France and her reproduction of ideals of a traditional rural France in *Cousin Honoré* – embodying simultaneously what she sees as both most laudable and most troubling about Europe's past – is compounded by her fear of what the unknowable future may hold, her hope and her dread that the war might well be the epitome of human progress in Europe.

Moreover, it is the inhabitants of these regional spaces who must be convinced of war, who must come to feel the repercussions in their own fields and streets of events that seem to take place worlds away. These two novels can be seen to draw these worlds together to explore positive and negative reverberations of war for those removed from the capital cities, those who would be expected to fight or to contribute, but whose lives could not be further removed from the decision-makers of London or Paris. The movement to France at the end of the 1930s with *Cousin Honoré* is crucial to understanding what sets Jameson's writing apart from her contemporaries. Through examining her letters and autobiographical writing during this period, it is possible to trace Jameson's movement towards Europe through her break with pacifism and move to a pro-war stance. Always a passionate European, she shaped these novels to demonstrate her own identifications beyond England and the connections she came to make between the Nazi threat to European life and its repercussions for Britain. This ability to use her experience of the English region to empathize with life in rural France allows her to explore what might be at stake in both countries and the ways in which war might offer not only a way to defend these traditions but a way to improve the lives of ordinary people across the Continent.

'A good little Englander': From Yorkshire to Europe

Jameson observes in her first autobiography, *No Time like the Present* (1933), that 'it is my great good fortune to have been born in Whitby, so that the scenes which lie under the others I have kept are incomparable' (12). From her earliest memories to her love of international travel later in life, Jameson's formative experiences in this northern English coastal town informed her life and a great deal of her writing. There was only one other country which stood this comparison in Jameson's affections: France. As Birkett notes, Jameson's great love of France grew 'to become as much part of her conscious definition of herself as her Yorkshireness [sic]' (2009: 3). Both *The Moon Is Making* and *Cousin Honoré* are characterized both by Jameson's 'Yorkshireness', by her later love of France and, in particular, by the relationship between a sense of regional identity and her desire to identify more widely with other nations and communities.[1] For Birkett, by the end of the 1930s 'Jameson had refreshed herself and her [Yorkshire] landscape by reinvesting both in the landscape of France' (2009: 4): France symbolized not only the rustic goodness of the Yorkshire landscape; it symbolized all that was good about Europe, from culture and wine to tradition and rural life. The movement between these novels of the late 1930s is essential to understanding Jameson's political convictions during this period: this relocation from Yorkshire to France indicates Jameson's movement from a parochial pacifism and desire to protect her family (symbolized by Whitby's rolling landscape and local characters) from the coming war to an outward-looking conviction that Britain had to acknowledge its part in Europe to save both the country and the Continent from Nazism.

In fact, Jameson's identification with Yorkshire relates to her sense of identity or multiple identities and informs every level of her work. David M. Smith and Enid Wistrich have a helpful turn of phrase for characterizing the formation of these multiple identities (the national, the regional and the European), describing how 'collective identities are the rooms through which we pass on our biographical journey which help define belonging' (2007: 10). To borrow their analogy, Yorkshire is a room through which Jameson has passed, as is France, and from each she has drawn elements which inform both her writing and her sense of self. She identifies passionately with Yorkshire throughout her life because she grew up there; she understands its people, its customs and its feelings of separateness from the rest of Britain. She comes to identify with France later in life, primarily because she sees some reflection of Yorkshire's characters and rural lifestyle in that country, but also because she sees it as central to the European civilization and culture she admires. In setting *Cousin Honoré* in Alsace, she evokes a similarly entrenched independent spirit, one attributable to repeated occupation and proximity to a contested national border, both characterised by the hardiness and wilfulness she attributes throughout her work to the regional identities of northern England. It is this sense of regionalism which allows her to draw parallels between these two areas and to explore the relationship between Britain and Europe in a way that helps her to work through her anxieties about the war and to realize what might be at stake for Britain and for Europe.

This sense of indecision between an instinctual pacifism and a more considered pro-war stance can be traced through her critical writing of this time. In the mid-1930s, Jameson assembled and edited a group of writers, journalists and politicians in a collection of polemics dedicated to making the case against war, *Challenge to Death* (1935). Featuring West, Brittain, Julian Huxley and Edmund Blunden, among others, it encompassed the key voices of contemporary pacifism in Britain. In it, Jameson herself describes war as 'the collective suicide of nations, the last triumph of the irrational' (1935: 16). *Civil Journey* (1939), a collection of her writings from throughout the decade, for Jameson, 'mark[s] the stages of a mind, my mind' (1939: 5). Here, her ambivalence is pronounced. In the 'Introduction', she warns that 'the collapse of civilisation [...] would be accelerated by another war' (1939: 21), and she seems throughout *Civil Journey* unable to reconcile her personal 'fear that another [war] will kill my son as brutally as the last killed my brother in his nineteenth year' (1939: 53), with her conviction that the fascist forces within Europe must be stopped. Like the other contributors to *Challenge to Death*, her response to this war was mired in the very recent experiences of the First World War, just twenty years before and an utterly formative experience for writers such as Jameson, Brittain and Blunden. In this Jameson's fears reflect the grief and anxiety still being felt across Britain and Europe, as well as illustrating the strong desire not to relive those traumatic memories by entering into another and seemingly more wide-reaching conflict.

At the end of the 1930s Jameson makes, as the title suggests, a *Civil Journey* in which her civic duty, as both a Briton and as a European, overpowers the more emotional elements of her pacifism. In 1941, writing to Basil Liddell Hart, she describes her pacifism as 'of the emotional type – that is I loathed the waste and cruelty of war' (21 December 1941); however, events were beginning to overtake this emotional response and she goes on that she had no choice but to 'abandon [pacifism], after Munich' (21 December 1941). The Munich Pact of September 1938 marked a key turning point in her beliefs not only about the war but about European culture itself, as she realized the scale of Hitler's ambition and the implications for countries and for friends across Europe. A year later, she is more certain in her conviction that 'I do not know how, in September 1939, war could have been avoided' (1941: 11). By this point, Jameson had come to view the war as a clash of cultures, a necessary evil to combat what she saw as 'the Nazi contempt for the individual soul' (1941: 14). However, this change of heart was not without its own casualties: Jameson's break with pacifism caused a rift between Brittain and herself which lasted many years.[2] Nonetheless, her commitment to Europe eventually overcame her initial emotional response and led Jameson in the late 1930s to mobilize her fictional and journalistic work in making the case for war.

She did so by examining the shared cultures between Europe and Britain and making the case for a European way of life. Thus, at the heart of both of these novels is an affection for the countryside and a depiction of these two rural landscapes which seeks to draw out the commonalities of the regional rural cultures in both Britain and France. *The Moon Is Making* is set in the northern coastal town of Wik, Jameson's fictionalization of Whitby, with Over-Wik and Under-Wik representing the real town's cliff and harbour areas. The novel centres on local eccentric and intellectual Handel Wikker and his brother Ezekiel, a farmer. Whilst Handel is highly critical of the parochialism of Wik, Ezekiel relishes the sense of tradition and conservatism which characterizes his isolated rural life. In *Cousin Honoré*, the protagonist is also an elderly man, Honoré Burckheim, a rich landowner living in the isolated village of Burckheim, in Alsace, built up around his family farm and vineyard over hundreds of years. As Sonia O. Rose has noted, 'Landscape whilst often symbolising the whole and something generic, is necessarily the depiction of certain locales, since all the various geographic features and style of living that exist within the nation state cannot be portrayed simultaneously' (2004: 198). Both of these landscapes then come to stand for the wider nation, their traditions evocative of years of British and French life and even their regional charm something of a testament to British and French eccentricity.

The countryside is, of course, the bearer of national myth *par excellence*, hence its deployment throughout the interwar period and into the early days of the Second World War.[3] As Sarah Neal notes, 'In World War Two it was again the *Southern* counties of England that provided the rich ruralist propaganda of the home/nation that was being defeated' (2009: 26; emphasis added). In Jameson's work, it is neither the southern landscape of England nor, at times, England itself which is represented as this home territory: in *The Moon Is Making* it is not the soft hills of the home counties which symbolize England, but the harsh moorland around Wik, where 'the stream pouring through the gully to the harbour is deep, swift, tree-shadowed; the rough fields turn steeply to the limestone cliff, hollowed with quarries, with moors above' (1939: 3). Jameson displays her own sense of Britishness, which, like that of a great many other writers from that area, from Winifred Holtby to J.B. Priestley, is coloured by her identification with Yorkshire and the Yorkshire landscape. This identification, informed by the otherness and remoteness of the regional, allows her to embrace and to understand the Alsatian countryside: both landscapes are in many ways estranged from their home nation through this underlying sense of difference and of otherness – Yorkshire through its rugged landscape and Alsace through its proximity to Germany and its frequent movement between the two countries. Jameson deploys these romanticized associations of rural landscapes with nation not to make the case for an exceptional or isolated England, as many of her contemporaries did, but to make the case for an England that is indelibly tied to the landscapes and customs of the continent. She does so through a deliberate decentring of the mythical landscape of England away from the soft and rolling southern territories invoked by Woolf, and others, towards a rougher and more hostile northern locale, calling attention not to a quaint or parochial Englishness but to a hardier and more inviolable landscape holding more in common with the border areas of France. This is an empathetic engagement with landscape as territory but also as a common space, epitomizing the shared traditions and concerns of rural life not across Britain but across the Continent itself.

Jameson is also able to illustrate what she imagines are the factors that might lend Alsace its particular regional flavour. Honoré explains that 'everything the French do well we do better. We Alsatians. Every civilisation in Europe has left a drop of its pure essence in our cup. We are as supple as the French, as orderly as the Germans' (1940a: 71). Alsace is always 'proving herself to be what she had always been, neither French nor German but greenly and strictly Alsatian' (1940a: 4). Even Honoré feels 'a cool affection for France. A much warmer one for Alsace' (1940a: 58). Similarly, the opening page of *The Moon Is Making* informs us that 'the fishermen of Under Wik can make themselves understood on the coast of West Freisland to this day' (1937: 3), because the dialects of the north-east coast of Britain are often more easily understood by inhabitants of the Nordic nations than their own southern countrymen, emphasizing a commonality with the Continent which undermines national identity. Wik, she writes, stands with 'its back to the rest of England and its face to the sea and to the coasts and harbours of strange lands there' (1937: 273), and both regions are characterized in each novel by the need to identify beyond the nation and often with other nations. These regional identities are, for Jameson, part of the 'living nerves which bind nation to nation' (1935b: 11) and which join all European nations in times of threat. In another reversal of the traditional wartime emphasis on the national rather than the international, these novels draw on the regional to make the case for a shared European culture, one which must recognize its similarities in order to save itself.

It is these regional landscapes, then, which symbolize points of identification for the characters, an identification far more visceral than their feelings of duty or loyalty to either France or England. In *The Moon Is Making*, Ezekiel has far more compassion for his fields and their produce than for his family. He neglects his children, quarrels with his neighbours and ignores his brother Handel. Ezekiel's land is 'the only creature – he thought of it as a living being – on whom he was prepared to spend money' (1937: 16). His emotional attachment to this land expresses itself in an intimate and almost extra sensory knowledge – 'he boasted that he had known the thunder was coming three days before it came' (1937: 300) – one missing entirely from his human interactions. Honoré shares this same compassion and knowledge of the land, advising his neighbour that the shorter the vine 'the longer they'll hang in a good year, until they're rotten-sweet' (1940a: 146), and displaying a sensual attachment to his vineyard as, eyeing it greedily one day, 'he seemed to want to roll all the goodness of the vineyard on his tongue' (146). Both men enjoy a physical and emotional connection to the landscape of their home which far exceeds any human connection either to family or to nation as community. This is a territory which they wish to embrace, possess and protect, and this sense of territory as both a living thing and a possession dominates both narratives, uniting both characters across national boundaries.

Beyond this visceral physical connection to the land, Honoré and Ezekiel also reflect each other's temperaments and attitudes: Ezekiel has more in common with the unreasonable, penny-pinching French landowner than with the rest of Britain. As Jan Marsh notes, during the nineteenth and early twentieth centuries it was the peasant who underwent an immense transition in popular culture, 'from a dumb boorish fellow to a loved and respected figure bearing the weight of all of the wisdom and virtue ascribed to the English countryside' (1982: 71). Although both Ezekiel and Honoré certainly command respect and show a great deal of skill and knowledge, they are far from demonstrating either wisdom or virtue. Both men refuse to pay their workers properly, hoard their money, abandon their children and avoid serving their countries in the First World

War in order to make greater returns from their businesses. Their affections towards the land, then, can be seen to stem chiefly from their own greed for the financial and social rewards afforded them by their ownership of it. Both men's ruthlessness and, most importantly, their individuality and indifference to the rest of the nation are reflected in the other inhabitants of Jameson's rural idylls: Wik-born Merry Jordan tells her southern husband that 'you don't know yet what the Wik character is – or you would come among them as a strong man armed. They have so much courage and force of life that one only wishes they could be civilised' (1937: 129). The exaggeration of this greed and cruelty represents an ironic undercutting of the idealized countryside and the simple-minded peasant metaphor, but the affection which remains in each portrayal serves primarily to emphasize the similar personalities at work on either side of the Channel, both of which seem to have more in common with each other than with their countrymen in Paris or London. Moreover, each man's refusal to acknowledge the world beyond his land, his needs and his prosperity provides a damning indictment of the shortcomings of an isolationist viewpoint, one reflective of attitudes in both England and France to Nazi aggression elsewhere in the continent.

Through the traditional rural identities that they represent, Honoré and Ezekiel support a romanticization of rural life which enables the maintenance of feudal power structures. Both rich landowners, they enjoy a certain level of status in their respective regions through their continued subordination of the peasant and working-class population. Theirs is not always a patriotic commitment to nation and tradition, but one which maintains their own power and the subordination of others: Honoré openly refuses to believe his colleagues who inform him that 'we are living in a new age, an age where justice has to be done to all classes' (1940a: 120), rejecting the requests of the union of workers at his factory for better conditions. Just as Honoré rejects France in order to make money from his German business interests, so too Ezekiel is content to turn his back on his own countrymen and indeed, his own family, viewing himself not as English or even British, but as a Yorkshireman. This is what underpins both men's visceral connection to their land: it is the source of their livelihood, their power and their social standing. Ezekiel may only spend money on his land but that is because that land makes a more tangible financial contribution, through the animals and crops which it produces and nurtures. The human inhabitants of each man's life are of little monetary or political value and are therefore discarded and ignored. Honoré and Ezekiel are not presented uncritically, nor are the traditions they represent; what Jameson's novels point toward is that even the flaws in their ways of life are held in common, creating parallels between English rural life and French rural life which hint at a Europe-wide sense of inequality, of a conservatism which is not benign in its clinging to tradition but is avaricious, inward-looking and self-serving. The negative characteristics shared by these two men, and the ways of life which they represent, offer another motivation for European cooperation – the building of a fairer, less materialistic society – as I come to discuss in the next chapter.

It was Jameson's acceptance of the Europe-wide nature of this threat of war, coupled with her conviction even as early as 1935, that 'I am a good little Englander on one side [...] and on the other I try to be a good European' (1939e: 253), which caused her to abandon her pacifism and prompted her to set her novels for the rest of war in occupied Europe. She wished to combine her regionalism and her desire to defend her England (Yorkshire) with her long-standing sense of what it meant to be 'a good European' and saw these not as exclusive identities but as mutually informing. Jameson came to stand, like Wik, with her back to the rest of England facing out to sea and towards the coasts and strange harbours of Europe. Her work of the late 1930s demonstrates not only her personal interest – since her childhood trips on her father's ship she had been a fascinated and frequent visitor to the Continent – but a desire to show her fellow 'Little Englanders', those who resisted foreign influence and expansion, that theirs was a shared struggle. Jameson employs the same rural idylls and peasant characters as English isolationist rhetoric to draw comparisons between Britain and Europe and to promote a sense of mutual threat, reflecting her own changed attitudes to war. She was not a political conservative perhaps, yet, like her Yorkshireness, her Englishness and her Frenchness, her conservatism appears to be an identity through which she passes and which leaves certain indelible marks on her writing of this period. If, as Light asserts, conservativism might involve 'a commitment to family life, to the idea of nationhood, to the notion of necessary authority' (1991: 18) then there are stirrings still of conservative tendencies in these novels in particular; the romanticization of the Yorkshire and Alsatian landscapes; the fierce libertarianism of two central characters whom the author regards with some distaste but also, in some sense, with a degree of respect and even admiration for a simpler more authentic way of life rooted in the landscape of home. It is not only her pacifism but in some sense the latent conservatism exemplified by her romanticization of rural life which is displayed as it is dispelled in her novels of this period and which demonstrates her ambivalence towards the coming war.

'France was in the greatest danger since the Marne': Territory and tradition under threat

This French landscape was not only a point of commonality between a rural and regional Britishness and a rural and regional Frenchness; it was also the physical territory over which the war would be fought. This was an anxiety prominent in the minds of both the French people, and of Jameson herself, as the fall of France became increasingly likely. It was particularly troubling in light of the First World War, which had taken place on French soil just twenty years before and which still scarred the landscape and the minds of its inhabitants. In *Cousin Honoré*, this French countryside and its inhabitants become the point of origin for the nation itself, which, as Raymond Williams explains, is widely viewed as 'the land from which directly or indirectly we all get our living and the achievements of human society is deeply known' (1975: 9). This is the oldest element of the nation, the territory which defines its traditions and its identity, encapsulating all of the qualities which Jameson most admires in France and in French culture. The German threat was both to this territory and to the customs and traditions it engendered and which defined the nation in the eyes of its people. Alongside this understanding of national and regional identity, Jameson conveys in *Cousin Honoré* the threat from Germany to Europe through her rendering of French territory and French bodies. Furthermore, through the ways in which Honoré relates to the landscape and defines himself and France against these threats, Jameson expounds her own sense of the relation of one individual citizen to nation in these times of personal and national threat.

The main element underpinning Honoré's connection to this French landscape is his family's long-standing presence in the area. For Honoré his primary duty is 'first and foremost as bailiff to land that had belonged to Burckheims for centuries' (1940a: 3). The novel reflects this and is divided into sections across his lifetime in order to better explain this long-standing relationship and the changes it underwent in 1939 in the approach to war. The novel begins: 'When Honoré Burckheim was a child of eleven years, the city he lived in ceased to be French and became German. In December 1918 he was fifty-nine, Strasbourg had been French again for almost a month and he had forgotten the intervening years' (1940a: 3). Honoré's indifference to the manoeuvrings of the modern nation stems from an allegiance to the land and produce with which he is in constant physical contact in his role as winegrower. This land is his nation and his identity, and he is little troubled by the nationality of its occupants, provided it does not interfere with his own traditions and customs. The Alsatian landscape forms a crucial aspect of his sense of self and of belonging. This is informed by Jameson's own understanding of French notions of statehood: more than a decade later, she still believed that 'the French nation could survive even if the French state broke down on the people's indifference to its health' (1954: 450). His indifference to the well-being of the French state demonstrates Jameson's sense that the nation is not defined or even represented by the state but is a much less tangible and more instinctual concept. This provides an interesting contrast to Jameson's socialist convictions, which of course foreground the responsibilities of the state to support and bring together its citizens, showing another tenet of the latent conservatism which runs through this novel. Jameson is not wholly in favour of Honoré's indifference to the state, one suspects, but rather admires something of his wilful simplicity, one familiar from her experiences in Whitby as I have discussed.

Honoré's attachment to the Alsatian landscape stretches far beyond his personal history: he feels that the close relationship he enjoys with the land through his work among the vines means that his own fate is tied to that of the French landscape as an extension of his own body. This bodily connection to France is such that, in 1939, he can sense that 'France was in the greatest danger since the Marne, and that he himself would not live forever' (1940a: 148). Jules Reuss, his closest aid and employee, echoes this sentiment as 'his own mind, confusing himself and Alsace, was paralysed by the danger approaching both of them' (1940a: 261). The link between the landscape and the human body is a familiar trope in Jameson's writing of this period: the French Officer Aubrac in *The Other Side* (1946) also describes the roads of one's home country as 'the continuation outside you of your nerves' (1946: 56) and the British soldiers in *The Fort* (1941) feel a close connection to the French landscape in which they once lived and fought, suggesting that it is easy in times of threat to identify bodily with a landscape similarly threatened with physical destruction by the same guns and armies of conquest. For Honoré, as for the men in *The Fort* and *The Other Side*, it is this connection between the landscape and its inhabitants that feeds the sense of a 'danger approaching both of them' (1940a: 261) and which anchors the citizen's bodily safety, through landscape, to the threatened nation.

Of course, it is not only male bodies which are associated with this landscape. Honoré's referral to France in the feminine 'she' and 'her' illustrates prevailing attitudes to nation as both woman and subject to male protection. This is a familiar cultural discourse during times of war in which, as Gill Plain describes, 'the nation is feminised as an indicator of its vulnerability and its need for protection' (1996: ix). This is also reflected in government policies: French women did not receive the vote until 1946, yet their bodies remained a territory to be policed within the nation, not an active agent in its political or social life, but a valuable possession. This association of the female body with territory or landscape is a long-standing area of discussion for feminist scholars, creating a link between woman and nature which problematizes women's relationship to systems of political and military power. The female is, as scholars such as Ruth Lister note, never accepted as a full citizen because 'behind the cloak of gender neutrality that embraces the idea [of citizenship] there lurks in much of the literature a definitely male citizen and it is his interests and concerns that have traditionally dictated the agenda' (1997: 3). The female citizen is thus always problematized in times of war, as I have discussed elsewhere (Cooper, 2014), while her body is simultaneously deployed as a symbol of the nation under threat.

In *Cousin Honoré*, and in the eyes of Honoré himself, the French landscape is frequently associated with the body of the French peasant woman and vice versa. Honoré sees his love for one reflected onto the other, as he describes seeing a woman in a field one day and deciding that the reason 'he must have her [was] because suddenly she gathered into herself the warmth of the day, the scent, the hills [...] he wanted to enjoy in her Alsace' (1940a: 17). Like the countryside itself, she embodies the 'authentic' and 'traditional' France, one which he, the French citizen, wishes to preserve but also to possess. As Anne McLintock observes, 'Women are represented as the atavistic and authentic "body" of national tradition (inert, backward-looking, and natural) embodying nationalism's conservative principle of continuity' (1993: 66). This female body represents not only a racial but a cultural continuity, one which safeguards both the purity of the nation and its traditions. Through this long-held association of women with landscape and, indeed, with nature, the novel plays upon the patriarchal associations of territorial conquest and of national identity itself: the French woman must be protected, as the landscape is, from possession or contamination by invaders.

Feminist criticism has long noted this conflation of female bodies with territory, not only in wartime but also as a metaphor for nation, fertility and control.[4] In Luce Irigaray's seminal study *Elemental Passions* (1992), like the landscape itself, 'the mother is seen as the earth substance which must be cultivated and inseminated so that it may bear fruit' (1992: 2). For Irigaray, the female body, through its ability to reproduce, is always regarded as a territory for production and cultivation, and thus for control. During wartime, and even times of national threat, this association can severely curtail women's reproductive and political freedoms. As Michael Burleigh observes, 'Anxieties about a decline in birthrate and the need for pronatalist state policies were commonplace in interwar Europe' (2001: 229), a point which impacted upon women's rights during this period and which was both informed by and informed a growing tendency to associate female fertility with both territory to be defended and with the ability of the nation to defend itself.[5] Throughout the 1930s, as another war became increasingly likely, French social policy also began to reflect these concerns. In the latter years of the Third Republic and the early years of Vichy, pro-natalist policies were introduced to try to encourage French women to reproduce: the French state had outlawed abortion and contraception in the 1920s, perhaps as a reflection of anxieties about population following the First World War and in 1939 launched financial incentives to reward those having families. In fact, part of Daladier's Family Code of this time promised loans to young couples buying land and reducing payments each time they had a child, further enforcing the association of fertility and family with the possession and maintenance of territory.

Honoré's daughter is particularly emblematic of this association. Anne-Marie Eshelemer, is, by 1939, and the main section of the novel, middle-aged. Honoré sees in her 'the wide throat of the young peasant' (1940a: 17), but her now forty-year-old body bears even more of the marks of the French landscape and he describes how 'the lines of Anne-Marie's face seemed to darken, as though they were rivers cutting deeper into the French soil' (1940a: 215). In the eyes of Honoré and others, Anne-Marie's body represents the French national community, just as the landscape of France is a physical manifestation of the French nation as territory. The fruit that it bears is the future of the French nation itself, its children. The 'fertile earth' (1992: 2) of the female body to which Irigaray refers in her discussion is, in this novel, always a site for contamination by other races and nations and must be protected. Where his land provides Honoré with a lucrative livelihood, his wives and his peasant lover have brought him produce in the form of children, making *their* valuable bodies similarly worthy of defence against the German threat and racial contamination.

As if to actuate this anxiety about French female bodies, and in an echo of the repeated invasion of the Alsatian landscape she represents, Anne-Marie marries a German. This is, for Honoré and the other Frenchmen, both a pollution of the national community *and* an invasion of French territory, representing an incursion in both bodily and literal terms. Honoré harangues her repeatedly for allowing herself to be possessed by such a historic enemy and one whose occupation was tied to the power of the state over the individual: 'Why, if you had to marry a customs official, did you pick a German one?' (1940a: 104). He is doubly aggrieved that the closest approximation he has to a male heir, Anne-Marie's son Henry, is half German: 'if there's anything of our family in him, he thought, it's been overlain by Germany – that ugly German father of his' (1940a: 104). For Honoré, this represents a loss for France, as Anne-Marie has failed to provide both Honoré and France itself with a sufficiently French grandson. As a consequence, Anne-Marie and her son Henry are ostracized from the Burckheim community. The employment, and indeed the enjoyment, of Anne-Marie's body by this foreigner makes her an alien within the conservative rural village. Her legal and bodily possession by a German serves as a constant reminder to the villagers of the threat from what Honoré refers to as the 'yellow-haired rank-smelling savages ferrying themselves across the Rhine to descend on the swirling fields and vineyards' (1940a: 159) – this colonizing of Anne-Marie's 'French' body by the enemy serves as a reminder of the vulnerability of the physical territory of the French nation.

Whilst, as Jane Garrity points out, British women writers during this period often sought to play upon these associations of women's bodies with national territory. The use both of French countryside rather than British and of Honoré's gaze upon both the female body and the French countryside it represents, complicates Jameson's portrayal. This serves to distance her from this discourse of woman as nation, whilst simultaneously preventing her from being able to deploy it, as Garrity suggests other female writers do during this time, to 'invert the dynamic of female passivity and male action' (2003: 19). Instead, the French nation is mediated and understood through the male gaze, enforcing stereotypes of man as the idealized citizen and undermining the agency of Jameson's female characters. I would suggest that this does not function as a critique of the position of the male citizen but in this novel represents another point of latent conservatism in which Jameson seems to unquestioningly deploys traditional associations between the feminine, the rural and tradition as a reflection of her own ambivalent feelings towards nationhood, belonging and the war itself.

Honoré's sense of this belonging, the connection he makes between natality and nationality, means that, as war approaches, he becomes increasingly distrustful of those not born in France. Although he was initially charmed by the novelty of taking an American wife, Caroline, when he feels the French nation to be vulnerable he becomes hostile towards her precisely because of her difference and the threat which her foreignness symbolizes. In lacking this natal connection to the landscape she is lacking in the ethnonationalist qualification which acts as a populist definition of nation in Europe in the early twentieth century.[6] For critics such as Walker Connor, nation is synonymous with ethnonationalism, as a 'group of people who believe they are ancestrally-related' (1994: xi). The civic inscriptions of nationhood as based on statehood and shared experiences sought to efface this link with birthplace and race; however, the ethnonationalism of the modern nation, especially in the early twentieth century, sought to trace these connections back again to descent from specific bloodlines and geographical locations. Caroline shares many scenes in the novel with Anne-Marie and the Englishwoman Blanche Berthelin, because they all exist outside Honoré's French nation, as foreigners, as contaminated by the enemy, and as women. As the likelihood of German invasion grows, Caroline gets 'her first taste of that impulse the French feel to turn on the stranger within their gates – any stranger will serve – in the shock of danger' (1940a: 93). Honoré believes that she does not understand what it is to be European and under threat, telling her that 'you know nothing about Germans looking at their vines and fields and praying' (1940a: 21). In setting his wife up in opposition to France, the novel highlights Honoré's change of heart as the threat increases. He watches his wife enter the room on the brink of war, describing her as 'this big, barren woman: the American woman, he thought, stripping her in one second of thirty years of marriage, and of all her anxious honourable wish to become French' (1940a: 252) even referring to her as a 'foreigner' and telling her that she 'better clear out of France'(1940a: 253). As Caroline comes to represent a threat to this nation, to this landscape, through her nationality, Honoré comes to accept that he belongs to this landscape and to France in a way that he will never belong to his wife because she does not share this bond.

As an American, Caroline is regarded as an alien and a threat to traditional life within the village but her husband's description of her as 'barren' evokes another key concern and perceived threat to Europe during the 1930s, not only in Jameson's work but in other popular discourses, from literature to politics. Using a comparison with Anne-Marie, already established as the embodiment of the French countryside, Caroline's body is marked out as sterile and asexual, and she feels inadequate and unfeminine: 'beside the soiled body of the peasant woman, mis-shapen, deformed by work, by her single hard child-bearing, Caroline's own body, smooth and powdered after a bath into which she poured pine essence, seemed feeble, like dough set to rise' (1940a: 62). Anne-Marie's body is both abject in its decay and emphatically natural, whereas Caroline's seems incomplete, like 'dough set to rise' because it is smooth, unblemished and, crucially, unproductive. Caroline's failure to have Honoré's French child represents another way in which she has failed to enter into a relationship with the French landscape through maternity. Her inability to do so seems to represent a bodily rejection not only of motherhood but of France itself.

Caroline's infertility comes to symbolize anxieties about falling birth rates linked to an industrialization and a modernity emblematic of the rural conservatism at the centre of *Cousin Honoré*. The comparison between Caroline and Anne-Marie immediately sets out the differences between the two nations as Jameson saw them: America, the future, as modern, sterile, over-sanitized, and France, the past, as natural, fecund and productive. Caroline's affiliation with the modernity of her homeland, and her independence from the land and from domestic work, sets her apart from her French counterparts, echoing contemporary fears that increased female independence, city-living and industrialized modernity, associated with America in the popular imagination, was responsible for falling birth rates across Europe. This anxiety, not only about fertility in and of itself but of the ability of the nation to reproduce itself and, crucially for this particular period, to produce future citizens to defend it and to maintain levels of production in times of both war and peace, is precisely what France's interwar pro-natal policies were designed to address. It was also a familiar trope in the literary work of the period.[7] Jameson writes in *A Challenge to Death*:

> Apart from the certainty of war, it is worth remembering that the latest and most trustworthy investigations into population growth discover a startling decline in fertility in industrialised nations – as if, despairing of any other solution of the paradox of wasted food and wasted individual lives, nature was preparing to solve it by the death of the species. (1935: 12)

This industrialization, encapsulated by America and at odds with the traditional rural life depicted in *Cousin Honoré*, forms another element of the threat to Europe which Jameson detected in the 1930s, as I discuss in the next chapter. For the purposes of my reading of this novel, these links between female bodies and national decline further cement the association of the female with the French landscape.

Even Honoré's death emphasizes this relationship between nationhood and natality, his desire to return to the earth with which he shares this emotional and physical connection, emphasizing the trope of nation as mother. As war approaches, and Honoré approaches the final days of his life, he visits the local priest, chanting under his breath that 'they shall sit every man under his wine and under his fig tree; and none shall make them afraid' (1940a: 258). This biblical quote, taken from the Book of Micah, is not testament to Honoré's acceptance of God in his final hours but to his spiritual connection to the landscape and his convictions about his rights and place within it. Even in death his respect for this landscape far exceeds that which he holds for his banished wife or his daughter – the mourners at Honoré's funeral remark that 'it was probably his greater respect for the vines that kept him from demanding to be buried at the other side of the low wall separating the vineyard from the park' (1940a: 273). Moreover, there is a sense here of the nation as mother earth to which men might return upon death, enacting a different kind of control and invasion. Irigaray writes in *An Ethics of Sexual Difference* (1993) that woman, mother, is typically understood in terms of place and, in particular, of home and belonging (1993: 35), that the child 'belongs to that body and is fed by the body until it comes into the world' (1993: 46). This return marks a re-making of the land in the image of Honoré but also a return in which he, for a final time, enacts his possession of it, this final bodily union with the French landscape making his Frenchness inviolable.

In the novel, physical threat to the nation is also combined with an ideological danger, one which reflects Jameson's own fears for Europe and European civilization as she understands it. France is under attack, not only from the modernity epitomized by American progress and urban living, but also from Nazi politics. For Honoré, the French nation is a matter of ideology, of attitudes and of characteristics, many of which can be seen to stem from his own ideas about the Alsatian landscape. He believes that the French character naturally lacks the 'servility' he attributes to the Germans (1940a: 91), where 'the very injustices that make a Frenchman or an Englishman rush into the street or into Hyde Park, or form societies, or refuse to pay income tax, send a German into an ecstasy of self-sacrifice' (1940a: 91). The same hardy stubbornness which he feels in the fields and vines of Alsace and in its inhabitants naturally repels this will to obey. Servility or subordination of any kind contradicts, for Honoré, the principles on which the French state has been constructed (*liberté, égalité, fraternité*) and therefore represents a threat to the French nation as it was created and is perceived by its citizens. Without these ideas the Germans are primitive; they are 'not a people, they're a tribe, with a tribal leader and loyalties. One can't meet them on equal terms any longer' (1940a: 91). His cousin and close confidant Rene Hoffmeyer echoes this view, asking as war approaches, 'How can a country which sets the standard of freedom and equality be defeated by a nation to whom these dreams are unknown?' (1940a: 210). Hoffmeyer echoes Jameson's convictions about France as a nation which represents Europe's most highly-prized ideals, but he also expresses a French arrogance about its invincibility, an arrogance which it is suggested might lead to France's undoing.

For the Frenchmen in the novel, just as for the historian A.J.P. Taylor in his controversial contemporary study *The Course of German History* (1945), Germany's fall to Nazism represents a fundamental flaw in their national character, one which the rest of Europe does not possess. Taylor asserts a view shared by many historians and commentators at the time on the first page of his *The Course of German History* (1945): 'The history of the Germans is a history of extremes' (2001: 1). For Taylor, Nazism could not have happened to any other nation. Despite significant pressure from other writers and historians, he maintained this view in his 1961 edition of the book, arguing that, in terms of German history, 'it is no more a mistake for the German people to end up with Hitler than it is an accident when a river flows into the sea' (Taylor, 2001: xvii). Later historians have refuted this view, arguing that what happened in Germany after the First World War can be seen 'paradoxically, in some way as a modernisation crisis within a modernised country' (Kershaw and Lewin, 1997: 347) akin to that which took place in other European countries around this time. In light of this, Jameson's analysis of the French and their attitudes both towards Germany and the French nation itself seems very much of its time. Further the novel's exploration of French attitudes towards Germany and towards French defeat seems particularly well placed in light of that defeat. Jameson suggests, perhaps, that in the case of these nationalistic and nostalgic Frenchmen, pride comes before a fall.

Furthermore, her discussion of France's own uneasy relationship to the modernity which Honoré associates, by turn, with the Germans and with the Americans points to France's own crisis of modernization during this period. Honoré's obsession with the rural and with the landscape represents a clear parallel with the myths perpetuated by the Frenchman's purported enemy. The Nazi regime was founded on ideas surrounding a return to rurality, concerns over modern femininity and female independence and declining birthrate, and the nation as a feminized territory to be regulated and protected by men, reflecting many of the concerns of the conservative Frenchmen in the novel. As Roderick Stackelberg suggests, Nazi Germany 'romanticized a rural agrarian lifestyle and inveighed against the insidious consequences of rampant industrialism and urbanization' (1998: 125), just as Honoré does in the novel. While Honoré associates Germany with a threatening modernity in which German people are 'working twenty-four hours a day, seven days a week in armaments factories' (1998: 91), Germany itself was deploying alongside this more conservative principles of nationality, blood and soil. Blood and soil, *Blut und Boden*, formed the basis of Hitler's figuring of the Germans as a unique and superior race. These ideas stemmed from the nineteenth-century *Volkisch* movement, which believed that 'Aryan blood was superior to alien blood and German soil was superior to foreign soil [...] and the full greatness of the German Volk – biological and moral – came from the special connection between Aryan blood and Germany's soil' (Victor, 2000: 136). Honoré's associations of the natal with the national, along with his allegiance to the soil, in many ways tie him to this aspect of Nazism. Here, the novel draws a telling parallel between the myths of nation at work in Europe during this time, suggesting perhaps Jameson's instinctual sense of a compulsion, in both herself and others, to return to the myths of the rural in the face of a growing and threatening modernity.

It also serves to illustrate some of the problems inherent in Honoré's own conservatism, a conservatism in which Jameson herself is at least partly complicit. Just as many of the images of idealized France are characterized as Honoré's point of view, the prevalence of these attitudes in the book hints at Jameson's own lifelong love of France and her admission in her autobiography that 'my France, still only half industrialized, out of step with less sane, less human neighbours, can keep the savour of civilisation founded on good bread, four hundred different cheeses, and heaven knows how many different wines' (1984a: 263). These romantic yearnings for a France shrouded in tradition and rustic charm highlight again Jameson's ambivalent attitude towards the nation as both a site for continuity and also a landscape ripe for potentially revolutionary socialist change. While, as I discuss shortly, Jameson was committed to socialist change and to the improvement of Europe, perhaps through the destruction of war, there remains within her writing a tendency to laud tradition and to partake in certain national and imperialistic myths surrounding European superiority and a particularly Western European idealism about certain nations and their values.

These two novels move through a national and isolationist viewpoint, which can be linked directly to Jameson's pacifism, and then to a wider empathy with Europe, from France to Hungary, which reflects her decision to support the war and to defend Europe at all costs. Jameson argued in 1935 that 'only to live, and to grow to full strength, [Britain] must make advances to become part of a larger family' (1935a: 328), and by 1939 she had come to realize that Britain's presence as part of this family meant acting in defence of it and all of its constituent parts. For Jameson, becoming part of Europe was essential to Britain's survival and it is, in many ways, her sense of the regional that underpins this readiness to identify beyond Britain, particularly at this time of threat. Her strong identification with Yorkshire, articulated through her sympathetic and indulgent depiction of Yorkshire's idiosyncrasies in *The Moon Is Making*, enables her to distance herself from isolationist rhetoric about Englishness and to look beyond this to the Continent, sounding out her sense both of shared culture and of shared challenges in *Cousin Honoré*. The use of the pastoral and the invocation of the rural to advocate for greater British involvement with the European cause, and particularly the French cause, marks a reversal of the tendency for this sort of imagery to be adopted to isolationist and pacifist ends more in keeping with such a conservative viewpoint. As a result these novels both support and critique the pastoral as a model for isolationist and pacifist thinking, perhaps in an attempt to encourage readers to think sympathetically of their European neighbours and to defend shared though imperfect ways of living. The ambivalence towards these conservative tropes represents the push-pull of Jameson's own attitudes, to peace and war, tradition and progress, even the regional and the centre. As such, they mark a crucial turning point in Jameson's own intellectual journey, gesturing towards more than two decades of work which would engage, not only with Britain and the British, but with Czechoslovakia, Germany, France, Austria and even Cyprus, and which would embrace more progressive attitudes towards modernity, nationhood and citizenship.

2

'The tide of cruelty': *Europe to Let* and the path to war

Just as *Cousin Honoré* explores the nature of the threat to traditional and rural life, in *Europe to Let: The Memoirs of an Obscure Man*, also published in 1940, Jameson presents the sense of threat within a number of urban settings. Here, her vision of Europe expands beyond Britain and France to take in Germany, Austria, Czechoslovakia and Hungary and, as a result, the sense of threat is much more multilayered and far more wide-ranging. It is insidious, existing within the European city both in the guise of fascist mobs and a technologically-advanced modernity, in poverty-stricken slums and the endless flood of refugees and displaced persons through the bedsits of Vienna, Prague and Paris. It comes, in the minds of the characters, not specifically from a militant and aggressive Germany, but from an all-encompassing rot within modern progress itself. This preoccupation with progress and with civilization which grows throughout Jameson's work of the 1930s culminates in *Europe to Let* but appears in various forms in *The Moon Is Making, Here Comes a Candle* (1939) – set in a decaying London slum – and *Cousin Honoré*. As Jameson wrote in an article in the *TLS* in 1939, 'If France and England were defeated in this war, civilisation would recede in Europe' (47). Her sense here that England and France are the last bastions of a dying European culture and civilization, as Nazism moves across the Continent, emphasizes her sense of this as a cultural war, far above and beyond its territorial implications. Her concern is for the cultures and values which might be lost and it is these which she reflects upon in her most ambitious and wide-ranging novel of the period.

It is the cities of France and England which she links most clearly to civilization. As Desmond Harding has noted, the city has always been linked to civilization, both etymologically in the Latin roots of *civis* (citizen) or *civitas* (citizenry/citizenship) and as a 'critical mass which produces civilisation' (2004: 5). Harding draws upon Lewis Mumford's vision of the city as 'both a container and transmitter of culture' arguing that 'the idea of the city for Mumford constituted possibility, with civilisation passing on from one generation to the next the fruits of human achievement' (2004: 6). This association is particularly important in terms of Jameson's portrayal of the cities of Europe in *Europe to Let*. In the novel she scours these cities for answers to the questions which plague her writing – and the writing of many others during the late 1930s – about the nature of progress and civilization and whether both are at an end or are indeed linear processes at all. Paul Saint-Amour writes similarly of an 'anticipatory syndrome' in the interwar years in which 'early twentieth century military practices, particularly the aerial bombardment of civilians and population centres, fundamentally altered the temporality of urban experience, turning cities and towns into spaces of rending anticipation' (2015: 8–9). *Europe to Let* brings together five of these anxious cities, fresh from the experience of the First World War to explore them as sites for anxiety, trauma and alienation. The novel circles endlessly the question of whether the city is the full expression of civilization or is the architect of its downfall. In *Europe to Let*, Jameson traces through Europe the signs and symptoms of disease and its probable causes, with the city as both instigator and victim of the decline or even the reversal of human progress.

As I have discussed earlier, Jameson partly attributes this decline in civilization to what she refers to as 'the Nazi contempt for the individual soul' (1941a: 14), to her unease with the fascist ideal of man (or woman) as part of an amorphous and inexpressive mass, dedicated simply to fulfilling the duties of the state and without free thought or speech. She comes to advocate war because the only other option 'is submission, the concentration camp, the death of our humblest with our best, the forcing of our children's minds into an evil mould' (1941a: 25). This submission, an abnegation of democracy and justice and the suppression of individual thought and expression, would mark the end of all that Jameson values in European civilization. *Europe to Let* explores different perspectives on European civilization through comparing the viewpoints of a range of different characters across a number of countries and in doing so gives a sense, not of an English or French isolationism, but of experiences of threat, occupation and invasion across the Continent. It foregrounds the links between European cities and nations, the shared nature of European culture and history, and the validity of European claims to be civilized at all. Furthermore, this novel presents a case not only for what was under threat in Europe by the end of the 1930s, but also for what may be gained from the destruction or partial destruction of Europe. The outbreak of war in this novel offers both despair and loss, but also hope for a better future, particularly for Britain, which Jameson describes as a 'bad mother', adding, 'Let her treat us better when it is over' (1941a: 45). Jameson hopes that war will improve Britain and will make it more equal and more compassionate towards its citizens, particularly the poor and disadvantaged. Indeed, she hopes that this transformation will not be limited to Britain but that war might offer not only victory over the Nazis, but also the transformation of a failing Europe.

It is this sense of Europe as a flawed whole, and of the interaction of the nations therein, which characterizes all of Jameson's war novels and which undergoes a crucial evolution in the novels examined here and in the previous chapter. Birkett writes that 'Exploring the European dimension of Englishness, from the early 1930s, [Jameson] came to see in the fostering of European loyalties and European structures, beyond the deadly straightjacket of national identities the chance to create a new and better community for the future' (2009: 4). Jameson remained critical of nationalism itself, but she viewed national identity as far more than a 'straightjacket': she regarded it as a tool for mutual understanding, for cultural advancement and for democratic progress. In fact, *Europe to Let* is the first to hint that beyond the 'European dimension of Englishness' that Birkett suggests, there may be better possibilities for Europe, and for Britain itself. The novel is the first of Jameson's oeuvre to stand in direct opposition to the wider literary climate of this period, which concentrates chiefly on an inward-looking examination of England and Englishness as both Esty and MacKay point out, pushing to describe conflict from a range of European viewpoints. Discussing Jameson's work in light of that of her contemporaries, from historians such as R.H. Tawney and A.J.P. Taylor to writers such as Aldous Huxley, George Orwell and Katherine Burdekin, this chapter uncovers the ways in which her work interacts with discourses around threat at the time, engaging with her growing unease about how Europe might be saved and even whether it is worth saving at all.

'Something must be done to stop the rot': Capitalism, civilization and the threat to Europe

Jameson's sense of the Continent in *Europe to Let* and her criticism of Enlightenment ideas around progress and modernity echo the widespread belief that there was a 'gradual ruin spreading like a stain' (Auden, 1930: 26) across England and even Europe during the interwar period.[1] In a reversal of traditional associations of civilization with modernity and with progress, this sense of decline stems from anxieties about the linear nature of progress itself and its implications for humanity's future. For Jameson, Europe has lost its moral compass, demonstrated by the rise of fascism, poverty and the 'tide of cruelty' (1947a: 46) which she detects engulfing the whole continent in the 1930s. For her Europe was 'to let' at this time because it was at the mercy of whatever ideology offered to fill the vacuum left by this declining civilization and the liberal ideologies which it espoused. The novel begins in Cologne with a section entitled 'The Young Men Dance', as the city's inhabitants struggle through the effects of the First World War and rail against the economic sanctions imposed by the Allies at Versailles, leaving them vulnerable to the angry rhetoric of the Nazi party. In the second section, 'Between March and April', it moves to Vienna as the city's inhabitants come to terms with the Nazism in their midst, as well as that brought by their German invaders, before moving on again to Prague, shortly after the Munich Pact is signed in September 1938. It ends in Budapest, as the city falls to Nazi forces in 'The Children Shall Fear'. Jameson visited many of these cities during the 1930s as part of her duties with PEN, and many of the experiences which the protagonist David Esk describes can be found in her autobiography, *Journey from the North*, such as her trip to Prague with PEN shortly before the Munich Pact (1984a: 374) and to Budapest (1984b: 387). What is at risk in this novel is a European civilization embodied by Europe's history, its architecture and its cultural achievements but which is being overrun by an indifferent modernity and an uncontrolled capitalism, both of which are paving the path to war.

The exact characteristics of this specifically European civilization differ slightly from account to account in the work of Jameson's peers and influences: for Max Weber it was linked intrinsically both to rationalism and to capitalism (Andreski, 1983: 7–8); for Leonard Woolf it was 'the social order secreted by men who are civilised' or certain 'standards of value in social organisation, judgements as to what ought to be the relation between the individual and the community' (1939: 72); while for the historian R.H. Tawney it was linked to social justice and Christian values (Winter, 1978: 24). For the French historian Fernand Braudel 'it would be easy to characterise Western civilisation simply by describing that society and its component parts, its tensions, its moral and intellectual values, its ideals, its habits, its tastes etc. – in other words by describing the people who embody it and who will pass it on' (1994: 16). For him, as for Jameson, this civilization is something which is embodied by its people and by their traditions and practice, and it is their responsibility to 'pass it on'. In the 1930s, it was widely felt that, from the 'bright young things' caricatured in Evelyn Waugh's novels to the inescapable urban sprawl which greets George Bowling in Orwell's *Coming Up for Air* (1936), society no longer embodied any of these civilized values and would therefore fail to pass them on.

This idea of European civilization inspires a multitude of feelings in Jameson's novels and in her characters, from loyalty to disgust, pride to disillusionment, reflecting her own ambivalent attitude to it. She writes in 1941:

> We are watching an attempt, made with a great equipment of science and machines, to destroy an order, materially imperfect, productive by its imperfections of injustice and misery, but constantly being called to book by both our reason and our consciences, and constantly compared with values and standards we did not forget even when we were denying them. (1941a: 24)

This civilization is, as she recognizes, 'materially imperfect' but is mediated by the ideologies, the 'values and standards' which underpin it. Her concern is that these 'values and standards' are being increasingly eroded by the forces of capitalism and fascism and their contempt for the Enlightenment ideals which she values so highly. Here, civilization is a not only a literary and cultural heritage but also a political and philosophical ideal, linked to an age of reason and rationalism. She argues in *A Challenge to Death* that 'in fact Fascism in Italy and National Socialism in Germany are marks of a spread of disrespect for reason which certainly did not begin with them' (1935: 9), echoing views expressed elsewhere in her fiction: that neither Nazism nor fascism is responsible for the demise of civilization but both are a symptom of it. Her novels of the late 1930s come to interrogate this idea, often examining the nature of civilization, its decline and the possibilities, or even desirability, of saving or reforming it. In *The Moon Is Making*, she presents the reverence Handel Wikker has for his books to suggest his sense of culture and humanity, whilst mocking Thomas Money's claim that Wik 'civilise ourselves' (1937: 282) by embracing modern tourism and building a spa for holiday-makers in the town. In *Love in Winter* (1935), she compares the self-sacrifice and commitment to social justice of intellectual Labour MP Louis Earlham with the political convictions of fascist leader Julian Swan, who wishes simply to crush 'the stale and stuffy brothels of democracy' (1935/1984: 122). Despite her clear commitment to the idea of Europe, this European civilization is something towards which Jameson remained deeply ambivalent throughout her life, and this period marks a particular struggle within her writing as she wrestled with its benefits and its pitfalls.

Whatever Jameson's personal attitudes to this civilization, her concern over its future was by no means new and, especially during this period, by no means unique. As Leonard Woolf describes, 'At almost every stage of human history many people have usually quite wrongly thought that the world – their world – was just on the point of coming to an end, that barbarism was breaking in and that civilisation was on the point of being destroyed' (1939: 35). This sort of speculation had begun afresh at the end of the First World War, originating in an article entitled 'The Crisis of the Mind' published by the French poet Paul Valéry in the British periodical *The Atheneum* in May 1919. For many economists, historians and philosophers, civilization, and indeed empire, was a cyclical process, as Marx had proclaimed in the previous century, leading to inevitable entropy and decay. Numerous works examined this possibility, from Oswald Spengler's *The Decline of the West* (1919) to Arnold Toynbee's *A Study of History* (1934). All predicted the inevitable fall of Europe, comparing the modernity of late capitalism to the Roman Empire in its final days. In Jameson's dystopia, *In the Second Year* (1936), the historian R.B. Tower remarks that 'I could draw a convincing parallel with the decline of Rome. There are many likenesses – the vast area of the old empire, the different nationalities it covered, and the standardised Roman culture taken everywhere with the conquerors' (2004: 129).[2] Jameson makes this comparison again in one of her letters to Liddell Hart, comparing Europe in 1939 to 'when Rome was broken' (14 September 1939). During the interwar period, the catalogue of catastrophes that befell Europe and America, from the First World War to the Wall Street crash, all taking place alongside fast-paced social and political change, lent credence to these theories.

For many left-leaning historians, the increasing power of capitalism – of capital as the chief means and motivator of human progress and human interactions – brought with it the inevitable decline of human society. For Tawney and Weber, in the latter stages of history in the West the link between the late-stage capitalism and the decline of a more ideologically-driven civilization was well established. Weber, in 'The Protestant Ethic and the Spirit of Capitalism' (1904), writes of capitalism as a mechanized and uncontainable force for continuous generation of profit because 'in a wholly capitalistic order of society an individual capitalistic enterprise which did not take advantage of its opportunities for profit-making would be doomed to extinction' (1983: 24). Other intellectuals had also made this connection. Walter Benjamin, for example, wrote in 1921 of capitalism as 'a religion which offers not the reform of existence but its complete destruction' (2004: 289). Jameson explains in *The End of This War* that 'the only social change worth working and hoping for involves the death of what R.H. Tawney named the Acquisitive Society' (1941: 40), something which she hopes the war can bring about. Tawney wrote in *The Acquisitive Society* (1920) of a society in which 'the individual enters the world equipped with rights to the free disposal of his property and the pursuit of his economic self-interest' (1920: 21), arguing that these rights to possess and acquire supersede any other interests or functions which that individual may perform, to the detriment of the individual and ultimately of society itself. It is this 'Acquisitive Society' which seems in this novel, as in many of Jameson's other fictional and non-fictional works, to be strangling European culture and through this European civilization itself.

However, the connection between the two is far more intertwined than may first be apparent. To place capitalism and Jameson's idea of a shared European civilization in direct opposition is to fundamentally misunderstand both processes. Jameson's own vision of civilization, as I have discussed, is itself imbued with the values which established the very imperialist hierarchies which themselves led to both economic and political oppression across the world. Its emphasis on European values as derived from Enlightenment thought was itself underpinned the early stages of capitalist progress and the growth of trade, which both sought to inflict European values – European civilization – elsewhere in the world and also worked to establish global flows of capital which would enforce and support these power structures. In Jameson's work, these systems do not exist in opposition to each other; the emphasis on capitalist values of greed, individualism and acquisitiveness seem instead to have subsumed her sense of European democracy, justice and freedom, leaving a vacuum both ideological and moral – forcing Europe to forget the 'values and standards' of European democracy. It was into this vacuum that the forces of fascism and the 'tide of cruelty' seemed to pour, threatening to drown what she saw as the laudable aspects of Europe's 'materially imperfect' cultural and political histories.

In *Europe to Let*, it is the cultural aspects of this shared European civilization which seem most at risk and which can often be seen to embody these shared values. In Prague, in the loggia of the Valdštejn Palace, Esk watches *Romeo and Juliet* and remarks on the 'irony that the purest flame of the Renaissance sprang up only a few weeks before barbarians in S.S. boots trampled it out' (1940b: 146). This flame of European culture and art is anathema to the barbaric forces of Nazism, the freedoms and values which it symbolizes can only be trampled by the indiscriminate barbarity of Nazism symbolized here by the uniformity of the S.S.'s footwear.[3] Similarly, in 'The Hour of Prague', emphasis is placed on another aspect of this shared European intellectual history: the Enlightenment.

Here, after being 'quickly and featedly murdered at Munich, the ghost of Europe squeaks and hovers over Prague from Hradčany' (1940b: 135). Another reference to Jameson's displeasure at the terms of the Munich Pact, this passage highlights the fact that this was an offering which did not appease Hitler, nor prevent him from taking Czechoslovakia as a German Protectorate on 15 March 1939. This ghost signifies the last hope of Europe, crushed when Chamberlain and Hitler agreed to sacrifice Czechoslovakia's sovereignty to preserve the rest of the continent. It returns – in darkly comedic form – after the Nazi invasion of Prague, when, according to the old women of the city, it 'appeared to Hitler's deputy in Hradčany, and scared him into his wits for an instant' (1940b: 135).[4] The ghost emphasizes the Nazi distaste for reason – while such an episode might normally be said to scare someone out of his wits, in scaring Hitler's deputy 'into his wits' it implies the unreasonable and irrational nature at the heart of Nazi ideology. It takes the ghost of Europe, as the (dis)embodiment of Enlightenment thought, to fleetingly return the deputy's critical faculties, before the un-reason of Nazism possesses him once more. This weaponization of Enlightenment ideals to combat Nazism shows the power Jameson sees in Europe's shared past but also its futility in a new world in which witlessness pervades.

However, not all of this shared history is so worthy of pride and celebration. In Mâcon, France, whilst visiting Czechoslovakia's Jan Stelík in exile, Esk remarks that in light of the bloody history of the area through the centuries, 'it had the air of a person violated by torture. Events of this sort, repeated too many times, haunt Europe' (1940b: 150). Mâcon – in Soane-du-loire – had a long-held strategic importance within France and during the Napoleonic wars saw Austrian and French forces engage in a bloody battle to take control of the land. In referencing the centuries-old conflict between European powers, Esk's comment undermines any pretence that Europe, and France itself, might have to being civilized. Despite its cultural achievements, this Europe remains trapped in an endless cycle of war and oppression as its duelling nations vie for power and (economic) superiority. Even within Europe's apparent ideological commitment to democracy and justice, to reason and culture, the 'tide of cruelty' remains irrepressible as a natural expression of human nature and of the drive towards profit and progress.

Yet, against the backdrop of this shared and idealized culture and the communities united by it, it is the negligent and amoral capitalism which Jameson critiques most vehemently in the novel and which remains the most pressing threat to European culture and values. For Jameson, the marked inequality within the cities of Europe is inherently uncivilized and un-European. Capitalism has, as Jameson writes, 'heaped up great riches and great rottenness.

It made magnificent technical advances and used them to dehumanise whole classes' (1941a: 41). Europe has become the backdrop for spivs, profiteers and arms dealers, usually denoted through their exuberant eating and drinking habits in the finest restaurants each city has to offer. Esk describes his disgust at these journalists, political leaders and industrialists, remarking that one 'eats so much that, as my nurse used to say of greedy eaters, I think he must have a worm' (1940b: 116). Even this diagnosis belies a greed and corruption at the heart of those who would profit from Europe's destruction. In a restaurant in Cologne, Hesse and Esk observe a Trade Union official lunching with a rich industrialist, 'though in the Ruhr a few hours away the workers are half starved' (1940b: 17). Similarly, during a brief stay in Paris, Esk frequently dines with corrupt officials who work solely so that 'the bankers, certain rich industrialists would feel safer' (1940b: 162) and who confirm to him the rumours that 'the German steel trust pays Bonnet a salary to preach submission to Germany' (1940b: 159). The reference here to Georges Bonnet, French Foreign Minister between 1938 and 1939, emphasizes another element of this corruption, in which political events might also be influenced by the flows of capital throughout the continent. Bonnet was a controversial figure who strongly advocated French surrender to the Germans, prompting suspicions that he was on the Nazi payroll. Historian Julian Jackson writes in his *The Fall of France: The Nazi Invasion of 1940* (2003) that 'Bonnet was convinced that France, being too weak to act as the policeman of Europe, should extricate itself from its treaty obligations and allow the Germans a free hand in the east' (64). The implication here is Bonnet's loyalty to France, to Europe, is a commodity which might be traded. Not only do these capitalists and profiteers embody the worst excesses of capitalist greed, they also represent a more tangible threat – their corruption spreads into the political systems of Europe, evoking a further and perhaps more troubling aspect to Jameson's title – that Europe may not be simply 'to let'; it could also be convincingly described as 'for sale' to the highest and least scrupulous of bidders.

Indeed, this sense of the pollution of political systems by flows of capital is also expressed in the novel through a sense of bodily corruption or contamination in Europe. Throughout the 1930s and 1940s Jameson repeatedly employs a vocabulary of disease, symptom and cure. Richard Overy describes 'the medicalisation of the language of crisis' (2009: 4) at this time, as writers and intellectuals increasingly sought metaphors of disease, torture and particularly cancer to describe a sense of decline of democracy of the integrity of the nation-state and society at large.[5] *Europe to Let* designates Europe as a body and its inhabitants as a body politic, drawing on a tradition of referring to a people, a community or a continent in bodily terms dating back to ancient times and to early philosophical renderings of the state. In the novel, Esk observes that 'when the cells in our bodies alter, and corrode their neighbours, it's called cancer' (1940b: 269), comparing this bodily corrosion to that of European civilization in 1939, in which nations infected with a 'disease' began to 'corrode their neighbours'. Jameson also writes to Liddell Hart that 'the normal predatory and cannibalistic instincts of men in groups or classes or nations have become abnormal, much as the normal sub-hostility between the cells and tissues of the body can become abnormal and malignant' (19 April 1941). This malignant disease, one characterized by the severity of its treatment and its tendency to spread throughout its host, could be interpreted as either fascism or as capitalism. In either context the prognosis for Europe looks bleak.

Nonetheless, these disease metaphors also necessitate a cure: for the young Nazis living in Cologne in *Europe to Let*, 'something must be done to stop the rot' (1940b: 21) which they see in Europe. For them, conversely, only a fascist (German) state can heal Europe. This possibility of cure and of redemption is also represented in the novel through characters such as Emil Wolf, the surgeon whose hands were destroyed by Nazi torture, the healer who is unable to work not only because of his Jewishness but also because of the barbarity of his fellow men. Wolf, despite his injuries, is filled with hope, telling Esk that 'the world, I tell you, is due to shed a skin [...] half Graeco-Roman, half Christian' but, mindful of his own likely fate as a Jew, adds, 'Ah, how I should like to see these new cities' (1940b: 76). The city for Wolf still marks the zenith of civilization, and the renewal of these works of progress will define Europe's future as they have defined its past. In Cologne, Esk too remarks that 'ahead of us there must be something as primitive as the past, and as green and hopeful' (1940b: 58). This primitivism offers an antidote to the endless pursuit of progress – a reflection perhaps of Jameson's desire in *Cousin Honoré* or *The Moon Is Making* to return to a simpler time, it might represent a stripping back of so-called progress to reveal a new world. That the past might be 'green and hopeful' offers a panacea to the machine age, in which the industrialized city marks the pinnacle but also the demise of modern progress, echoed in the title of this section of the novel: 'Between March and April'. The invocation of these spring months seems to suggest a possibility of cure or renewal as part of a natural cyclical process in which the city and the civilization it represents might be destroyed in order to be remade as a purer and less malevolent expression of human progress.

Moreover, whilst echoing Jameson's sense of the nature – and the imminent demise – of European civilization itself, these novels also indicate the possibility that Europe may be remade as a more equal civilization. In *Here Comes a Candle*, the fire in the slum New Moon Yard at the end of the novel represents another part in this cyclical process. Here, the destruction of Europe acts like a forest fire, generating new growth by trimming back the rottenness of the old world and giving hope that a new Europe will rise phoenix-like from the ashes. Looking out over the ruins after the fire, Pop, the old drifter who lives in New Moon Yard – the name itself is another reference to a cyclical process of waxing and waning – emphasizes this point: 'they say we're all done for, he thought cheerfully: it's the end of the world; England's finished' (1939f: 281). In this novel, as in *Europe to Let*, the dialectic of destruction and rebirth fuels hope for a better European civilization in the future.

Esk expresses not only trepidation through his experiences in Europe at this time but also hope that 'we may return to a civilisation that grows from the earth instead of rushing over it' (1940b: 79). Reflecting fears that, as Esk admits, 'the climate of the world is changing, and it breeds these organisms, blind, destructive, greedy' (1940b: 77), it depicts these 'organisms', their surroundings and their habits to express a sense of shared threat across Europe, demonstrating that what was really at stake at this time was Europe itself, as well as the possibilities for its survival or rebirth which these catastrophic events may yield. For Jameson, the fate of Europe was tied to war itself and the choice, as she saw it, between 'two types of civilisation' (1941a:12). She seems undecided, however, as to which aspects of this civilization constitute the most threatening to European life, the pull towards fascism and extreme politics or the pursuit of profit and productivity tied to the capitalism which she sees as wholly indifferent to and in contravention of European values. *Europe to Let* then becomes a way of depicting this civilization, her ambivalence towards both it and the processes which threatened it, and its own destructive tendencies, as well as a sense of a hope for transformation which would justify another war in Jameson's eyes. This sense of European civilization as 'to let' in the coming war, informs her depictions of Europe at every level and certainly influenced her desire to look outwards towards the Continent in her writing of this period.

'Per me si va ne la città dolente':[6] The city, modernity and progress[7]

In *Europe to Let*, the threat to Europe is characterized by the anonymity, criminality and poverty of the modern city, but it is also threatening to that city itself, as the zenith of modern progress. R.J. Holton observes in *Cities, Capitalism and*

Civilisation (1986) that there exists always an 'association of the city (or at least some cities) with innovation, social change and modernity' and that this often 'is interpreted in a positive way with cities and those who live in them portrayed as agents of "progress," "civilisation" and "enlightenment"' (1986: 1). Yet this association with progress is also often tied to anxieties about the city's nature and usefulness, wherein this same city can also be seen to 'produce social pathology, moral disorder and the destruction of community' (1986: 1). Jameson's city is evoked by this epigraph taken from Dante's *Divine Comedy*, where it appears as the first line of Canto Three of *Inferno* inscribed on the gateway to the outermost layers of Hell. It translates as 'through me you enter the woeful city' (1990: 25). Her use of it here references Jameson's association between the city and, in particular, its slums, and purgatory, or even Hell itself. However, I suggest that in *Europe to Let*, Jameson explores the opposing viewpoints which Holton describes, reconciling her desire to associate the modern city with cultural achievement, with decades of shared European history and culture but also with an unease about the inhumane conditions and processes which it represents and facilitates.

The novel explores the ways in which, as Leonard Woolf wrote the previous year, 'it is not the barbarian at the gate, but in the citadel and in the heart who is the real danger' (1939: 169). In *Europe to Let*, Jameson not only focuses on the threat from outside the city, the storm troopers marching into Vienna or the Allies starving out the Germans in Cologne, for example, but also reflects a Europe-wide anxiety about modernity, poverty and progress taking root in every city she describes. For Ugo Rossi, writing as part of a wave of critiques of the city in the early twenty-first century, 'Cities are no longer viewed merely in relation to capitalism but as its constitutive element' (2014: 10) and Jameson's ambivalence towards the city both as the apparent pinnacle of civilization and culture and also as an expression or constituent of capitalism underpins her portrayal throughout the novel. Rossi goes on that 'ambivalent attitudes towards the urban phenomenon reflect those towards capitalism itself, which is a socio-economic system historically oscillating between hope and despair, between a promise of prosperity and development and an experience of inequity and injustice' (2014: 10). Jameson's sense of hope, stemming from her belief in the artistic and cultural achievements often centring around the modern city, is problematized by the links she makes between capitalism and the acquisitiveness which she sees as undermining these very achievements. For her, the barbarian is indeed at the gate and already inside the citadel, because that citadel has been honed and formed in part by these processes.

These urban spaces are characterized throughout *Europe to Let* as machine-like, corrupting their inhabitants, and encouraging them to embrace the mechanical qualities celebrated by fascism and its artistic and philosophical wings in the futurist movement and the German philosophy of Friedrich Nietzsche and Georg William Friedrich Hegel. For the German Kurt Hesse in the first part of *Europe to Let*, this threatening mechanized metropolis is just as intimidating as the fascist gangs which patrol its streets. The city, for him, is the centre of a new mechanized society. He worries:

> It must take every ounce of strength a man has now to resist the machine. Society has become one immense, greedy machine, without a heart, without intelligence, without humour. How is a man ever to be himself, to be alone? He has to work for the machine. He has to let it feed and clothe him. Unless he is careful he will grow to love it. (1940b: 27)

For Hesse, the city as a machine threatens the humanity of its inhabitants, luring them away from the values and ideologies of Europe's liberal or Enlightenment traditions and towards a future of enslavement and unquestioning subservience. The fact that this observation is made by a German character also provides a contrast to the images of Germans as Nazis, or as *willing* automatons, which characterize *Cousin Honoré* and many of Jameson's other novels of this period. In this, the naming of the character is crucial, invoking a great German literary and cultural tradition which Jameson struggles during this time to reconcile with the country's embrace of Nazism.[8] Hesse's concern – in part reflecting Jameson's – is that the war is a veil, distracting from another threat which has already invaded Europe's bones: 'Instead of rushing about conspiring against the French, against the Separatists, against employers of Communists or Jews, one should be turning one's soft flesh to bone and gristle. The harder, the more self-contained one is, the less chance there is for the machine' (1940b: 27). It is the processes of capitalism or modernization and mechanization which seek to draw the people of Europe further away from their humanity. For Hesse, the city is both the manifestation and the purveyor of these dehumanizing processes.

Despite Jameson's sympathetic portrayal of Hesse, there remains a sense that it is Germany which epitomizes both this inhumanity and its embrace of the machine. The war, then, represents another means through which these processes might spread throughout Europe, obliterating the cultural heritage which Jameson treasures. Germany is repeatedly associated with this drive towards progress of a different kind, a true expression of capitalism's impetus towards efficiency, profitability and homogenization. While in *Cousin Honoré*, the protagonist is haunted by a Germany in which modern production values are all-pervasive, in *Europe to Let* this is epitomized by the German landscape itself: 'When I think of the Rhine, I see it heavy and full-flowing, the colour of dirty steel, just as I see the Loire sparkling in a clear early morning light' (1940b: 2). Even the most natural of features of the German landscape are defined by their associations with productivity, 'steel' and heavy industry, whereas France is light and natural, more evocative of freedom and romance. Indeed, fascism, and its association of man and nation with machine, emphasized this association of progress with a productivity and profit. As Stackelberg describes, policies such as Hitler's Four Year Plan, announced at Nuremburg in 1936, drove forward Germany industry from steelmaking to armaments manufacture.[9] In contrast many of 'the social changes that actually took place moved Germany further away from the *Volkisch* utopia of blood and soil' (Stackelberg, 1998: 125) and towards a more industrialized future.[10] Though this threat is already within the cities of Europe, the German embrace of this particular mode of modernity and its dehumanizing properties symbolizes another element of this threat, marking a convergence between the threat from capitalism and the threat of war.

There are numerous examples of this anxiety about modernity and the future of civilization in interwar literature, from the futuristic dystopias of Yvegeny Zamyatin's *We* (1920) to Aldous Huxley's *Brave New World* (1932), Orwell's *Nineteen Eighty-Four* (1949) and Katharine Burdekin's *Swastika Night* (1937), all of which engage with that the idea of modern progress is detrimental to human values such as democracy, equality and freedom. Zamyatin's *We*, in particular, draws out this tension between reason and freedom. From its opening pages, it contrasts 'the savage state of freedom' with 'the beneficial yoke of reason' (2007: 3), using irony to call into question the post-Enlightenment fixation with reason at the expense, perhaps, of all else. While Jameson is concerned by the move away from reason exemplified by the Nazi mobilization of feeling and untruth, she is also concerned with reason's own dehumanizing elements, its links to modern obsessions with progress and efficiency. Invoking the language of progress and reason to justify the control and authoritarianism of the one state, Zamyatin – writing twenty years previously and from the standpoint of revolutionary Russia – also expresses an ironic discomfort with the modern values of reason, progress and productivity as counter to humanity and freedom. Like *Europe to Let*, the novel deploys imagery of man as machine and the dehumanizing effects of modern production systems to further these ideas: 'I saw: people below, bending, straightening, turning, like the levers of one enormous machine, on the beat, rhythmically and rapidly' (2007: 73). Here, music is evoked but not as a free or individual expression of self, but as a means of facilitating production and the building of the state, raising the question of culture itself falling victim to these modernizing practices, a point particularly relevant to Russian society at this time.[11] The difficulty, throughout this novel, is for the protagonist to reconcile his belief that everything can be explained and expressed by reason, mathematics, progress, with his inability to understand and explain certain of his own behaviours and reactions to living within this highly restrictive and dehumanizing system. Drawing on Zamyatin's work, over the subsequent two decades, writers such as Orwell and Huxley and Burdekin explore similar issues around a dehumanizing modernity, inflicted by a modern state attempting to reduce life to a means of production. Jameson's engagement with similar issues in *Europe to Let* marks out not only a shared discomfort but also the extent to which, in 1940, the coming war was exacerbating these concerns.

In Jameson's novel the city itself is characterized by these dehumanizing properties, not only through its association with capitalism and mechanization but also through the alienating effects which it has on its inhabitants. Where Hesse's 'machine' is a society in which men fulfil automated roles in a production line of streets and buildings, Jameson characterizes the city as itself a destructive force through its capacity to gather its human inhabitants and to amplify their more destructive behaviours. Echoing the concerns of earlier modernist writing, Jameson's cities are busy, fast and noisy, alienating and dehumanizing their inhabitants. For Richard Lehan, 'two kinds of urban reality emerged from literary modernism: the city as constituted by the artist, whose inner feelings and impressions embody an urban vision, and the city as constituted by the crowd, which had a personality and urban meaning of its own' (1998: 71). As Esk observes in Vienna, 'The streets between the Ringstrausse and the Danube were solid with people going through all the stages of moral drunkenness: lorries filled with armed storm-troopers and police tried to force a way through, hooting ceaselessly' (1940b: 90). This plays on the city as an immoral space of crowded, claustrophobic streets – a familiar trope in the work of philosophers such as Elias Canetti, Georges Simmel and Friedrich Nietzsche who interrogated, in their respective ontological explorations, the influence of the crowd on the individual psyche. It is the city itself, and *not* the invading storm troopers, which threatens its inhabitants, driving them into 'moral drunkenness' (1940b: 90) just as the doors in Budapest with 'no one knows how many people behind them, in every room, poisoned the air' (1940b: 237). The cramped conditions within the city combined with the alienation of being part of a crowd have diminished its inhabitants' conception of empathy with others, driving the sense of panic just as much as the invading forces. For Jameson it is living within the unnatural and over-crowded environment of the city that has diminished their humanity.

This 'moral drunkenness' is often encapsulated in the living conditions in Jameson's cities, where the closed doors of crowded rooms housing whole families 'poisoned the air'. Although this is evident in Jameson's earlier novels, from the unemployed former soldiers in *Company Parade* to the poverty-stricken lives of the strikers in *None Turn Back* (1936), the emphasis in the novels of the late 1930s moves from the hardships of working-class life in British cities to those same problems in a wider Europe. It is not only British but European poor who live squalid lives with an emphasis on disease, claustrophobia and hunger. In *Europe to Let*, Esk is shocked by the cramped poverty of Therese and Emil Wolf's attic rooms in Vienna which smell of 'drains and caraway seeds' (1940b: 70) and by the child asleep in the street in Budapest 'naked except for a rag with sleeves. Its hand was awake. Scratching without pause. Its bones were slightly deformed through hunger' (1940b: 237). This child is dehumanized; 'its' qualities are animalistic, driven by poverty and deprivation. This is reminiscent of Jameson's most evocative depiction of the over-crowded, poverty-stricken city as it appears in *Here Comes a Candle*, wherein London's New Moon Yard 'throbbed like an ant-heap with human, animal, and insect life' (1939f: 11). It is not only a repulsion at the conditions of poverty stemming from Jameson's middle-class upbringing which manifests itself in these descriptions of working-class life, but her horror at the industrialized modernity which creates these conditions by attracting low-paid labour to cities in the name of modern progress.

This destructive and threatening side of the city is expressed throughout the novel through the use of a chiaroscuro effect, deploying the artificial lighting and shadowing of the modern city to underline its unfamiliar or menacing qualities: For Esk, the darkness accentuates the sense of inevitability of violence, particularly in Vienna in 1938, as 'dusk had thickened in the streets. I had every anxiety that one has when waiting to hear of a death' (1940b: 87). In Prague, moths rush 'through the weak patches of light into the darkness between the street lamps' (1940b: 151), while in Vienna 'anything may be shaping itself in the darkness, and it may be any hour of any century' (1940b: 75). Street lamps are characteristic of the modern metropolis, but here they also only light a particular area, casting another in shadow – it is these artificial shadows which come to characterize but also to disguise the threatening nature of the cityscape and its inhabitants. In Budapest, Esk looks into the street where 'the streetlamps on the Pest side of the river stretched left to right like a grin disturbing the features of the darkness' (1940b: 236). This unsettling image adds to the otherworldly appearance given to the city at night by this artificial light. The street lamps create both a commonality and an unfamiliarity which both disorientate the reader and universalize the threat to Europe – the presence of the same artificial lights which cast shadows in London and in Budapest emphasizes the threat to every city in Europe. Furthermore, these lights can be linked directly to modernity and to the progress which allowed each city to light its streets for the safety and convenience of its inhabitants. However, like much of the modern progress that Jameson describes throughout, they can have the opposite effect, making the city more alienating and more unfamiliar.

It is not only the cities of Europe that are affected by this modernity in *Europe to Let*, it is also their constituent parts, the people who inhabit them. This darkness hides the deeds and misdemeanours of the city's more corrupt citizens, but it also accommodates their avaricious excesses. Criminals, fascist gangs, treacherous arms-manufacturers and profiteers all lurk in the shadows, making use of the bars, restaurants, parks and vehicles for clandestine meetings and deal-making. Here, the city is both complicit and indispensable, giving these characters the anonymity, the locales and the contacts necessary to their criminal enterprises. In her later novel *Before the Crossing* (1947) – which is also set in the late 1930s and is able to express, with the benefit of hindsight, a more nuanced version of the threat which characterizes these earlier novels – the city's corrupt inhabitants move about shadowy streets and houses which conceal their misdeeds, making the city itself seemingly complicit in their corruption. In the section of *Europe to Let* entitled 'The Young Men Dance', Esk pursues two men through the dark, shadowy streets of Cologne, where 'a shaft of light crossed a wall, like a staircase leading to nothing' (1940b: 53). These shafts of electric light create shadows adding to an increasing feeling of paranoia as Esk chases the other men through the streets. Highly evocative of the iconography associated with classic film noir, these scenes make use of 'images of the dark, night-time city [...] where deep, enveloping shadows are fractured by light from a single source' (Spicer, 2002: 4). Using a similar formulation to classic noir's characterization of the city as a site for corruption, violence and criminality, these moments denote the threatening nature of both the city and its inhabitants. The noirish sensibility leant to this scene by the city setting and the theme of alienation and paranoia is repeated throughout the novel: in the suspicions and skulduggery of desperate men in Cologne, the death squads of Vienna and the repressive evening heat of Budapest.

The suspicious activities of these characters culminate in the death of Kurt Hesse at the end of the first section of *Europe to Let*. That Hesse, who represents throughout this section the civilized European and the good German, is driven to suicide by a death squad consisting of his former friends is not only another noir-esque climax – the body in the badly lit room – but also testament to Jameson's fear that in the shadows of these modern cities the civilized body of Europe was being sacrificed. Esk, who finds him, suspects immediately that Hesse has been murdered because of the atmosphere in the city. When he enters Hesse's shadowy lodgings, he describes 'a sensation of cold, as though an icy plain began at the door of the room, covering Germany' (1940b: 55). The darkness and the 'intolerable cold' add to Esk's feelings of alienation from a city which once seemed friendly and welcoming. They also indicate, as does Hesse's death, an escalation in violence in Cologne and a movement from discussions about changing the face of politics to the drawing and enforcement of political battle lines. The darkness which has taken over the city on the night of Hesse's murder is not only literal, it also signals the turning of the tide in Cologne towards a greater darkness to come.

However, not all of Europe's cities are depicted as unnatural and dehumanizing in this way. For Esk, the city is not only alienating or claustrophobic but also compelling, beautiful and familiar. He remarks one evening, regarding Budapest from his hotel balcony, that he 'should like to embrace this city but it is too close and too alien, as though we were brothers who had been brought up separately' (1940b: 237). Furthermore, Budapest, Prague, Vienna and Cologne are intrinsically linked through their shared histories – Esk is 'intimately aware of Europe beating in the darkness, the Danube a vein' (1940b: 237). The city is also an organic, living part of Europe, as much so as the romanticized landscapes of *Cousin Honoré* or *The Moon Is Making*. The presence of these links – historical and cultural, seen and felt – marks out the city as part of Europe and of its shared heritage, rather than simply the source of its corruption. This contradiction is characteristic of Jameson's treatment of the modern European city in the novel: the city is, by turns, purveyor of this modernity and its organic victim, as in Vienna when 'a frightful dullness had eaten deeply into the bones of the city' (1940b: 92). Evoking the discourses of disease and bodily contamination elsewhere in the novel, the city is corrupted as it corrupts, representing another element of Jameson's ambivalence about its role in Europe's decline.

Jameson's city has elements of the palimpsest, with earlier incarnations, histories and cultures existing beside its more modern, menacing features. These historic or cultural elements, etched beneath the surface of the modern metropolis, contain repeated references to past achievements in art and culture, conjuring more positive visions of shared European history. As well as being disgusted by the poverty of these cities, Esk is staggered and impressed by the architecture, the history and the music surrounding him. In Cologne, he is fascinated by the history of the city as 'the memory even of the Romans is close to the surface' (1940b: 58), while in Prague he is awed by the architecture of Hřadcany, flood-lit one evening 'lifted up on its hill on the left bank of the Vltava, the castle, incredibly long, seemed to be pierced by the towers of the cathedral, floated in the air' (1940b: 136). This reflects Jameson's own sense of wonder at Europe's great cities and their rich histories. Her use of a cast of writers (Esk) and journalists (Tithaneth) placed within the mediaeval buildings and ancient architecture locates each city firmly within this great intellectual and classical tradition. Even in her novel, *In the Second Year* (1936), the protagonist is anxious that 'if there is a war, and London is bombed, and Paris and Berlin, not to speak of Vienna, which would be a greater loss than all the others put together, a greater part of the civilisation of six centuries will be engulfed, burned or scattered' (31). The modernity that the city embodies threatens even the history and traditions which created it, as both its inhabitants and the progress it symbolizes threaten constantly to reduce it to rubble. Jameson wishes to preserve this sense of a shared culture and history at all costs but cannot reconcile this wish with her anxieties about the modernity or the capitalist processes ingrained within the city's different manifestations, ancient and contemporary.

The four sections of this novel represent an analysis of the threat that, for Jameson, modernity and urbanization posed to Europe during the 1930s, yet each of the cities represented is also remarkable for its sense of history, tradition and culture, and each of these civilized qualities, as Jameson sees them, represents some sense of the shared European culture she prizes so highly. However, as the metaphors of disease and degeneration and even some of the descriptions of the mechanized city itself indicate, within the novel the threat to the city comes also from within its own walls. The city is both the victim and the architect of its own decline, corrupting its inhabitants and desecrating its own history and culture. Jameson's concern is as much with the processes of capitalism and urbanization embodied in the cities she depicts as it is with Nazism during this period. The depiction of a London slum set alight in *Here Comes a Candle* alludes to her sense of the war as an opportunity to abolish poverty and poor housing in Britain just as Esk's descriptions of the streets of Budapest or Vienna point to the prevalence of inequality and injustice throughout Europe. Poverty, inequality and the unchecked 'acquisitive society' of late capitalism have poisoned Europe's heart and now threaten its claim to be civilized at all. If the city is the pinnacle of European civilization, marking out a shared history and a shared culture, this novel asks what it means that it is also a site of extreme poverty, of mob violence and of avaricious and immoral forces. The novel seeks to ascertain whether European civilization as Jameson understands it deserves to be saved in its current form.

As *Europe to Let* completes its journey across the Continent as it falls to war, fascism and other corrupting influences, it represents not only despair but hope. This stems not only from the voices of the characters, such as Emil Wolf, the surgeon who has lost the use of his hands through torture, Jan Stelík in his hope that he will return to his native Czechoslovakia to re-build the country after occupation, in Hana Čarek – another hopeful Czech – but also through Esk himself. As Mumford writes in the first pages of his seminal study *The City in History: Its Origins, Its Transformations, and Its Prospects* (1961), published twenty years after *Europe to Let* and against the backdrop not of Nazi invasion but Cold War politics, the city is the space in which mankind might make or destroy his future, the choice being 'whether he shall devote himself to the development of his deeper humanity, or whether he shall surrender himself to the almost automatic forces he himself has set in motion and yield place to his dehumanised alter-ego "Post-Historic Man"'(1961: 4). In Mumford's analysis abandoning 'his deeper humanity' and embracing his alter ego 'will bring with it a progressive loss of feeling, emotion, creative audacity and finally consciousness' (1961: 4). His words evoke an ongoing struggle which stretches beyond *Europe to Let*, but which embodies some of its central concerns, namely that the city represents a site at which contemporary civilization is at stake, threatening to rob mankind of its humanity but also offering an opportunity, through its expression of more positive aspects of human culture and tradition, a sense of the possibility of rejuvenation and renewal. In Jameson's novel, the fears articulated by her contemporaries are offset by a sense of hope that both the city and the coming war could provide a clean slate for Europe, rejuvenate European civilization and culture, and encourage new political systems based on equality, democracy and justice.

3

'The memory of sacrifice': Culture, myth and the occupied nation in *Then We Shall Hear Singing*

Jameson's vision of Europe as a unique civilization united by common cultural and political heritage permeates her work both before and during the war. Despite her commitment to a united, transnational Europe, one country in particular came to epitomize European values for her during this period: Czechoslovakia. Her love of this newly formed country and her commitment to its nationhood led her to embrace many of its national narratives, forging an allegiance to it which surpassed in its idealism even the ambivalent admiration she held for France and Britain during this time. Her commitment to Czechoslovakia stemmed in part from her sense of guilt and outrage about the occupation of the country by the Nazis and her sense that the other European nations were complicit in these processes. This chapter examines *Then We Shall Hear Singing: A Fantasy in C Major* (1942), 'The Hour of Prague' in *Europe to Let* and extracts from her autobiography *Journey from the North* (1969) in order to trace the evolution of her idealized representations of this country and the political motivations which underpinned them. Employing both nation theory and postcolonial understandings of the value and use of national culture in shaping the fledgling nation and in maintaining that nation under occupation, I explore her renderings of Czechoslovakia and the ways in which her glossing over of the more contentious aspects of Czechoslovakian identity help her to further her vision for about the wider European project.

Nation in these novels functions both in terms of 'the immemorial past' out of which each nation looms according to Benedict Anderson, but also as the result of myth-making processes in the present which seek to deploy this past, creating a narrative which justifies the existence of the nation (1991: 12). Arts, culture and even domestic tradition can be seen to enforce these myths in order to create a sense of continuity and through this a justification for the future existence of the nation. With reference to the postcolonial struggles of the 1960s, Frantz Fanon writes that the claim to a national culture of the past has the capacity to 'rehabilitate the nation and serve as a justification for the hope of a future national culture' (1963: 209). This conviction that culture has the ability to 'rehabilitate' the nation, to find a past on which to build a future, runs throughout Jameson's novels of occupied nations. Fanon's postcolonial account is of course at odds with Jameson's imperialist privileging of European culture during this period, but his analysis of the power of national culture as a force for resistance, and the desire of occupying forces to obliterate this culture in order to establish dominance and weaken the nation, rings true. This is particularly pertinent to Czechoslovakia following the First World War, after which the nation was ostensibly constructed following centuries of domination of the Czech and Slovak peoples by the Hapsburg Empire. During the Second World War, this sense of a shared national culture was deployed again as a rebuttal to Nazi domination and a plea for survival by the beleaguered Czechoslovak nation. However, as I go on to explore, the forging of this nation was difficult, particularly in light of the diverse racial and linguistic groups within Czechoslovakia and the necessity to create a false sense of homogeneity in order to make the case for the united, historical nation. This makes the Czechoslovakian nation – short-lived and under constant pressure to project a coherent and unassailable image of itself to both its enemies and friends, internal and abroad – a potent symbol of the power of national myth-making and the role of cultural production within it, more especially when viewed from the perspective of a sympathetic outsider, in this case, Jameson.

As I have described, conflict often acts as a rallying point, through which the nation must continually renew itself. This may not be violent conflict, such as war, but may be another mode of challenge stemming from a rival nation or community, be it economic, cultural or social. Czechoslovakia's ongoing struggle to first create and then continue to regenerate the nation in the face of increasing adversity is central to Jameson's idealized representation of it as a plucky, youthful nation, imbued with Europe's best qualities. In his work on the borders and interstices between national cultures, the postcolonial scholar Homi Bhabha argues that it is only through encounter with otherness – other nations and races – that national identity can really express itself. These borders, Bhabha writes, function as 'the space of intervention emerging at the cultural interstices that introduces creative invention into existence' and lead to 'the performance of identity as iteration' (1994: 12), where the nation is forced constantly to define itself against an other. Czechoslovakia's repeated encounters with this other, through invasion, through its shared borders with more influential powers within Europe, and even through its own diverse population and landscape, make this definition particularly pressing. The attempts by the Nazi occupiers to suppress Czechoslovak national culture are, as I come to describe, testament to its perceived power. Ironically, perhaps, in *Then We Shall Hear Singing* the safeguarding of this national culture, of the nation's songs, arts, tradition and even language, falls chiefly to the female citizen. As Elleke Boehmer notes, male nationalists, particularly in postcolonial settings, still 'establish the female domestic sphere as a storehouse for traditional attitudes' (2005: 8). Despite woman's problematic relationship to the nation, it is women who nurture and pass on national culture, through song, language and domestic practices becoming the agents of resistance against Nazi rule.

This chapter explores the power of this female-led resistance and its significance for national myths usually associated with male protectors of territory. The use of a female-led resistance movement places cultural and domestic practices seen, as Boehmer describes, as the 'storehouse' for tradition, at the centre of the narrative. This view of nation both echoes Jameson's earlier representations of women as guardians of more conservative modes of nation-building, such as racial purity and national landscape, and inflects her female-only insurgency with a home-spun agency which shrewdly undermines and challenges male structures of power. The novel also locates nation and national identity differently to her previous novels, looking at the roles of ritual, memory and craft as effecting national modes of belonging and bonds of community. The second half of this chapter steps outside the implications of Jameson's own representations to look at the impact of Czechoslovak national myth-making on her writing and to explore the ways in which her belief in a liberal and united postwar Europe led her to deploy certain narratives of national unity and pride promoted by the Czechoslovak government. In comparing these to her own ideas about a liberal, democratic Europe, with a dedication to freedom, the arts and social justice, it is easy to see why she found them so compelling. However, as I show, her view is sometimes rose-tinted and these novels occasionally lapse into propaganda for the Czech government-in-exile. Both cultural practice and national myths become useful for her own political purposes as she strives to present certain favourable elements of Czechoslovakia to a wider world, whilst continuing to assert for each the right to a national identity and a role within her idealized Europe. Here, in the case of Czechoslovakia, national culture and shared European culture become no longer a way of defining oneself and one's country against threat, but a mode of resistance both against an occupying force and against the collapse of European civilization itself.

'A nation lives from mother to daughter': Domesticity and resistance

If occupation forces citizens to place greater emphasis on their national identity and their own sense of nation, then it also blurs the boundaries between the public and the private. The movement of troops into a country brings the (historically male) political arena and battlefield into the (historically female) home. In addition to this physical movement into private/home territory, occupation often constitutes interference by the occupying force in cultural and traditional practices, from language and communication to domestic work and crafts. This represents a merging not only of public and private space, but also of public and private forms of cultural and national expression. By this I mean that, as invaders seek to control the private spaces of the nation, they also aim to control its private national habits and culture – the domestic habits of the home. In *Then We Shall Hear Singing*, Jameson explores the impact of occupation on the private, the domestic and the traditionally female spaces of the nation to draw attention to the effects of war on the lives of those beyond the traditionally male battlefield. Jameson's novel, in its representation of occupation, not only depicts the collapse of gendered spaces under enemy control but also challenges the associations of traditionally public processes of war, resistance and nation-building with maleness. It demonstrates the importance of sustaining national culture and identity through domestic practice under occupation.

The historian Melissa Feinberg has observed that 'historians interested in the problem of collaboration and resistance tend to neglect places like kitchens, seeing the domestic world as somehow removed from the harsh realities of war and occupation' (2006: 95). This is a consequence of the traditional gendering of the nation, which is influenced by understandings of the nation as 'a loved woman in danger or as a mother who lost her sons in battle' (1989: 315), as Nira Yuval-Davis, Flora Anthias and Jo Campling describe. They go on to explain that this characterization 'is a frequent part of the familiar nationalist discourse in national liberation struggles or other forms of national conflicts when men are called to fight "for the sake of our women and children" or to "defend" their honour' (1989: 315). Through turning the female-gendered space of the home into the battlefield, Jameson represents an alternative, as her female figures enact their resistance not through traditional weaponry but through the domestic arsenal of housework, traditional craft, childbearing and storytelling. These practices come to provide a valuable resistance movement in themselves. As Lassner notes of *Then We Shall Hear Singing*, 'The language of women's domestic lives is not only the novel's dramatic centre but an effective resistance movement since their lullabies, recipes, and needlework never become worthy of Nazi attention' (1997: 106). Indeed, the key to their success is the familiar assumptions about women and their domestic domain as passive subjects, unlikely to offer up significant resistance. I explore Lassner's observation further, reading this resistance movement through analysis of national culture as a purveyor and preserver of national identity and problematizing the ending of the novel which undermines the power of this female-led resistance movement.

Set in a village in an unnamed country which, as I discuss shortly, can convincingly be read as Czechoslovakia during German occupation, the novel follows the lives of the village's women as their menfolk are repeatedly abducted for medical experiments by the invaders.[1] These experiments, through 'destroying the higher functions of the brain without affecting the body in any way' (1942b: 17), rob the men of the village of elements of their memory, emotions and, in particular, their sense of national identity. They ensure that, as their inventor describes to the Civil Governor of the Protectorate, only 'the body is left fit for work [...] amiable, obedient, docile [...] you can imagine yourself directing a zoo' (1942b: 19). This technology turns the men of the village into serfs, echoing Jameson's earlier portrayals of both Nazism and modern capitalism as dehumanizing forces. Furthermore, in removing these memories, the Nazis not only free the men up to work without protest, but also remove their sense of the history and culture of the nation and therefore their resistance to the occupiers. Dr Hesse, the inventor and practitioner of this operation, hopes that it will guarantee that 'the memories of a nation of perpetual servants will be buried with its old people and their gossiping tongues' (1942b: 21). Hesse's words imply that the root of the nation is in the memories and identifications of its inhabitants and that it is a mythic and imagined concept relating to emotion and shared experience. However, the operation cannot remove the memories carried by these landscapes and domestic settings, which are preserved by the women of the village. Thus, it is the women in this novel who safeguard the nation, constructing a covert but effective resistance to the occupiers.

The resistance movement takes place chiefly in the women's homes, although, as the novel shows, these private spaces are still not safe from the occupiers' attentions, emphasizing the movement of the war from the public spaces of the battlefield to the private sphere. Hesse and his men repeatedly transgress the boundaries between the public and the private in order to maintain their power over the inhabitants of the village. They occupy public buildings, such as the old school house, as well as taking over private homes and insisting that residents do not lock their doors, even at night. This signifies the occupiers' understanding of the nature of national resistance and their willingness, in this case, to erase all sense of national identity, memory and privacy in order to achieve complete domination. Hesse himself often visits residents in their homes, usually unannounced, to gather the men for their operations and to check on their progress. Just before he calls suddenly to take her husband for his operation, one of the women of the village, Liba, complains, 'I hate not being able to lock my door. The first thing I shall do when we're free is go indoors and lock myself in' (1942b: 130). The irony of her words – that the first thing she will do when she is free is to confine herself – conveys the need to reclaim the private from the occupier. Under occupation, both private and public spaces must be invaded and controlled in order to limit resistance and establish dominance.

Built upon the familiarity of home, and the rituals of domestic practices, these spaces come to represent in the novel the birthplace of the nation. The furniture bears memories of family, tradition and ritual far more implicitly than the monuments of nation such as the president's statue, which the enemy soldiers destroy as soon as they arrive (1942b: 41). In the houses taken over by the invaders, the women tell of how the nation's 'forefathers spoke through their old chairs and bed-steads' (1942b: 31). The villagers feel that, even in those houses occupied by the invaders, at the touch of a native of the village, 'a chair, a wooden step, would come suddenly and thankfully to life and begin to tell all it knew' (1942b: 31). As the invaders ban the speaking of the Czech language in schools and public spaces, the women painstakingly care for tables and chairs, beds and mats from generations past, all imbued with memories of nation and time-worn domestic rituals. It is these handcrafted and hand-maintained items, passed through generations, which bear the hallmarks of the nation in the novel. They sustain it in the minds of the women as they go about their daily tasks, unbeknownst to the occupiers who are not privy to these whisperings of national solidarity and resistance.

Other domestic practices are also ingrained with a sense of nation and nationality: Jameson's characters resist the invaders by continuing to prepare traditional Czechoslovakian meals. Stepanka and Vera bake together as they always have – 'you could have guessed it from the natural way in which Vera kept an eye on the other woman's bread in the oven' (1942b: 83). Another young woman remarks that 'when I'm making a salad and chopping herbs and I see the old marks on the board and smell the parsley […] I feel free then' (1942b: 122), marking out these traditional tasks, textures and smells as reminiscent of better, freer days before the German occupation. According to Feinberg, one women's group in occupied Czechoslovakia published books and pamphlets of recipes and other domestic advice for women living under German occupation, showing them how to 'mould unfamiliar ingredients into old Czech culinary standards' (2006: 105). Ironically, the books were published at the expense of the Nazi government in Prague. Such cookbooks and domestic manuals had been a popular tool in Germany for mobilizing housewives for the Nazi cause and were supported by right-wing women's groups. For Feinberg, through this work, this group of Czech women was 'assisting women in preserving the most basic elements of Czech culture' (2006: 106), whilst outwardly assisting the occupiers in encouraging women to carry out the domestic work necessary to feed and clothe their families, freeing the men up to work more effectively for the Third Reich. Like the frequent references in Jameson's novel to the experience of preparing food and the evocative physical sensations of the kitchen, these offer an implicit mode of resistance, a way of preserving national memory and of maintaining the nation which appears innocuous to the male invaders and which may even be seen to be assisting the smooth-running of the occupied state.

Like these cookbooks, acts of explicit collaboration in the novel are underpinned by genuine, though perhaps somewhat negligible, acts of resistance. When the Nazis come to admire Czechoslovakian lace-making and embroidery, they force the women to produce traditional Czech items for export back to Germany. The women of the village make sure that 'no perfect garment left the hands of the most skilful worker. There was always a flaw, known to the maker' (1942b: 31), duping the Nazis (male and female) who do not possess the skill to recognize the defects. That the oppressors wish to take the fruits of this domestic labour, such as lace and embroidery, as 'the wives of the invaders wanted these things' (1942b: 31), emphasizes the curious double-bind between the oppressors' need to wipe out national practices in order to control subjects and also to appropriate exotic or desirable elements of this culture and absorb it into their own. This process of cultural looting by the occupying Nazis is also depicted in *The Black Laurel*, as the art historian Gustave Leist oversees the pillaging of museums and galleries in occupied countries, and his German officers send furniture and national heirlooms home or to 'the [German] colonel who wanted furniture for his rooms in Warsaw, or to send his wife or some other woman at home' (1947a: 83). Like the furniture mentioned earlier, these items hold memories of the Czech nation, bearing the marks of Czech tradition and crafts(wo)manship. In removing these cultural artefacts, the German occupiers not only furnish their homes with items from the Protectorate, but they also prevent the Czechs from using these objects as symbols of nation.

When her handiwork is seized by the occupiers, Stepanka is hopeful that 'perhaps this other [German] woman would be a little ashamed, and in trying to put her own memories into the things, she would leave some room for the past; she would try to copy a darn or she left the initials undisturbed in a corner of a pillowcase' (1942b: 46). There is a sense that the shared domestic experience of Czech and German women creates empathy between the two countries and the hope that this sort of work might be appreciated by other women in its new context. The Czech women see themselves as holding certain values and practices in common with the German women through their domestic work, which sets them apart from male citizens and their public pursuits of politics and war. Although Stepanka shares a good deal with German women in terms of domestic practices and daily routine, she also shares their position within patriarchal national structures. While the German woman is free in national terms, she is required to work to further the German state, through a sense of duty and tradition and without economic reward. As Nancy Ruth Reagin writes, since the late nineteenth century, 'women – especially in their roles as housewives – served as vehicles for the expression and maintenance of German identity' (2007: 71), and, particularly after 1914, their domestic tasks became a crucial element of state control and indoctrination.[2] In this sense, both of these groups of women function as subalterns, subjects of the nation but not party to the rights and privileges of citizenship, yet both are the purveyors and the guardians of national cultural identity. However, as Dr Hesse points out, 'No one can come into my country and order the washerwomen about, but I can come here and do exactly as I like' (2007: 114). For the Nazis, the superiority of the German Aryan race places all its citizens in a position of privilege. This is a privilege which will always place the German woman above her Czech counterpart, even if the terms of Hesse's insult do illustrate perfectly the Reich's policy on women and domesticity – the washerwoman to Hesse is clearly the lowest German citizen, being both a domestic professional and a *woman*. Nonetheless, in creating a parallel between the lives of ordinary women in Germany and the Protectorate, the novel draws attention to the inequalities perpetuated by the nation in both contexts, wherein women are always subject to the patriarchal underpinnings of citizenship.

These Czech and German women also share another potentially subversive and highly-influential characteristic, one which is indispensable to the nation:

the ability to bear children. Through childbirth and childbearing, these Czech women both resist the Nazis in their continuation of the occupied nation and collaborate with them, as their children provide the workforce for the Reich. During times of occupation, 'a nation lives from mother to daughter' (1942b: 148), as male family members are frequently killed or imprisoned by occupying forces. For these women and their daughters, childbearing is truly a political act, removed from the home life of the family during times of occupation in order to serve a wider political purpose, as feminist critics such as Adrienne Rich have described. In *Then We Shall Hear Singing* it serves another purpose, uniting women in their suffering and strength because 'a woman carries her child nine months. During these months she is every woman; she remembers the gestures she learned from then, and they serve her in place of a common language. Forgotten in anger, they return in suffering: poverty uses this language, and so do happiness, death and childhood' (1942b: 46). Here, the process of childbearing binds a woman to the nation but also to hardship, and it is this hardship which makes her a formidable adversary for the occupiers. These women have not only endured childbirth for their nation, but they have carried its progeny within them for nine months and will never lose this attachment to its future, an attachment which stems from their love of their children. In *Then We Shall Hear Singing*, these children represent the freedom of the future, epitomized by the prophetic words of the young boy Milan: 'One of these days we shall hear trumpets and marching [...] Then we shall hear singing. Then we shall come running out of our houses, and run home from the fields, and we shall see our men come in marching or laughing or riding' (1942b: 43). That Jameson gives the title of the novel to one of the young boys demonstrates her own sense of hope for the occupied nation and her feelings as a mother herself towards children as symbols of faith in Europe's future.

In an attempt to prevent these children from growing up to be members of the national community and not subjects of the Reich, they 'are forbidden to learn to read [...] [their own] language, or to speak it' (1942b: 34). Language has a long history of communicating and even delimiting the nation itself. As Anderson notes, 'The nation was conceived in language, not in blood' (1991: 145) and later countless scholars of nation from Tony Judt to Gayatri Chakravorty Spivak and Judith Butler have continued to trace these associations through diasporic and migrant communities.[3] Sheila Grant-Duff writes in 1942 that '[the Czech's] refusal to speak the language of the conquerors was an obvious method of passive resistance' (1970: 198), even after the Nazis' suppression of the Czech language in public life in 1939. Grant-Duff describes how, on 20 August 1939, the Nazis released a decree stating that German must take precedence over Czech in every aspect of civil and political life, including street names, theatre and cinema tickets, official documents, and meetings and court proceedings (1970: 196). The refusal of the occupying force to allow their subjects to speak their own language in the novel illustrates its importance as a force for uniting the oppressed, alienating the oppressor and providing, alongside the furniture and domestic practices, one of the surviving symbols of the nation. As the women teach their children their own language they plant the seeds of resistance, continuing the cultural heritage of the nation, and this becomes another element of their resistance, for 'a man's own tongue is his only way back to his ancestors, to all that store of memories, commands, certainties they left for him' (1942b: 53). In a reflection of the title, song plays a major role in the continuation of this language and of discourses of resistance throughout the novel, and the Czech anthem 'Where is my home?' appears to indicate a resistance to the Nazis hold on the country, just as it provides a stirring sense of national mourning and of solidarity as the Nazis enter Prague in *Europe to Let* (1940). The significance of these songs is demonstrated by the description of songs which 'teach [the occupied people] the habits of their race' (1942b: 70). Its power is compounded by the Civil Governor's declaration that for the occupiers 'songs are as dangerous as rifles' (1942b: 25). Like the Czech language, these songs are taught and passed along from mother to child in a domestic setting and represent another area of private resistance to occupation.

The nation, then, is a product of collective memory and is perpetuated and, to a certain extent, created through the real and imagined memories of its citizens. The German Civil Governor, Baron von Rennensee, is more attuned to these subtleties of national identity: '"Dr Hesse," he said seriously, "if you take away every other weapon, and leave this country its memories, it will use them to defeat you"' (1942b: 20). For older men such as General Helmuth von Lesenow and Rennensee, veterans of the First World War, Dr Hesse embodies a new generation of Germans, driven by science and technology, who they feel have lost sight of basic human values. Dr Hesse's misunderstanding of the non-scientific human qualities of culture and memory will, for the General and the Governor, lead only to the failure of his scheme. As in *Europe to Let*, this is a reflection of Jameson's own concerns about civilization and the decline of liberal humanism in the face of ideologies more occupied with science and progress, here epitomized by Hesse's experiment. Lesenow, a representative of a previous, more civilized generation, knows that it is not the statues of the president of the country or the guns or the deliberate violent resistance of the men which will overcome the occupiers: 'if, he thought, it happens, it will probably be through the most commonplace, the least exalted of memories' (1942b: 156). These 'least exalted of memories' are held, in this novel, by the women – arguably, the least exalted of citizens: *Then We Shall Hear Singing* shows that 'the weapons for resistance are in women's hands' (2009: 238).

However, this is drawn into question by the fact that the women only preserve these memories and practices as a *gift* to their menfolk. Months after having the operation and, as a direct result of the guidance and guardianship of their memories by the women of the village, the men recover their faculties and join in a national resistance movement. The mission is coordinated in Anna's home and builds upon her surveillance work and the women's covert maintenance of the memories and practices of the nation, but victory belongs to the men. Although the women of the nation preserve these national memories they do so only to pass them forwards to the 'natural' defenders of the nation. This somewhat undermines the novel's concentration on women as the cultural guardians of the nation. In doing so, it can be seen to destabilize any attempt within the novel to assert the importance of women's role during occupation and resistance. Here, as in *Cousin Honoré*, Jameson seems almost to undermine or question her own feminist principles – another expression perhaps of the ongoing interplay between her conservatism and her more revolutionary impulses.

The novel's ending, aside from the role of these women and their domestic practices, is crucial in maintaining the nation and forms an important tenet of resistance during occupation, largely because their work and their lives are so obviously undervalued by the occupier. As Hutchinson's theory of nation as a product of conflict expounds, this occupation has strengthened ideas of Czech nationality by forcing the people to define themselves against an adjacent culture and by forcing them to rise up against this culture in the name of preserving their own national traditions and identity. Nation survives, as Anderson argues in *Imagined Communities*, through a memory and an idea, pulling citizens together. It is this idea, this memory of nation, which in this novel gives the men of the occupied village their pride and their desire to resist the occupiers and which drives Dr Hesse's desire to remove it. However, Hesse significantly underestimates the nation's women. As Floya Anthias and Nira Yuval Davies note, 'The role of women as ideological reproducers is very often related to women being seen as the "cultural carriers" of the ethnic group' (1994: 315). Jameson draws particular attention to women's role as 'cultural carriers' and to the value of this role during times of occupation, particularly as women are often disregarded as passive non-combatants by occupying forces. This novel represents an exploration of the sufferings but also of the victories of women during wartime to demonstrate, as one of the women in the novel observes, 'history, accurate history, is the affair of poor women' (1942b: 83). Here, national memory is located within the homes of the nation, the private domestic territories which are largely ignored by the invaders, but which, as this novel shows, become the battlefields on which the struggle for the occupied nation takes place.

'The happiest country in Europe': The building of Jameson's Czechoslovakia

It is not only these domestic traditions that can preserve and shape the nation in times of occupation. As I have discussed, culture, art, literature and music are also recognized as nation-building tools, and the importance accorded them by the occupier in Jameson's work is testament to her acknowledgement of this.[4] Jameson is aware of the political qualities of her work and, as a former advertising copywriter, of the impact that words and propaganda can have in galvanizing populations under pressure.[5] I examine throughout this study the elements of her fictional work which deliberately embody, perpetuate and propagate myths of nation, of both individual nations and wider Europe, and which further her vision for the European continent. This is particularly true of her writings on Czechoslovakia and I argue here that her work stands as both a product and purveyor of Czech nationalist propaganda.[6] This is not to disparage the power or authenticity of the Czech nation, nor Jameson's work, but to demonstrate the ways in which, as Smith argues, 'these meanings and visions are encapsulated in distinctive myths which, like all myth, bring together in a single potent vision elements of historical fact and legendary elaboration to create an over-riding commitment and bond for the community' (1999: 56). This representation of Czechoslovakia, its national myths and Jameson's relationship with them and the nation which they represent, is an example of their power to maintain, protect and regenerate the nation during times of occupation.

As I have discussed, Czechoslovakia is something of a recurring theme in Jameson's novels of the Second World War. *Europe to Let* is dedicated to 'J.T. in Prague, In the hope that when the curtain lifts again we shall see her/And to Her great country, the country of Masaryk and Beneš Czechoslovakia'.[7] It is also clear that Czechoslovakia is the unnamed country represented in *Then We Shall Hear Singing* for three main reasons, not to mention a whole host of other clues within the book itself. Firstly, the dedication of the book is to 'Líba Ambrosová and her country', one of Jameson's Czechoslovakian friends. Secondly, the fictional country shares elements of Czechoslovakia's history: 'before the invasion, the country had had twenty years of freedom [...] [b]efore then, three hundred years of conquest' (1942b: 30). This draws immediate parallels with the three hundred years of Habsburg rule over the territory that would become Czechoslovakia in 1919 and with the 'twenty years of freedom' which ensued until 1938 when the country was divided up by the Allies as an offering to Hitler.[8] Thirdly, the occupied nation in the novel is referred to repeatedly as 'the Protectorate' by the occupiers, which is what the Nazis declared Czechoslovakia on 15 March 1939, when the Czechs were forced to sign an agreement which, as Mary Heimann describes, 'confidently placed the fate of the Czech people and country in the hands of the Führer and the German Reich' (2009: 107).[9] These parallels would be evident to any reader of newspapers in Britain and almost certainly in America too, where Czech immigrants worked hard to keep their nation in the news (Heimann, 2009: 137). It is possible that Jameson chose to anonymize this country in order to universalize its experience and to continue her work to promote European unity by identifying shared experience and a sense of mutual empathy.

This desire to depict the Czechoslovakian nation is underpinned by Jameson's own fears and hopes for the future. The political preoccupations discussed earlier, such as Jameson's concern for civilization, her anxiety about the future of European culture in the hands of the Nazis, and her ultimate desire for a free, equal and democratic Europe, map neatly onto the stated aims of the founding fathers of Czechoslovakia, Tomáš Masaryk and Edouard Beneš. Masaryk was a liberal academic and Czech nationalist who had been working since the late 1890s on plans for a democratic Czech republic, underpinned by the same socialist intellectual concerns which lie at the heart of Jameson's own polemics.[10] He and his younger associate Beneš had been engaged during the First World War in a process of heightened political activity, ensuring that when the Allies restructured Europe in 1919, they made room for a new Czechoslovakian homeland at its heart.[11] In order to maintain and popularize this homeland among European nations and their citizens, they created what historians and their contemporaries came to refer to as the Castle (Hrad), named after Prague Castle (Hradčany). The Castle was a network of intellectuals and prominent Czechs who would serve as spokesmen and propagandists for Czech national myths, both at home and abroad. Andrea Orzoff describes the creation myth promoted by the Castle:

> Under Habsburg rule, the innately democratic, peace-loving tolerant Czechs were viciously repressed by bellicose, authoritarian, reactionary Austrians, under whose regime the Czech language and national consciousness almost died out. Czech identity was rescued by a heroic, devoted group of intellectuals, dubbed the Awakeners, who brought the dormant nation back to life by recrafting literary Czech, retelling Czech history, and making political claims on behalf of a 'Czech nation'. (2009: 11)[12]

The Castle Myth, as Orzoff describes it, uses the same vision of a nation supported by shared culture and a liberal humanist political tradition to make the case for the future of Czechoslovakia as Jameson employs in making the case for the future of Europe.[13] This Castle Myth and its later evolutions can be seen throughout both *Europe to Let* and *Then We Shall Hear Singing*, influencing Jameson's representations of the nation just as it echoes her own ideas and attitudes.

One key point of contact between this myth and Jameson's work is the sense of the Czech nation as innately tolerant and democratic, with a natural desire for freedom. Masaryk told Karel Čapek in *Masaryk: On Thought and Life Conversations with Karel Čapek* (1938) that 'we are a democratic nation in body and soul' (1971: 182). The Czechs believed that, as a result of their repeated hardships at the hands of authoritarian oppressors, 'in virtue of our history and nature, we are destined for democracy' (1971: 194), and this is an idea on which Jameson draws repeatedly in her polemical and fictional writing. Even a contemporary scholar of nation and nation-building, Hans Kohn, referred in 1944 to 'the pioneer work of the Czechs for humanity and liberty' (1945: 437), and this was a popular view for left-leaning intellectuals and journalists at the time, as evidenced by the work of Sheila Grant-Duff and Martha Gellhorn. Gellhorn writes in her novel, *A Stricken Field* (1940), also set in wartime Czechoslovakia, that 'the Czechs were notoriously honest and filled with a passion for citizenship' (1986: 34). Gellhorn, however, seems to regard this as somewhat naïve and longs for a 'nice crooked country' (1986: 34), perhaps like France or Italy at the time where corruption and capitalism meant that wealthy foreigners could buy their way out of trouble and out of the country, though this seems more likely a humorous reference to her tendency to be on the wrong side of the Czech authorities in her journalistic work. For Jameson though, it is precisely this idea of Czechoslovakia's purity and honesty which makes it such a compelling victim of Allied manipulation and Nazi expansionism, and an ideal blueprint for the new Europe.

In *Then You Shall Hear Singing*, the old woman, Anna, describes how even during the three hundred years of occupation 'the memory of freedom remained so near the surface that to come on it a man had only to thrust a spade into the ground' (1942b: 30). In this novel, the villagers cannot live under oppression and, despite the gruesome means employed by the occupiers to remove their national consciousness, resist authoritarian principles in every aspect of their daily lives. Before the Munich Pact, the wider European population had, like Jameson, been convinced 'that Czechoslovakia, alone in East Central Europe, was a true democracy, whose leaders were devoted to democratic ideals and practice' (Orzoff, 2009: 57). Yet, as Feinberg notes, this was not necessarily the case in terms of minorities such as Magyars, Slovaks or Hungarians. She points out that for the young Czechoslovak nation, 'their inability to come to terms with the problems of difference rendered them incapable of creating the kind of political culture that would support these [democratic] institutions in times of crisis' (2006: 8). As Feinberg's work shows, what Jameson presents here is a somewhat romanticized Czechoslovakia, one seen in precisely the terms that its leaders wished, in order to justify its existence to the rest of the world. Furthermore, Jameson's presentation reveals her own motivations for preserving Czechoslovakia as, for her, an integral part of Europe and a symbol of its future potential as a more liberal, democratic collection of states.

This romanticization stems largely from the Castle's use of the First Republic, and particularly popular memories of it, both within and outside Czechoslovakia. Lasting from the founding of Czechoslovakia in 1918 to the Munich Pact in 1938, it represents the 'twenty years of freedom' frequently referred to by older characters such as Anna. The First Republic was Czechoslovakia's first youthful foray into nationhood, epitomizing, in terms of the Castle Myth at least, a democratic, socialist utopia: David Esk describes in *Europe to Let* how 'in June 1938 Prague was a young man, a boy, a young woman, drawn taut before the dive, yet smiling, unable not to smile' (1940b: 132). Four months later, the state would eventually crumble, in part as a result of the Munich Pact and subsequent claims for autonomy by many of the inhabitants overlooked in the mission to establish a nation-state in 1919 – such as the Slovaks who established their own state, with Nazi support, on 14 March 1939.

Nonetheless, Jameson repeatedly associates this vision of Czechoslovakia with youthfulness and hope. She consistently emphasizes the youthful nation by referring to it as a 'young man, a boy, a young woman' or the 'young republic' (1940b: 132), and by using as a symbol of the Czech nation the irrepressibly youthful Hana Čarek in *Europe to Let*. As Hana explains to Esk on their first meeting: 'You haven't time for the past – there's too much of it – you simply must see our present and our marvellous, endless, tomorrow' (1940b: 132). The motif of the youthful, hopeful nation appears again in *Then We Shall Hear Singing*, in which Czechoslovakia is described as 'the young Republic' (1942b: 103) and its future symbolized by the young boy Milan, and his conviction that his country would be liberated (1942b: 43). Jameson continues to expound the youthful virtues of the Czechoslovakian nation in her non-fiction work, writing in *The End of This War* (1941) that 'I knew Czechoslovakia: It was the happiest country in Europe; Its people were consciously proud of it and its living culture, young and fed by centuries' (1941: 15). As an outsider, Jameson seems attached to this image of Czechoslovakia as Europe's child, epitomizing its hopes for the future, and seems willing to overlook the inconsistencies of this national myth in the hope that the fortunes of this young nation might be tied to those of Europe itself.

Jameson's sense of the Czechoslovakian nation is paradoxical: it is both young and old, new and rooted in an enduring and incontrovertible past. This statement offers an example of the tendency, pointed out by Anderson, for nations to play upon the exuberance and idealism of their youthful vigour whilst at the same time asserting that their nation 'loom[s] out of the immemorial past' (1991: 12). The novel describes this past as deeply engrained within even its most youthful members, as epitomized by 'what each individual remembered of the past, and in what each child dreamed' (1942b: 103). This history constitutes what Alison Landsberg has referred to as a 'prosthetic memory' (2004: 10), passed on even to citizens not born when the Republic was thriving.[14] Jameson's sense of organic memory is in keeping with the Lamarckian paradigm described by Laura Otis in *Organic Memory: History and the Body in the Late Nineteenth and Early Twentieth Centuries* (1994), in which memories could be inherited from ancestors along with physical features. These inherited memories, the innate conviction of national-belonging, connected to ideas about birth and natality, tie its inhabitants to the Czechoslovak nation and underpin their hopes for its future. However, these memories are wholly constructed and highly problematic. For historians such as Orzoff, Feinberg and Heimann, looking back on these events sixty years later, 'Czechoslovakia's brief period of democracy, however good it may look when compared with German Nazism or Italian Fascism, was seriously flawed from the first' (Heimann, 2009: 49). Czechoslovakia's need to make the case for its future led often to the manipulation of the past, a level of national myth-making in which Jameson unwittingly partakes.

One key element of this myth-making and its political deployment was the offering of Czechoslovakia as an Eastern bastion of liberal European values. This, of course, was extremely appealing to other European nations. They saw, and the Castle worked to support the view, that 'East-Central Europe had been re-made in those allies' idealized collective image, trumpeting the ideals of democracy, transparency, cooperation, and peace and their triumph over absolutism' (Orzoff, 2009: 51). Masaryk helped to create this idea when he said that 'the history of our nation was to me a part of world history' (1938: 159), emphasizing 'that our politics must be cosmopolitan' and that being a good European as part of the Czech national character (1938: 164). Indeed, for Jameson, as for many others, 'in Czechoslovakia the idea of Europe lived as it lives nowhere else' (1940b: 134). There is a repeated characterization in Jameson's novels of the Czechoslovaks as perfect Europeans. Esk notes that 'there is an almost extinct race of *Europeans*, of which Czechoslovakia has bred the noblest living members, each worth a hundred Nazis and what not' (1940b: 113; original emphasis). This idea was crucial to any chance Czechoslovakia had of survival at the time, as it established it, despite its location among the alleged enemies of the Allies in the East, firmly within the European context. As Grant-Duff writes, when the Germans occupied Czechoslovakia, what they 'could not allow was that the Czechs should pretend to be European' (1970: 199), because this may encourage the rest of Europe to defend them. For Jameson and others like her, Czech ideas of Europe were perfectly attuned to her own sense of a continent with an inherent understanding of democracy and one steeped in culture, and it seemed imperative that the rest of Europe defend them on this basis.

The Castle also set out to establish Czechoslovakia as a leading light in terms of European culture. Heimann explains that, during the First Republic, 'culture flourished [...] opera and concerts were of the highest standard. Villas, factories and municipal buildings were built in as boldly Cubist, Constructivist or Functionalist style as any to be found in Berlin, Vienna or Budapest (or, for that matter, Paris, Brussels or New York)' (2009: 48). The leaders of the new nation were keen to establish themselves as artistic and cultural leaders, whose tastes and talents had been oppressed during years of occupation by the Habsburgs. In Jameson's work, this Czechoslovakia plays a key role in defining the nation, not only in opposition to its barbaric occupiers but also a part of a great European cultural tradition. During the performance of *Romeo and Juliet* in Prague in *Europe to Let*, Esk speculates that 'Elizabethan actors must have played with this energy, this untameable, vigorous youth' (1940b: 146).[15] The Czechs, then, owing to their idealism and the youth of their nation, are more able to identify with Shakespeare, being as they are, unspoiled by the cultural rot which she sees as undermining every type of progress in the more established nations of Western Europe. Here again, the Czechoslovakian nation represents an earlier, purer nation, one whose embodiment of Europe's humanity and its cultural values is worthy of protection from Nazi forces. This assumption, and indeed the overall privileging of Czechoslovakia above other threatened countries, implies that certain European nations where these qualities were not as evident were unworthy of defence in Jameson's eyes.

In *Europe to Let*, it is European intellectuals who must make the case for the defence of Czechoslovakia. Čarek even asks Esk to 'find writers to explain to the English nation that something must be done for these victims. Poor Hana, she still imagined that England, more than other countries, has writers burning to expose lies, injustice, cruelty' (1940b: 217). This is clearly an expression of Jameson's own feelings of powerlessness and her disappointment at the lack of political engagement with European issues among her contemporaries. Her guilt is manifest as she rehearses her own trip to Czechoslovakia in 1938 with PEN. Esk himself meets and describes the PEN party, invited in the hope that they might deploy their pens and their resources to further the Czechoslovakian cause. The episode is characterized by an extravagance of food, accommodation and entertainment, which serves to juxtapose the hungry desperation of its Czech hosts with the thoughtless gluttony of the English writers, who are 'swollen horribly with goose and slivovitz' (1940b: 139). In fact, the cultivation of Europe's literary elite was a popular strategy within the Castle set and its contemporaries: As Orzoff describes, 'Writers from Habsburg successor states, jockeyed for power and wooed Great Power intellectuals in PEN just as their diplomatic corps did Great Power politicians in Geneva, Paris, and London' (2009: 160) and 'the Castle paid the expenses of the Czech chapter of the PEN Club, which Beneš and the writer-members viewed and used as a propagandist forum' (Orzoff, 2009: 19), hoping that membership of this influential writers organization would further the Czech cause.[16] The aim of this trip is made abundantly clear in the novel, as 'excited by plum brandy, the writers were swearing to defend Czechoslovakia' (1940b: 190), yet their alcohol-infused convictions seem unlikely to yield any tangible political benefit for their hosts. As if to emphasize this point, the scene ends as a young peasant shouts to the assembled and, by this point, inebriated, writers, '"Next time bring your rifles"' (1940b: 139), underlining Jameson's misgivings about the real power she or any of her contemporaries held in influencing Czechoslovakia's – or Europe's – fate.

Jameson's novels reproduce many of the myths of Czechoslovakia in circulation during its early years. From her depictions of the innate affinity for freedom, democracy and European solidarity within the Czechoslovakian nation, she makes a case for Czechoslovakia's protection. Most crucially, novels such as *Then We Shall Hear Singing* and *Europe to Let*, published in both Britain and America, emphasize a sense of shared culture and shared ideology between Europe and America, and Czechoslovakia. The reproduction of these myths can seem uncritical, and largely, Jameson seems blinded by her own convictions about Europe and by Czechoslovakia's possession of certain qualities and values that she admires, from being 'uniquely democratic' to a dedication to both a national and shared cultural heritage. However, she is aware, even in 1941, of the processes at work behind these national machinations, describing the 'intriguing that sickens me among the Czechs and the French' and referring to the (then exiled) President Beneš, as 'the central point (if that) of a scramble' (3 April 1941), the 'scramble' being presumably to gain favour among the free countries in the hope of securing political or military support. While Jameson seems aware of this manipulation, her novels at this time play upon these myths because her goals and motivations chime with the wider goals and motivations of the Czechs – to secure a democratic and free postwar Europe. Though her failure to grasp her privilege as an English woman who does not have to take part in such a 'scramble' for her basic freedoms seems thoughtless, her use of Czechoslovakia during this period is, then, largely instrumental: it stands as a blueprint or guide to her future hopes for Europe, and its fate at the hands of the Nazis comes to embody her fears for the whole continent. Her reproduction of its national myths does represent a real sentimental affection for the country but also an alignment of interests and even an expression of guilt.

These novels do much to support Czech propaganda, as I have shown, which happens to complement perfectly Jameson's own political commitments and ideals in the early years of the Second World War. Czechoslovakia is cast as victim, as uniquely innocent and idealized as uniquely European. In many ways, it is not the ghost of Europe which is sacrificed at Munich, but the hopes and future of this new nation, one to which Jameson is particularly attached, through both her friends and her politics. It is this nation which has, in Jameson's eyes, become symbolic of Europe itself. As the Czech leader Masaryk wrote, 'Nationality and internationality are not exclusive but they compensate each other' (1938: 202). For Czechoslovakia in Jameson's work, these processes of occupation are also used as a way of defining the nation in the minds of those outside it – from individuals to other nations – through processes of national myth-making and the invocation of empathy and sympathy for the suffering of nations under occupation. In *Then We Shall Hear Singing*, this manifests itself through the domestic practices and traditions of the women of the village, which are identified as the devices which define and perpetuate Czech nation and

Czech culture in response to the Nazi occupation. Read alongside a novel such as *Europe to Let*, this work can also be seen to advocate the cultural and political value of Czechoslovakia, reiterating the ideas of Czechoslovak nationhood propagated by the Castle organization and its affiliates. Jameson deploys these myths because they are in keeping with her own desire to translate wartime and postwar feelings about nationhood and national suffering into Europe-wide discourses which may inform not only reconciliation, but real social and political change across the continent. The links she makes within these novels between the Czechoslovak nation and Europe place Czechoslovakia and its values as central to Jameson's vision of this new postwar Europe.

4

'Two sorts of human beings': Culture and myth-making in the German nation in *The Other Side* and *The Black Laurel*

Czechoslovakia is not the only country whose national myths become a cultural commodity during the Second World War. Germany's national identity was also dominated by popular myth during the interwar and the Second World War years. Jameson deploys some of the myths of German nationhood to explore parallels between the German experience of war and those of other countries in Europe in her novels of this period, as well as to make the case for Europe-wide postwar reconciliation. This constitutes an evolution in her thinking about Germany, as she moves from the dehumanizing myths of German aggression in 'the yellow-haired rank-smelling savages ferrying themselves across the Rhine to descend on the swirling fields and vineyards' (1940a: 159) of *Cousin Honoré* to the highly-sensitive literary Germans who 'grow wine' and 'read French' (1946: 53) in *The Other Side* (1946). In part, this stems from her anxieties that after the First World War the Allies sowed the seeds for a second conflict years later through their aggressive punishment of Germany in the Versailles treaty of 1919 – in *Company Parade* (1934) the protagonist David Renn describes how 'a bad Treaty doesn't settle anything – except the causes of the next war' (1984: 97). Renn returns in *The Black Laurel* (1947) as a former soldier and sometime spy, whose experiences in Allied-occupied Berlin come to expound some of Jameson's ambivalent feelings about the treatment of Germany in the immediate aftermath of war and to investigate her own feelings about the need to balance justice for the victims of Nazism with the need to build a fairer and more hopeful postwar world. In this novel, she channels her sense of the defeated German nation into a nuanced analysis of the capacity of international systems of justice to interpret and account for the crimes committed by the Nazis. In her representations of the immediate aftermath of war in Germany, she comes to express her hope for a united postwar Europe by calling for a measured and empathetic approach to Allied victory and to postwar justice, one which can heal the wounds of war-torn Europe.

Although a small number of British authors sought to depict – to both understand and represent – the Germans, this was a rare and controversial undertaking for a British writer, even in the later stages of the war.[1] There is an absence of depictions of German characters in texts of this period, in contrast to the propaganda of the First World War, pointing towards a need to generalize but not to perpetuate these national myths. In her study of the representations of Germans in English modernism, Petra Rau describes 'the necessity of the German other for the construction of Englishness for the period in question' (2009: 10). Rau here asserts that a dialectical relationship existed between Britishness and Germanness in interwar texts in which contemporary anxieties about Britishness were projected onto the German characters. Jameson's novels of the postwar period can be seen in similar terms, channelling her anxieties about the future of Britain and of Europe itself, onto Germany and German characters. Jameson writes to Liddell Hart in 1941, 'I don't hate the Germans, how could one hate a whole nation?' (Letter to Basil Liddell Hart, 19 April 1941), and it is this question to which she returns in 1944 whilst writing *The Other Side*. In contrast to her previous deployment of Germany as the symbol of the malevolent nationalism and even of modernity, she moves to consider more compassionately the German nation, its people, its past and its future. This change of heart is certainly tied to her growing fears for the future of Europe itself following the war.

In *The Other Side* Jameson depicts Germany immediately after Allied victory, setting the novel in a German home occupied by French and English troops. The novel – written in 1944 as the war drew to an end – serves to reconcile her own feelings about Germany with the popular discourses surrounding the German nation in both her own earlier work and that of her contemporaries. In the novel Germans are educated but proud, resistant to occupation but lacking the inhuman characteristics of the 'savages' of *Cousin Honoré*. The von Galen family in *The Other Side* – like the occupied Czech characters in *Then We Shall Hear Singing* – use their furniture, stories, culture and memory to resist their occupiers and they are represented throughout as reasonable, polite and even friendly to the Allied troops stationed with them. The novel seeks to draw out and dwell on these similarities, rather than the peculiarities of Europe's wartime experiences. By *The Black Laurel* (1947), Jameson's attitude to Germany has evolved further, and, although her representations of German life still focus on this desire to recuperate the German nation in the eyes of the British and other Europeans, the novel shows a far darker side to German life and German experience: It foregrounds the suffering of ordinary Germans in Allied-occupied Berlin. While Jameson herself had not visited Germany since the 1930s, she had visited Poland in 1944 where, as Elizabeth Maslen explains, her friend 'Jirina took her to the prison where she herself had spent many months, now housing German prisoners' (2014: 332). She had not visited Berlin in August 1945 where *The Black Laurel* is set but had seen it from the air (Birkett, 2009: 275) and had, through her reading and correspondence, worked to build a fuller picture of life there at that time. The novel expounds these experiences, probing Europe's physical and emotional scars to urge caution and compassion in the early days of Allied victory. From the Jew Heinrich Kalb, returning from exile in London to find his family dead, to Lucius Gerlach, a German man who punishes himself for the sins of his country, Jameson's characters come to enact on a personal level the national and international processes of justice and retribution preoccupying postwar Europe.

In this, Jameson seems, unlike Martha Gellhorn and other writers of the time, to step beyond a desire to 'imagine justice from within the stricken field of Nazi atrocity' (Stonebridge, 2011: 3), to explore more dispassionately the limits and consequences of postwar justice to respond to the events of the Holocaust and of the war itself. In *The Black Laurel*, she comes, as she herself describes to examine 'justice versus expedience' (1984c: 203), illustrating her concerns that a swift and decisive justice hinged largely on the political convenience of the forces trying to establish control over occupied Berlin might lead to a punishment of Germany which was immoral at best and murderous at worst. She sees this impetuosity as playing into Europe's tendency to create a cycle of violent retribution which perpetuated years of conflict. Rather, her desire for a new Europe cannot be one stained in the blood of the defeated, regardless of the horror of their crimes or of public clamour for such a spectacle. From her position of relative privilege – an Englishwoman in Britain – she raises many of the reservations which have since occupied scholars of the human rights and international law structures erected in this 'new moral and political beginning' as Stonebridge questioningly refers to it in *The Judicial Imagination: Writing after Nuremberg* (2011). Jameson asks, in line with later theorists such as Stonebridge herself, but also Samuel Moyn and Joseph Slaughter, who these new legal systems will really protect and punish, who might not be included within them and the extent and accountability of their powers. Certainly in *The Black Laurel*, as I come to discuss, she demonstrates precisely how innocent bodies might become embroiled within these *ad hoc* legal systems, leading to miscarriages of justice which might at best 'set the terms of the next war' and at worst propel humanity's further decline into murderous immorality.

The other side: Culture and resistance in the occupied German nation

A lifelong admirer of the founding fathers of German culture and philosophy, Jameson found it difficult to make sense of her hatred of Nazism in light of her love for the elements of German culture and philosophy which it frequently referenced. From her master's dissertation, *Modern Drama in Europe* (1920), submitted to King's College, London, in which she writes of 'the German tradition, half-fantastic, half held to the misty philosophy of the ideal' (1920: 91) and of 'the older writers of Germany Schiller, Goethe, Lessing and Kleist' (1920: 91), she remained a keen and knowledgeable reader of German literature and philosophy. She was forced to reconcile this vision of Germany and its scholarly traditions with the cultural barbarism that she associated with the Nazis. In a letter to the *Times* concerning their work with German refugee writers through the PEN Fund, Jameson and International PEN Secretary Hermon Ould write that these refugees are 'representatives of the *true* German culture' (Letters to the Editor, Saturday, 13 July 1940: 339; emphasis mine) forced to flee as a result of their opposition to Nazi ideals. A true inheritor of this German literary heritage could not, as she saw it, hold anything in common with the constraints on free will and free expression imposed by Nazism. However, as I have discussed, during the interwar period and the early years of the Second World War, the slippage in her work between Nazism and Germanness is tangible. In the later years of the war, as Allied victory seemed assured, Jameson's work came to concentrate more explicitly on the consequences of defeat for the German nation, in light of both her sense of Germany as a key contributor to the European culture of the past and her vision for a united postwar Europe. In *The Other Side*, in which German family home is commandeered by occupying Allied troops, she uses culture as a way of familiarizing Germany and of drawing parallels between ordinary German experiences of occupation and those of other countries under the Nazis. She also challenges the notion of victory and defeat, showing how easily occupiers become occupied, victors become victims. The novel can be seen as an attempt to explore German experiences of war, to represent the views of the other side and to rehabilitate Germany through exploring her own feelings of ambivalence and anger, vengefulness and compassion.

The interplay in the novel between the cultural Germany that Jameson admired and the savagery of the Nazis is perfectly encapsulated in Paul von Galen, the head of the von Galen household, whose home has been seized by the conquering British and French soldiers.[2] Von Galen remains coldly courteous to the soldiers staying in his house, reminiscing about shared experiences in the First World War and retaining a quiet dignity in the face of national defeat. He is described as 'tall, excessively thin, with a long nose and bright pale eyes: when he smiled which he did readily, his eyes became still brighter, almost merry, and his face, sunken, a bad colour, had a charming kindness' (1946: 13). This thinness and pallor is a characterization used by Jameson in other novels to signify intellect and idealism.[3] It stands in direct contrast to the Nazi Germans whom she described previously as greedy or overweight, or at least broad and tanned, such as Anne-Marie Eschelemer's 'ugly German' husband (1940a: 104) and the tall blond 'German[s] of caricature' (1940b: 6) in *Europe to Let*. Von Galen is an affluent and even aristocratic intellectual. He represents Jameson's desire to associate Germany, not with the hysteria of Nazism but with what she refers to as the 'bony rationalists' of German intellectual history such as Herder, Fichte and Hegel. Ironically, as Roderick Stackelberg points out, it was arguably Goethe, alongside Kant, Schiller and Hegel, who gave Germany 'a legacy of acquiescent political attitudes, attitudes that reflected subservience to authority and the futility of political action to affect political reform' (1998: 45). It is this subservience, this bony rationalism and the ways in which it undermines the human which she rejects so fervently in novels such as *Europe to Let* and *Cousin Honoré*, but which comes later to stand as an expression of Germany's contribution to the wider European intellectual culture through which she hoped to restore Germany to its former position at the centre of Europe.

Paul von Galen might be seen as a manifestation of this 'true German culture' which Jameson had hoped to protect from the Nazis through her work with German refugees. Her depiction is of von Galen as the inheritor of his culture, as well as the inheritor of the von Leyde family home, built in 1899 and marked by the same dishevelled grandeur as its owner. This characterization of the shabbily elegant educated middle class as the guardians of 'true German culture' hints also towards an association of Nazism with the German working or lower-middle class, which can be seen in the soldier savages of Jameson's other, earlier novels. This is quite at odds with, for example, Phyllis Bottome's rendering in *The Mortal Storm* of the aristocratic Von Röhn family and of even a Jewish Brownshirt, Olaf Toller, who dreams of Germany being 'born again' (1937: 6) through Hitler's election, unaware of the danger he and his family might face under Nazi rule. While Bottome's constitutes a more balanced representation of the different classes of Germans who might be drawn to Nazism and why, Jameson's portrayal of the von Galens fulfils a more simplistic desire to recuperate something of German intellectual culture from the trappings of Nazism and to create a 'Good German' character whose middle-class standing is more attuned to the intellectual traditions which she associated with Germany's history as a crucial component of the European cultural landscape. The establishment in this novel of this distinction between Germans and Nazism, between German intellectual culture and Nazi barbarism, is crucial in making the case for a more measured and compassionate response to the German nation following its defeat.

Von Galen is also, rather remarkably, characterized as English. In the first description of him in the novel Jameson writes that 'he was fond of pointing out that caricatures of an Englishman, of the lean and stooping degenerate variety, might have been drawn from him' (1946: 13). Furthermore, 'he liked to stress the resemblance by wearing shabby clothes, he wore them with a placid elegance' (1946: 13). These allusions to Englishness can be read as a way of humanizing the Germans for an English reader, in this case by making them recognizable and removing their associations with the otherness that Rau describes. The novel draws attention, using words such as 'lean', 'stooping' and 'placid', to his unthreatening nature – this is a German above the physicality and aggression often associated with Nazism in the work of Jameson and her contemporaries: in 1936, Stevie Smith writes in her *Novel on Yellow Paper* of Germans as possessing a 'vicious cruelty that isn't battle cruelty, but doing people to death in lavatories' (1936: 104), and Grant-Duff claims in 1942 that 'Nazism is the narrowest, most destructive and most pitiless creed which has ever made young men into fanatics' (1970: 20). She goes on: 'The Nazis have a terrible guilt upon them, not only in this part of the world but in every country they have occupied, and indeed in the greater part of the world at large. They have roused up a real hatred of the Germans which has never existed before' (1970: 240). Jameson addresses this 'real hatred of the Germans' as she defines her good Germans against stereotypes of machismo, aggression and brutality through her language and characterization. Von Galen is in fact never over-wrought with emotion like the hysterical Nazi conjured up in the popular imagination by Hitler's apoplectic speeches, the characterizations of Smith or Grant-Duff, and even Jameson's earlier work. Before the occupying troops even arrive at his home, von Galen tells his family calmly that the occupying soldiers may wish to evict them all: 'When I was in France I usually found it more convenient to turn the owners out of a house where I intended to live. It saves awkwardness!' (1946: 13). His sense of calm understanding draws attention not only to the ease with which occupier may become occupied, but also to his philosophical approach to the occupation itself.

Even the von Galens's home marks a point of commonality with the rest of Europe, as well as an example of a more refined and cultured Germany of the past. The décor of the house is appealingly reminiscent of prewar standards and decorum, but also somehow ineffably English: it is grand, filled with antiques, but falling into disrepair, as were its English aristocratic equivalents at this time. The attachment of these Germans to their home and its traditions draws parallels with more sympathetic nations represented by Jameson, such as Czechoslovakia. Just as the Czech nation is hidden within the home and its traditional furnishings, the German nation lingers in this occupied home, in the memories stored within its furniture, books and family memories. This is most noticeable, as it is to Caroline in *Cousin Honoré*, to the foreigners navigating these objects. For Marie, a French girl who married into the von Galen family before the war, it is only once the French soldiers arrive that she is struck by the 'Germanness of the things in the room' (1946: 29). She is told by her mother-in-law: '"You don't hear what any of those things say Marie [...] it's not your fault [...] they talk about people you never knew, and only in German"' (1946: 32). Here again, the nation defines itself against an invading force, responding immediately to the presence of foreigners by re-establishing itself in the eyes of citizens under occupation. It does so in a way that is, like the Czech furniture, undetectable to both invaders and other foreigners. Although this is much more problematic in a German home in light of the racial preoccupations of the Third Reich, it nevertheless draws parallels between experiences of occupation Germany in 1945 and the states which Germany occupied during the war.

Similarly, the idea of these homes as having, like the nation itself, a long history that still echoes through their walls is a trope familiar in Jameson's other novels, from the stones and walls of Alsace in *Cousin Honoré* to the homes of the villagers in *Then We Shall Hear Singing*. A description on the first page of the novel recounts how the von Galen house was built by George von Leyde in 1899, after a fire destroyed the original house, which had itself stood for centuries. His widow decorated the rooms with family heirlooms and antique furniture, expressing longevity and a link with the German cultural and intellectual traditions of the past. For their daughter Anna, the household also holds many memories, including the last 'English mission which had occupied the house' in the First World War, and she tells her son, 'I remember everything that happened that year' (1946: 11). Anna's words emphasize the fact that the experience of occupation is not new to Germany either. Just as Europe's wars have dominated the lives of the Czechs, the French and the Austrians, they have also dominated the lives of Germans, leaving its marks on their buildings and their memories. The house is still, for Anna, a monument of sorts to family and national history. As in Czechoslovakia and France, these private, domestic spaces have become the setting for very public experiences.

These comparisons emphasize the precariousness of the nation at war and the speed with which the victor can become the defeated. Marie, who shows the soldiers around the house, describes how 'the [von Galen] chateau was built to house two sorts of human beings. It could hardly be more up to date' (1946: 26). Not only is this evocative of the English class system, perhaps a joke Marie hopes to share with the English and French soldiers, it is also an allusion to the Nazi desire to categorize and divide citizens along racial lines. By commenting that 'it could hardly be more up to date', Marie draws attention to the constructedness of the social and political systems which differentiate between these 'two sorts of human beings', in terms of either class or the eugenics and race politics of Nazism. The implication is that the crimes of the Nazis stem from a similar desire to establish hierarchies, leading to the subjugation of certain groups on the grounds of class, race or gender, and is part of a wider human tradition aiming to categorize or divide for economic or ideological reasons. For Jameson, this is a compulsion which must be overcome if European civilization is to survive. Ironically, of course, these notions of political and social hierarchies form the very basis of the civilization Jameson so admires. Her sense of intellectual culture certainly creates two sorts of human beings, the educated and the uneducated, cultured and un-cultured. In spite of their class and culture, the relegation of the von Galen family to the servants' quarters when the English and French soldiers arrive creates an additional testament to their weakness and to their defeat. The fact that this division 'could hardly be more up to date' demonstrates the crucial difference between the occupiers and occupied, and the precedent set by the ongoing state of war during the first half of the twentieth century for two other sorts of human beings, one the victor and one the defeated. There is no triumph in this depiction, only Marie's sense of the continued suffering inflicted by this constant striving for power and dominance.

It is within this space, and in defiance of the occupiers, this family can also be seen to privilege German culture – not the Nazi culture of *Volk* and mythic traditions, but the culture of German intellectual life, from literature to art. This privileging of German high culture operates throughout the novel, in tandem with the portrayal of Paul von Galen as a reasonable and rational intellectual. Marie describes this as she tries to plead the case of her German family to the English and the French:

> You ought to know what sort of people you are dealing with. This is their family house, they used to grow wine, they were modestly rich, they used to read French, they travelled, they adore cactus plants, and strong black coffee with cream, they cry when they fall in love, they have a swarm of cousins, and the younger ones, even the plainest, can't enjoy a fine day without taking off their clothes, they are possessive, sentimental, nervous – in short. German. (1946: 53)

This categorization of Germanness creeps far closer to the agrarian leanings of blood and soil Nazism, in its invocation of naked Germans communing with nature, but it also emphasizes a cosmopolitanism, tied close to the rest of Europe in which Germans 'travelled', 'read French' or 'grow wine'. Through marking out their similarities with other seemingly cultured nations, such as the France which Jameson describes in novels like *Cousin Honoré* – a France of winegrowers, literary people with the ability to speak other European languages, and the perpetual coffee-drinking which characterizes her portrayals of almost every European city – Marie advocates for Germany's place among the Europeans as slightly eccentric or 'sentimental' cousins. The final scene in the novel emphasizes most explicitly Germany's position as part of a shared European intellectual culture and literary tradition, when Heinrich, the youngest of the family, reaches into the stove where his angry grandmother has thrown 'some rubbishy French book' (1946: 143), a collection of the poems by the French poet Pierre Ronsard, and picks it out. The book is unharmed by the heat and comes to symbolize hope that Europe's fate and particularly its literary traditions can be extracted from the ashes of war. It is significant that it is his grandmother, who symbolizes the past and has lived through two world wars, who throws the book on to the fire, and the youngest member of the family retrieves it, emphasizing Jameson's desire to see future generations move beyond the conflicts of their elders towards this united Europe, inspired perhaps by a shared literary past.

Despite the von Galens's calm exterior, they are unable to move beyond the occupation of their country by the Allies, and, like their counterparts elsewhere in Europe, they respond to occupation through their own acts of resistance. By the end of the novel, the outwardly reasonable and accepting Paul von Galen has been arrested for his part in an assassination attempt on some visiting English politicians. This action is portrayed not as a regression to traditional associations of Germans with savagery or unreasonableness, but as the natural reaction of a nation under occupation, as it is in Jameson's novels of Czechoslovakia or France. Von Galen justifies his attack, arguing that to him it is a matter of 'the difference between a vindictive peace and war' (1946: 126). He views the Allied victory and occupation of Germany as an unfair punishment and as a deliberate humiliation of his nation, a point which I take up in the next section. His reasons for fighting the occupiers are similar to those of the Czechs and the French: the result of years of German defeats and the desire to demonstrate to Europe the resilience and strength of his nation. Although Jameson certainly does not ask that her reader empathize with von Galen's murderous intent, his act of resistance represents another aspect of shared experience with other occupied populations across Europe.

The Other Side explores the flux between victor and defeated, occupier and occupied. The question raised initially by the title – it is unclear whether 'the other side' describes the Germans or the Allies; it depends, of course, on perspective – is its central concern. It also draws attention to the emphasis during occupation and wartime on otherness and difference as a means of dividing and conquering nations. As Marie, the Frenchwoman who becomes the conscience of the novel or its moral compass, admits, 'we all know in our bones that victory doesn't pay – after a victory the dead will still be dead, the war will have been a crime and humanity will have been poisoned' (1946: 78). Her very presence, as a French woman who married a German following the invasion of France in the First World War, draws attention to the futility of victory and defeat by shifting the emphasis of the novel from Allied triumph over Germany to the shared suffering of all of Europe in wartime. Through this, the novel depicts many of the issues in Germany immediately in 1945, as the Allies struggled to take control of the country and to assign responsibility, justice and even retribution for its crimes. The novel's failure to mention or even allude to the horrors of the Holocaust constitutes an oversight in terms of Jameson's clear intention to represent Germany following the war and to address issues of responsibility; however, this is something that she comes closer to addressing in *The Black Laurel*. That novel, written the following year, can be seen to move beyond the sentimental urges of *The Other Side* and its desire to understand and empathize with Germany and to record a shared experience, to explore the consequences of Allied victory, particularly in terms of the legal processes which might deal with the defeated. *The Other Side* is primarily dedicated to resurrecting the sense of a shared Europeanness which underpinned Jameson's commitment to the European project, of highlighting shared experiences and shared culture in order to make the case against severe postwar punishment for Germany. The novel can be seen as an attempt to prepare Germany, even in her own mind, for reintegration into European circles by marking out similarities, by re-establishing cultural links and by reconfiguring Germany's humanity through the experiences of one family.

'Now my child, I will hear your confession': Justice and retribution in occupied Germany

If *The Other Side* seeks to draw parallels between the German experience of occupation and other experiences of occupation across the European continent, *The Black Laurel* attempts a description of the human suffering which took place in Germany and particularly Berlin after the war. This is an unusual endeavour for an English writer, as Marina MacKay explains:

> German and Japanese war experiences were not only unspeakable in the familiar, colloquial sense that there seemed no words to describe destruction on such an unprecedented scale (Dresden, Hamburg, Berlin, Tokyo, Hiroshima, Nagasaki), but also politically unspeakable initially because their countries were occupied by the Victorious Allied Powers, and, in the longer term, because of the moral difficulty of saying anything that could be construed as 'we suffered too' – which risks eliciting the response that, first, 'they' brought it on themselves, and, second, that the crimes committed against them were dwarfed by those committed in their name. (2009: 4)

Jameson here seeks to give voice to this unspeakable German experience. This was an unusual undertaking for a British novelist in 1944 when Jameson was writing the novel, as the liberation of the concentration camps was beginning to reveal the true extent of the Holocaust. Jameson herself described the theme of the book as 'one of the oldest and darkest themes in the world, the problem of justice versus expedience' (1984c: 203). In order to encapsulate this problem, the novel presents a full spectrum of German suffering, from the ruined cities and their inhabitants to returning Jewish exiles and camp victims. In doing so it calls into question prevailing narratives which called for the wholesale punishment of the German nation for the war and for its complicity in the Holocaust. In fact, as Birkett discusses, this desire to depict German suffering and to pose 'questions which no one wanted to hear about England's collective responsibility for the devastation of Europe' (Birkett, 2009: 276) led to a hostile response to the novel from contemporary reviewers. The novel poses questions about the nature of justice, the limits of punishment and the fitness of the Allied victors to deliver either justice or peace. These themes of justice and retribution beginning in *The Other Side* run throughout Jameson's postwar works and on into novels such as *The Hidden River* which I discuss in the next chapter.

This examination begins with another good German – Lucius Gerlach. In *The Black Laurel*, Gerlach inhabits in 'a cell' outside Berlin, this description in itself evocative of punishment and sentence and even of Christian penance or contemplation (1947a: 51). The description offered of these living quarters enforce this sense of a self-imposed punishment and exile, wherein Gerlach lives in 'one room and a half room, held together by boards' and the 'living room was near empty' but for 'a stretcher he used for a bed, a table, a shelf, three or four chairs' (1947a: 51). Gerlach's sparse room is juxtaposed with the affluence of the 'great family house of the Gerlachs' with its 'avenue of lime trees', 'the wings, lower than that of the main building' and the great library inherited from generations before (1947a: 53). Like Paul von Galen, Gerlach is characterized by his thinness, his 'very long narrow face, the long finely arched nose, the eyes so deeply set that they looked out from their pits with the absence from the world of a gothic saint' (1947a: 50). Gerlach's suffering body also becomes a site itself for penance, its sparse surroundings enforcing his deliberate exile from bodily comfort as if to express solidarity with the rest of Germany, suffering following the Allied victory, and even with the populations of Europe wronged by his countrymen.

Gerlach's death at the hands of Nazi collaborator Dr Gustav Leist reinforces this Christ-like bodily suffering. In the moments before he is shot Lucius Gerlach 'imagines [a] familiar voice: *Now my child, I will hear your confession*' (1947a: 262; original emphasis). The confession, of his complicity as a German in the crimes of his nation, is implicit in this description. He is even referred to as a 'gothic St Francis' (1947a: 158), St Francis being the second person in the Christian tradition after St Paul to receive the stigmata and to bear the wounds of Christ's passion. Gerlach offers himself up to be sacrificed so that Germany may be absolved, may attain forgiveness and may begin the process of reconciliation and of rebuilding. He stands accused of 'preaching defeatism, of insulting the national honour by his talk of guilt, of denouncing people to his English friends'

(1947a: 257). As the charges are read by Leist in a deserted house within the 'blind lunar desert' (1947a: 256) of Berlin, the language is of a traditional court – 'the prosecution' 'your judges' (1947a: 257) – but the vigilante justice exacted by Leist and Gerlach's Nazi nephew draws out the inherent bias of victor judging defeated or vice versa. No trial in *The Black Laurel* is conducted in an atmosphere of fairness or justice – only revenge and prejudice. In keeping with his Christ-like characterization, as his death sentence is passed, Gerlach forgives his nephew – his Judas – for his involvement in his murder, arguing, 'I want you to remember that you're not responsible for this business, do you hear? I acted for myself. I did what I chose to do, you're not in any way to blame' (1947a: 261). Although it was Rudi Gerlach who lured him to the abandoned house, his uncle will not blame him for his misguided actions. The betrayal of Lucius by his nephew can be seen to express Jameson's anxiety about the corruption of youth by the ideologies which came in the preceding decades to contaminate the young minds of Europe and to motivate them in committing terrible crimes. Lucius Gerlach is dogged by guilt and not by vengefulness, but by a need to be absolved and for his nation to redeem itself in the eyes of the world. His death echoes that of Hesse in *Europe to Let* but, instead of symbolizing the descent of Germany into Nazism, becomes a Christ-like act in which this good German dies for the sins of Europe. It also stands for Jameson's growing scepticism that the judicial processes of postwar Europe are robust enough to dole out any kind of justice on its behalf.

Gerlach's is not the only suffering body in Jameson's decimated Berlin. Her highly-emotive rendering of the Jewish art historian, Heinrich Kalb, recently returned to the city, evokes the physical and emotional torment of the refugee, just as it gestures again toward the inability of the Allied military courts to contain or confront the horrors of Berlin's recent history. Kalb is knocked down in the street when he first returns to Berlin, a testament perhaps to his invisibility and his placelessness as a refugee: 'You forget, he scolded himself, you're no longer in London, and harmless, a harmless foreigner, here you're a German' (1947a: 42). His words and even his conviction that he remains 'a German' draw attention to his statelessness as the crowd in the street avert their eyes, although his Jewishness is not revealed until later in the passage. Kalb's body is also 'skinny', and his placelessness is epitomized by the physical shame he feels at causing embarrassment and inconvenience, 'the pain they gave him was so acute he told himself he must go away' (1947a: 42). Even in his lodgings he is uncomfortable and the barrenness of his rooms and the cold, as 'there was a faint click in the meter; the flames sank, quivered, died' (1947a: 42), forces him back out onto the hostile street. Kalb, like Gerlach, finds no comfort in this Berlin even if it is his home, and his suffering is encapsulated by the painful bodily responses he has to the city's coldness towards him.

Kalb returns to Berlin to find his friends and family dead and the city haunted by their ghosts. Despite being forced out of his job as an art historian at the University and his time as a refugee in England, he is ashamed of his survival of the Holocaust, his 'happy safe life' (1947a: 46). In Berlin

> A dark stream flowed behind his eyes: voices floated in it and broke when they reached him, like bubbles – his mother's, Walther's, anonymous voices from the black market and the cellars of dead houses. He tried to make himself deaf. Suddenly he thought: No! no!
> 'No,' he said, 'come, I'll shelter you all.'
> He opened his skinny arms widely. (1947a: 47)

Kalb attempts to console his murdered kinsmen, and to protect them in an attempt to assuage his own feelings of guilt and isolation. He embraces these ghosts as if to call them back to life and hold them there, offering them the protection he feels he could not offer them from the Nazis. They represent a Berlin lost to him on the day he left and which he can never reclaim. Kalb's need to feel a part of this lost community, to be part of Berlin, even if it means placing himself among the dead, further illustrates his estrangement from the living and from the nation to which he has returned, consolidating his position as a potential sacrifice for the Allied regime, which he eventually becomes.

Yet Jameson's description of Kalb is not wholly sympathetic. Other characters recoil from his Jewishness, perhaps repelled by its proximity to the horrors of the Holocaust, perhaps as an expression of the ongoing anti-Semitism within wider European society. He is a 'meagre little German' (1947a: 42), and later, when he firsts bumps into the young British pilot Arnold Coster in the street, Coster describes him as 'a skinny creature' and 'a man-sized insect' (1947a: 36). Even as he languishes in jail awaiting conviction for a crime he did not commit, he is described even by his sympathetic visitors as 'an unprepossessing insect' (1947a: 230). In the eyes of these characters, the nature of Kalb's exclusion is such that he is almost unhuman.[4] This preoccupation with the Jewish body as inhuman or as other is also visible in Jameson's other novels such as *Europe to Let*, in which Esk first describes Nicholas Tihaneth as having 'black hair, black sparkling eyes, a round white creased face' (1940b: 229) but, upon revealing that he is Jewish, offers immediately a new description, concentrating on his blunt features 'modelled in flesh the colour and texture of soft India rubber' and 'his mouth close and fine' (1940b: 230). While Jameson's portrayal of Kalb seems to evoke sympathy with his suffering and his symbolism of Jewish suffering, the ambivalence of her portrayal and other portrayals elsewhere in her novels points towards her characters' and wider society's discomfort with the Jewish other, elements of which she may share but which is overcome by her disgust with the crimes of the Holocaust as an attempt to exterminate *any* group of individuals.

This is supported in many ways by her Foreword to *The Diary of Anne Frank*, published almost ten years later in 1954. Here, she acknowledges the horrors of the Holocaust and the feelings of 'stupefaction' which acknowledging those crimes must arouse in her readers. However, she is cautious, describing it as 'wrong, unprofitable to ride off by throwing the whole blame on any nation or sect' (1954: 9). For Jameson, all Europeans were complicit in a crime which she soul-searchingly attributes to the tendencies of men to 'press a doctrine over ears and eyes, so that they could torture without being distracted by the victim's agony' (1954: 10). She comes to assign the actions of the Nazis not only to 'their merely murderous side – Hitler's obsessive hatred of the Jews' but to an overarching human desire to try to shape history 'to sacrifice a generation, two generations to the future they serve' (1954: 10). This desire to somehow absolve Germany of guilt for the Holocaust, as somehow only executing a human function within a perceived, though erroneous sense of historical progress, seems heartless, simplistic even. However, it points to a part of Jameson's wider worldview that man is politically and socially prone to cruelty and her sense is that this could have happened anywhere, in any nation, where the political and economic conditions could be deployed to justify and distract. That she still – in 1954 – following the Nuremburg trials – could attain this level of distance is remarkable, but also testament to her sense that Europe as a whole was complicit in the horrors of the Holocaust and that blaming and punishing a nation could create an unending cycle of retribution which could plunge the Continent into another war. Even the final line of the Foreword, which states that 'Anne Frank took with her, into a mass grave, every exquisite intellectual structure which allows its servants to torture, to work to death, to kill, for an idea' (1954: 11) seems to fall short. These tendencies had not of course disappeared, however much she might will them to do so.[5] Jameson's philosophical and humanist response to the Holocaust is, of course, underpinned by her privilege as a white British woman, but her instinct that European civilization itself must shoulder the responsibility for this event speaks directly to her earlier convictions that the cruel rottenness taking over Europe in the 1930s was not wholly a German problem, but a Europe-wide concern.

It is this sense of a universal moral decline which actuates her distrust of the very systems entrusted with recognizing and righting Europe's wrongs. Kalb is accused of spying for the Nazis in Britain, his very statelessness seemingly sufficient evidence for the prosecution because, as one observer of the trial notes, 'One definition of refugee is *bad citizen*' (1947a: 318). As Mankowitz describes, following the Holocaust, many Jews who returned from the camps to an Allied-occupied Europe came to describe themselves as 'liberated but not free' (2002: 45) because of their continued statelessness. Just as Carl Schmidt used the 'state of emergency' to remove protections from Jews and other citizens under the Nazis, so the emergency of the Allied occupation seems to allow for the killing of another Jew, placed outside the law by his former refugee status and the need for demonstrable justice.[6] As the same sorts of exceptions to proper legal process can be employed in light of the occupation and de-Nazification of Germany at the hands of the Allies, Kalb faces exactly the sort of 'inclusive-exclusion' (1998: 20) from the law that Giorgio Agamben attributes to the victims of the Nazi camps. Kalb is included in the law only so far as he is exempt from many of its protections, and this is as applicable under the military court system as it was under the Nazi regime. He is, as Adam Piette notes, 'the Jewish sacrificial victim of the novel' (2009: 20). He remains neither an enemy combatant nor a friend, a citizen nor a refugee. In this case, the legal circumstances and erosion of rights which forced Kalb into exile have not necessarily been alleviated by the Allied victory but have simply taken on different guises and different motivations. His fate illustrates, at this early stage, the inability of Allied judicial systems to contain the effects of the war or to fairly adjudicate them.

Kalb's punishment is evocative of what Walter Benjamin's 'Critique of Violence' (1921) views as an inevitable part of the law and particularly the contract between state and citizen. Benjamin writes that 'in the exercise of violence over life and death, more than any other legal act, the law re-affirms itself' (2004: 242). Himself later in life a Jewish refugee fleeing Nazism, Benjamin's insight here has clear parallels with Kalb's fate because, as the British command admit, 'whether he is guilty of murder or looting is less important than the need to be publicly and ruthlessly severe' (1947a: 199). Echoing Jameson's words from her introduction to Anne Frank's diary, here the British are themselves willing 'to sacrifice a generation, two generations to the future they serve' (1954: 10). The sacrifice of Kalb's Jewish body is deployed to preserve the law – to show that Allied justice is 'publicly and ruthlessly severe' – in order to consolidate British control of this sector of Berlin. Jameson here has perhaps come to share a concern which Stonebridge attributes to Hannah Arendt, that 'totalitarianism's rendering superfluous of human life has insinuated itself into the world at a fundamental level' (2011: 10). The parallels which Jameson draws between these two forms of state-sanctioned violence show her discomfort at deploying similarly faulty legal apparatus to that which had been manipulated to allow for the extermination of the Jews, in attempts to resolve the demands for retribution within postwar Europe. Any postwar system of justice must take care not to rush rashly into a retributive scenario which recreates the dehumanizing crimes of those it seeks to punish; justice must be fair not swift, measured and not vengeful.

This theme is continued elsewhere in the novel, when the main protagonist, English former soldier and sometime spy, David Renn, visits a hospital in which concentration camp victims are being treated and rehabilitated. He is appalled by the physical scars of a woman who was in Ravensbrück Camp for five years; he reacts angrily and tells her that 'there can't be any forgiveness', to which she responds: 'Oh, yes. There must be. So much cruelty can only be forgiven. You can't punish it, there was too much' (1947a: 131). Her doctor continues: 'If you're going to start punishment you'll have to bury as many more as are dead already; their children will want to avenge them; there'll be no end to it. I'm for food, clothing, mercy' (1947a: 131). The experiences of the doctor and the woman underpin their beliefs, giving them a moral authority over Renn's very English indignation. The voice of the female victim here emphasizes the natural role of woman as peacemaker and her desire for forgiveness when, throughout Jameson's novels women's lack of political power and personal agency often means that they are the ultimate victims of war, is all the more compelling.[7] Yet the underlying implications of this passage echo again Jameson's fears of the inability of Europe's judicial systems to sufficiently punish these crimes or to do so in a way which in any way constitutes a proportionate response to the horrors of the camps.

However, despite the inclusion of this camp victim, and of Kalb as a representation of the Jewish victims of the Holocaust, there is no in-depth examination of the Holocaust. While Jameson engages widely with ideas of guilt, forgiveness, defeat, occupation and suffering within the German nation, her characters never discuss what took place within those camps or, more specifically, to whom. In part, this can be attributed to Jameson's deep-seated desire to reunite Europe after the war – the horrors of the Holocaust perhaps presented a too greater barrier to reconciliation and the mass graves too great a scar on Europe's conscience to ever be forgiven. Furthermore, Jameson's commitment to realism and truth may have caused her some discomfort in presenting occurrences which she could neither imagine nor comprehend. However, this remains an omission from Jameson's work of the Second World War and one which certainly requires more critical attention.

On an intra-national scale, Jameson also fears that a swift and heavy-handed response on the part of the Allies will only settle 'the causes of the next war' (1984a: 97). The centuries-old conflict between the European nations has been perpetuated by hasty and brutal reckoning of the victors: as Captain Aubrac explains in *The Other Side*, 'I have everything against the Germans, you've invaded us three times in a lifetime, ruined our country, and deported or murdered more than a million young Frenchmen' (1946: 58). In fact, as the English Captain Long observes, 'Brutality is catching, but who was brutal first?' (1946: 53). The only option is reconciliation, as the French soldier Maulnier tells Paul von Galen, 'There's just one hope for the future, and that's for us to become friends, yes, friends' (1946: 91) because 'the day you forgive Aubrac for having mutilated him by torture – and the day when he decides to respect you for your modest efficiency as a farmer, a scientist, or an architect – anything you like except a murderer – that will be the first day of real peace' (1946: 92). Just as Jameson recognizes the horror of the Holocaust and the need for justice, she also recognizes that this cannot be confused under the terms of victor and defeated, nation and nation, citizen and citizen. For her, as the Lutheran pastor who meets with Gerlach in *The Black Laurel* expounds, 'you said too much about guilt, while taking too little pains to discriminate between guilty and innocent. To those of us Germans who are not guilty' (233). The pastor goes on that Gerlach should not use his fame as an intellectual 'to sadden many innocent people whose error – forgivable, like the errors of young children – was that they obeyed the criminals' (1947a: 233). While the Pastor's words can seem to forgive the actions of the Nazis, in light of the previous sentence about 'those of us Germans who are not guilty' it seems more likely to refer to the complicity of the German people in Nazi crimes, than to the actions of the criminals themselves.

The Allies, for Jameson, must also bear some of the guilt for Germany's crimes. Not only did they fail to take earlier decisive action which may have stemmed the violence, but they also settled the 'causes of the next war' with their harsh treatment of Germany at Versailles in 1919. In *Europe to Let*, one of the young fascists informs Renn in 1920 that they will destroy Europe: 'We shall burn it to the ground, with everything in it – Chartres, the Black Forest, Vienna, Prague, Cracow [*sic*]. How will you hate us then. And how in our hearts we shall blame you, for leaving us to play with matches in an icily cold room' (1940b: 36). Here, Germany is the unruly child of Europe and its punishment at Versailles simply amplified its destructive tendencies. This theme re-emerges in the immediate aftermath of the Second World War *The Black Laurel*, when British pilot Arnold Coster asks if occupation and defeat are really best to rehabilitate Germany: 'It's not the sanest place in the world, is it? Wouldn't it be better to leave them to pull themselves together? Give them the rules, no dangerous toys, no aeroplanes, no guns – then abandon them, with the R.A.F. as male nurses keeping an eye on them' (1947a: 116). Coster wishes not to punish but to rehabilitate, calling for compassion and empathy rather than retribution. If it is 'wrong, unprofitable to ride off by throwing the whole blame on any nation or sect' (Jameson, 1954: 9), then Germany cannot be abandoned or vilified. The only future for the German nation lies in understanding and forgiveness and a place within a new and peaceful Europe, rather than the 'icily cold' political isolation post-Versailles.

With these depictions of postwar Germany, Jameson moves away from her previous tendency to render Germany as the enemy of European liberal values and intellectualism and towards a position of rehabilitation and even forgiveness. As Smith explains, 'Identities are forged out of shared experiences, memories and myths, in relation to those of other collective identities. They are in fact often forged through opposition to the identities of significant others, as the history of paired conflict so often demonstrates' (247). In presenting characters with more complex relations to the German nation, Jameson attempts to move away from the 'paired conflict' which haunted Europe's past and which impaired its future. In jettisoning something of the national to enact a consideration of the individual and individual responsibility she seems to suggest that the punishment of whole nations is too much of a blunt instrument for the complex events which have taken place. Looking to a postwar world in which both Allied victors and victims sought swift and harsh retribution for the crimes of the Holocaust and of Nazi war crimes across Europe, Jameson in these postwar novels calls for calm and for reflection. She is mindful of the tendency for victors to seek vengeance as well as justice, and suspicious of the capacity of legal systems to cope with demands for justice when there was 'so much cruelty' that 'you can't punish it, there was too much' (1947a: 131). In recognizing, as she does throughout her oeuvre, man's capacity for cruelty, and the 'tide of cruelty' beneath the surface of Europe, Jameson calls time on the cycle of conflict in Europe in an effort to stop a vituperative postwar justice from enacting more cruelty still.

5

'The same tricks, the same corruption': Aftermath, resistance and reconciliation in *The Hidden River* and *The Moment of Truth*

Following the Second World War, understanding of the term 'nation' became further complicated and problematized as the effects of wartime displacement and occupation, the realignment of borders and the dissolution of empire made themselves felt around the world. The idea of 'nationalism' itself was, in the period following the war, burdened by associations with fascism and with genocide, and ideas of nation and belonging were further complicated as, for example, the Jewish diaspora began to seek a permanent homeland and inhabitants of the colonies were invited to come to live in colonial centres.[1] This period also marked a loosening of the bonds of nation or a disillusionment of writers with nation as a construct. As Marina MacKay notes 'Citizenship and the English Novel in 1945', 'If the embrace in 1940s novels of a specific version of the nation bespeaks wartime loyalties, in postwar fiction, by contrast, the state has no such attachments' (2016: 34). After two shattering conflicts, Europe was losing its political and cultural currency to the new superpowers, America and Russia. In addition to realigning and reconstructing themselves on a national level, postwar European nations were forming allegiances to East and West, to Russia and to America. Jameson's work of the 1950s and 1960s explores many of these issues, from communist threat to postcolonial violence. This chapter explores how novels such as *The Moment of Truth* (1949) and *The Hidden River* (1955) articulate these changes on both a private and a public level. Each novel presents the private crises of its characters, from a French family obsessed with the Resistance and with postwar retribution, to a young woman fleeing communist Europe for a new life in America with her child. Nonetheless, each takes place within a very public context: the Cold War and the postwar trials of Nazi collaborators. For all that these novels appear to look outwards from Europe, or forwards to another war or to another threat, each one is firmly entrenched in the Europe of the Second World War. Therefore, while these two novels represent an engagement with the postwar world and with postwar issues, they should also be understood as retrospective, continuing to foreground the wartime experience of European nations and even projecting it onto other countries and cultures.

As Jameson writes in 1950, only the most naïve writer imagines that he can go back to 1939 and that 'he is still being asked the precisely the same question, in precisely the same words. Only the most naïve of us imagine that there is no need to look at the words again, closely, to see what has been happening to them during these years – even a word like justice, a word like freedom' (1939: 5). In these postwar novels Jameson does precisely this, returning to the same concerns – Europe, civilization, justice, freedom – and re-evaluating them in their postwar context.[2] *The Moment of Truth*, in depicting a dystopian world in which all Europe seems defeated, remains rooted in Jameson's understanding of the previous two world wars, replicating many of her fears about European civilization from earlier novels such as *Cousin Honoré* and *Europe to Let*. This demonstrates not only a circularity in Jameson's novels at this time but also her own sense of the circularity of repeated European experiences of threat and war. Applying this to the more explicit examination of postwar France in *The Hidden River* and its return to *The Black Laurel*'s themes of treachery, retribution and justice, this chapter draws out the links between these postwar novels and Jameson's prewar and wartime fiction. For Jameson, the threat to Europe is reconstituted in the postwar period but the postwar world returns to the same prewar questions, questions which remain unanswered.

With that in mind, while the novels examined here are not the only ones that Jameson published during this time, they are the ones that engage most readily with her prewar and wartime ideas around resistance, collaboration and civilization. Jameson's other novels of this era most often depict incidents closer to home and are indicative of the narrowing of Jameson's vision into the mid and late 1960s.[3] Unlike this other postwar work, the novels examined here continue themes of 'justice and expedience' and of the future of European civilization and, viewed alongside others such as *The Green Man* (1952) and *One Ulysses Too Many* (1958), indicate not only the foresight but also the retrospective qualities evident in Jameson's writing during this period. *The Hidden River* continues *The Black Laurel*'s analysis of treachery, resistance and justice, by exploring acts of betrayal within the French resistance. Not only does this constitute an important and timely interaction with the myths of French nationhood in circulation across Europe during this time, it also interrogates the nature of the punishment deemed necessary for betrayal of family, of France and of the Resistance itself. The swift and brutal execution of the perpetrator, sacrificed for the good name of his family and for the future of France, echoes the themes of sacrifice in *The Black Laurel*, in which individuals are killed for political gain. *The Moment of Truth* engages with similar issues around the individual as part of a larger political project, in examining which bodies deserve to be rescued from a dying Europe and sent to live a new life in America. In this sense, Jameson can be seen to interact not only with ongoing discussions about justice and retribution, but also contemporary discussions around human rights, exemplified by the Universal Declaration of Human Rights, ratified in 1948, a year before the publication of *The Moment of Truth* and seven years before the publication of *The Hidden River*.

Through placing these novels in dialogue with Jameson's earlier work, this chapter also traces her disappointment with the postwar period in light of her hopes before the Second World War that another conflict would create a better world. Historian Tony Judt argues that the myths still circulating about postwar Europe at the end of the twentieth century hugely overestimate the success of its postwar recovery, belying undercurrents of anxiety and despair in order to present a 'miracle' in which 'post-national Europe had learned the bitter lessons of recent history' and 'had risen, "Phoenix-like", from the ashes of its murderous suicidal past' (2010: 5). Now threatened by communism and by Cold War politics, the Europe which Jameson prized seems outdated and outdone. From France's myth-making around the Resistance's role in liberation to the feared communist other of *The Moment of Truth* to the treachery and suspicion which characterizes these two novels, the politics of the postwar period can also be seen to represent a new cycle in Jameson's work, as much as it interacts with the old. This new cycle represents and intervenes in the same nation-building practices as her earlier work, using them to recover and reposition Europe in response to a new threat. However, these later novels are coloured by a pessimism not evident in her earlier novels. Here, Europe is defeated, rotten and consumed with hatred: in *The Moment of Truth*, Europe seems unequivocally without redemption and dialogue centres around the move to America. Just as each of the novels examined here can be viewed as a 're-wording' of prewar questions, so each conveys a sense of disappointment at the lack of progress in the postwar world in which such questions must be addressed at all. Furthermore, they are an expression not of the new Europe envisioned by Jameson in 1939, but of the demise of the old, a Europe unable to keep pace with the postwar world.

'All Europe is defeated': Russia, America and the end of Europe

It would be easy to assume that the end of the war and the triumph of the Allies in 1945 would assuage Jameson's fears about the future of Europe and the future of civilization. While novels such as *The Black Laurel* and *Before the Crossing* re-evaluate the war and its reverberations across Europe in the early years of peace, they only look back, never ahead to the future. By 1949, Jameson was beginning to look ahead to this future and to see not peace and prosperity, but further threats to her idea of European civilization stemming from the conflict between two new global superpowers. Like many other writers of the period she refers in a number of her novels of the 1950s and 1960s, most notably *A Cup of Tea for Mr Thorgill* and *The Green Man*, to communist threat and in particular to ideas of suspicion, treachery and espionage. However, it is *The Moment of Truth* which paints the bleakest picture of the Cold War – the triumph of Soviet Communism in the aftermath of the Third World War. This dystopian novel depicts a Europe overrun by Soviet armies, whose inhabitants are forced to choose between life under Soviet occupation or exile in America. This chapter explores the juxtaposition of America and the Soviet Union in the novel, its implications for Jameson's ideas about Europe and its links to the contemporary political situation epitomized by the increasing likelihood at this time of a global power struggle between these two former Allied powers.

The Moment of Truth engages very notably with ideas around territory, civilization and contamination in a way that suggests Jameson's continued inability to adjust to a peacetime world. This is the result of wider processes of national myth-making and the reconfiguration of international hierarchies taking place as the result of the early stages of the Cold War. While the Russians had been responsible, for the most part, for liberating Berlin in 1945, the city was now divided between France, Russia, Britain and the United States. Even before the war ended, each of these powers was acutely aware of the tactical value of Germany as a central point in Europe, as well as the political implications of control over Berlin and the future of Germany itself. Lenin had stated in 1921 that 'whoever holds Berlin, holds Germany. Whoever holds Germany, holds Europe' (Thody, 2000: 21), and Stalin remained mindful of this throughout the closing stages of the war. In February 1945, as Allied victory seemed secure, America, Britain and Russia met at Yalta to decide what course of action to take with postwar Europe and, in particular, with Germany. The conference not only involved the physical division of former Nazi territories, but it also led, ultimately, to the division of wider Europe into East and West, the East aligned with Soviet Communism and the West by American capitalism.[4] As Fraser J. Harbutt describes, the conference, though not reported in detail at the time, led to 'a generalised European sense of subjection to a United-States/Soviet hegemony' (2010: 2). *The Moment of Truth* presents precisely the concerns generated across Europe by Yalta, as the conference came to act as 'a symbol for the Europeans of their eclipse at the hands of the two supposedly hegemonic superpowers' (Harbutt, 2010: 3). The myths established around Yalta during this period, and the escalation of tensions which took place in the four years between the conference and this novel, inform its concerns regarding (and Jameson's well-documented interest in) the future of European civilization.

The Moment of Truth depicts the surrender of this European civilization from the perspective of a group of military personnel on an isolated military base in a Britain on the brink of Soviet invasion. They have already been ordered by their superiors to abandon their posts and to retreat to America, from where they hope to continue the fight against Soviet Communism and to retake Britain and Europe. However, the arrival of a convoy of civilians deemed particularly worthy of escape by military authorities forces the young soldiers to re-evaluate who will qualify for the last flight out of Britain. The majority of the novel comes to focus on discussions around who is most deserving of a seat on the plane and of life in Soviet-occupied Europe as opposed to exile in America. In placing this group of British people between Soviet aggression and an unknown and unfamiliar America, the novel acts as a metaphor for the struggle between the Soviets and the Americans for domination of Europe and Britain's position as ally either to Europe *or* to America. It depicts Britain under threat of invasion, transposing myths of the threatened nation from Jameson's earlier novels onto a British setting for the first time and combining these with the emphatically Cold War concerns about treachery, spies and fifth columnists.

The Moment of Truth presents Britain as the last bastion of Europe and its defeat as the final collapse of European civilization, as it had been in the last war. Dr Emil Breuner, an eminent scientist recently evacuated from occupied Austria, makes this link clear, admitting, 'It is true – England is defeated; and all Europe is defeated. The defeat has gone too far to be stopped' (1949: 46). However, repeating themes from earlier works such as *Europe to Let* and *Cousin Honoré*, he continues that 'Europe had collapsed already, before the barbarians began moving across it' (1949: 46). For Breuner, it is the Russians who constitute 'the barbarians', and not the Nazis so often described in these terms by characters in Jameson's earlier novels. Here also, these barbarians represent not the architects, but the symptoms of a wider decline. Breuner evokes, as characters such as Honoré did ten years previously, the same images of European culture under threat, declaring that the Russians 'will destroy out of suspicion and ignorance' (1949: 46), and emphasizes the loss of cultural sites such as historic cities, cathedrals and libraries. As well as echoing Jameson's earlier novels in its depiction of the demise of European civilization under Nazism, the association in the novel of the Russians with barbarism reflects contemporary political views on Russia's growing power and influence in Europe. In a broadcast on 3 January 1948, British Prime Minister Clement Attlee told the nation that Soviet Communism 'pursues a policy of imperialism in a new form – ideological, economic and strategic – which threatens the welfare and way of life of other nations in Europe' (*The Times*, 5 January 1948), and Ernest Bevin, then Foreign Secretary, wrote a paper entitled 'The Threat to Civilisation' evaluating the threat to Europe from an expansionist Russia. The Russians thus came to occupy the position of Europe's bogeyman, one borrowed from the defeated Nazis, but one which encapsulated the same threat to Europe's culture, its traditions and its heritage over a decade after the first signs of Nazi aggression against Poland and Czechoslovakia (countries in which communism had already taken hold). Jameson's novel captures popular discourses and myth-making concerning the consequences of Russian expansion for Europe, as well as revisiting her own earlier fears and preoccupations about European civilization.

This idea of a precious European civilization remains embedded in the European culture that defined it in Jameson's prewar work. As discussions regarding who will be chosen for the final flight from Britain intensify among the civilians and soldiers in the novel, the idea of cultural and intellectual preservation becomes increasingly topical. Two of the civilians who arrive at the airbase, the writer George Heron and the scientist Breuner, are understood as being of superior international importance to the rest of the group because of the contribution they may or may not make to the intellectual future.[5] Although Breuner profoundly doubts his own value and is critical of moves to save him, he also shares the group's concerns that 'there [is] anything, my God, more important than to save a few seeds of our civilisation and replant them in decent soil' (1949: 79). He is surprised at the soldiers' apparent indifference to European intellectual heritage. The writer, Heron, is less brave than Breuner and is almost hysterical about his own survival and the importance of his work. He tells his wife dramatically, 'I shall have to learn to detach myself from Europe – and the agony and despair of Europe' because 'you can't write properly about a death-bed when you can still smell it' (1949: 103). Heron is content not only to leave Europe but to forget it and to use its misfortune to further his own career in America. Cowardly and with delusions about his own success, he is an early foreshadow of Jameson's later novels and their focus on the arrogance and fickleness of writers, such as Geoffrey Mott in *The Road to the Monument*, the arrogant Mark Smith in *A Month Soon Goes* and the insufferable William Acker in *The Green Man*. Both Heron and Breuner testify to what is seen in *The Moment of Truth* as a political imperative to remove the intellectual 'seeds' of Europe to the relative safety of America, in the hope they will thrive in the soil of the new world. Each demonstrates the good and bad sides of European civilization that Jameson articulates throughout her work, representing its sense of justice, intellect and culture alongside its arrogance, selfishness and narcissism. Their presence engenders debates over the desirability, the morality and viability of preserving a European culture for transplant to America, as well as echoing PEN's attempts to preserve European culture in the face of the Nazi threat during the Second World War.

The novel also shares with Jameson's earlier works a tendency to depict Europe's occupation in terms of disease and contamination, as in novels such as *Europe to Let* and *The Black Laurel*. Breuner speaks with real empathy and warmth towards the idea of Europe, urging the others to do the same: 'You shouldn't despise Europe. It can still, I think, teach you a little it has learned before suffering [its final decline]' (1949: 58). This affective, sympathetic rendering of Europe falls just short of a personification of the continent as an elderly, wise, but distinctly human presence. Breuner's words echo contemporary concerns about the demise of Europe as an international or political power. The Continent and the nations within it are no longer capable of sustaining human life or even the type of European cultural life which characters like Breuner feel that it should, because even 'a country dies when its time comes – when the body ceases to renew itself: when the flesh is no longer warm, generous, able to love' (1949: 93). Not only is this reminiscent of depictions of the nation or continent as mother, a motif which I discussed earlier in relation to *Cousin Honoré*, it also gestures towards nuclear war and anxieties about the atomic bomb which, during this period, constitute another reason why a nation's 'body ceases to renew itself' following the poison of radiation. The growing spectre of nuclear warfare underpins this characterization and the novel's dramatic departure from the firm conviction in *The Fort* and other novels that 'you can't kill a nation' (1941: 7). Here, the organic body of Europe suggests not only disease and suffering as it has previously done, but the finality of death, reflecting the physical desolation of nuclear war, as well as the political impotence and irrelevance of Europe in the Cold War world. Even in *The Black Laurel*, the 'corpse of Europe' is 'flayed while still *living*' (1947a: 35; emphasis added). Here there is no question of life, just death and decline. Europe, in this novel, has passed the point of no return.

In this new world order, America stands as a symbol of hope in contrast to Russian aggression and barbarism. This is ironic, predominantly because America was often characterized in Jameson's earlier novels as symbolic of the forces of modernity and capitalism feared by characters such as Honoré and Handel Wikker. In fact, it was only after 1941, when Pearl Harbour made American intervention in the war inevitable, that Jameson, in response to her own convictions about the duty of a European writer, set about compiling and editing a collection championing American involvement. In *London Calling: A Salute to America* (1942), she and thirty-two contributors, including E.M. Forster, Liddell-Hart, E.M. Delafield, Macaulay and Priestley, draw parallels between America and Britain, seeking to explain British experiences of war and 'to repay [Americans] for the kindness on kindness on kindness, shown us since the beginning of the war' (Jameson, 1942a: 5), as well as encouraging further military engagement on the Allied side.[6] In this volume, it is American involvement which symbolizes hope for Europe, whereas in the fictional circumstances of *The Moment of Truth*, America is a much more ambivalent prospect, embodying not only safety and hope but also exile and defeat. In the postwar era, America's position as both saviour and safe haven represents not the cooperation of allies against mutual enemies as it once did, but a reminder of Europe's failure. As Breuner, the experienced exile of the group, tells the others, 'Don't pretend it's anything but humiliating to leave the country because we're defeated' (1949: 80). Here, the move to America is necessitated by the defeat of Europe and its occupation by Russian forces, but it is problematized also by the perceived differences between European and American life. Just as Jameson came to embrace America both personally and in her work, the characters in the novel must, in a reflection of the dilemma facing British politicians in the postwar world, appraise the future role of America as Britain's friend or foe.

Each character holds his or her own doubts and anxieties about abandoning Britain in the face of Russian invasion and about America as the future of defeated Europe. At first America is 'the bulwark, the hope, the only, yes, future, of our [...] deeds and words since 1945' (1949: 94). Heron worries that 'perhaps America is too far. Or the wrong kind of soil for seeds from Europe' (1949: 80), tying his concerns to difference and to the incompatibility of America with European ideals. He is sure that 'over there they don't know what it is to be European. They don't want to know. After all, why should they [...] why should they want a living corpse dragged into their rooms?' (1949: 103), echoing the concerns of Jameson's characters in earlier novels that America is too modern and too new for a decaying Europe. The best that Heron can hope for is to dupe himself that America can become a facsimile of Europe, telling his wife that they should move to California because 'the sea there would remind us of Antibes. There are hills, pine forests, cypresses. There'll be sand. In fact, very like the Mediterranean' (1949: 103). For General Thorburn, the very idea of transplanting European culture to America seems fruitless, as he explains to Breuner: 'I'm not sure you can save ideas by bolting with them. Either they're alive and kicking and don't need you to save them, or they're beyond anyone's help' (1949: 80). In the novel, America is a cultural receptacle to carry the hopes of Europe, and its inhabitants, into the coming century. What each character comes to question is not only the viability of this project, but also the desirability of sustaining what they view as a dying European civilization in a foreign land.

In a further interrogation of the importance of America for the future of Europe and its inhabitants, as well as to complicate the discussions concerning qualification for a seat on the plane, one of the military personnel discovers that she is pregnant. Cordelia Hugh-Brown is Jameson's only depiction of a female soldier (or in this case a member of the WRAF). She is repeatedly defined or understood in the novel not as a female combatant or as a woman, but as an expectant mother. Hugh-Brown conceals her pregnancy from her lover, eventually disclosing it to another woman, Elizabeth Heron, the writer's wife, as the reason she would like to be allowed aboard the plane. She begs Heron to give up her seat and to help to secure safe passage for herself and her lover, Kent. Her unborn child and this young family come to symbolize, for her and for the older woman, the hope of the British nation. Elizabeth Heron realizes this after their conversation, describing to her husband 'that boy, Andrew Kent – and the girl' as 'those children' (1949: 105). In her eyes, both herself and her husband are 'saving ourselves at the expense [...] of two younger people' (1949: 106). For her, this is inexcusable, and she makes it clear that she feels that they should give up their places on the plane. In the novel, these 'children', and the Herons' son Nicholas, represent the most important cargo to be taken from a dying Britain to America, where they will enjoy wealth, prosperity and, crucially, a safety that is not available at home. Although Kent refuses to travel in the end, preferring to execute his duty in Britain, the others travel onwards to New York to represent the future of Europe and the possibility of the continuation of European culture in America.

Here, youth – just as much as Heron's cultural achievements and Breuner's scientific reputation – is also seen as a qualifying factor. This constitutes a further reference to Jameson's earlier tendency to stress the importance of youth in preserving and renewing European civilization. It is also evocative of the First World War motif of the older generation murdering the young. Here, the tables are turned as young and old call into question the viability of transporting the elderly members of the group, who had been previously earmarked for seats on the plane. Hugh-Brown asks, 'Why should one of the old generals go?' when there are 'thousands of young women in this country, waiting for sons to be born to them' (1949: 69), while Breuner himself admits that 'the brigadier and I are both old men, tottering on the edge of the grave. One of us may easily drop into it before the aeroplane gets there' (1949: 90). In a reversal of the old myths of 'Class 1914' (1933: 102), it is the more senior members of the group who choose to sacrifice themselves for the good of the young and for the future of Europe. It is not the old – imbued as they are with the corruption of the dying continent – in whose demise they played a key role, but the young who, as in pre–Second World War novels such as *Europe to Let*, will carry the ideas of the European nation into the future.

This bleak vision for the future in *The Moment of Truth* is of a war to which all previous conflict has built and which will finally destroy the European continent whose decline has featured in so many of Jameson's novels of the previous decades. Despite the glimmers of hope given by the prospect of European youth and ideas flourishing elsewhere, an overwhelming sense of irretrievable decline and defeat dominates this novel. Framed within the juxtaposition of Soviet Russia and America at the beginning of the Cold War, the novel captures contemporary tensions and the precariousness of the postwar world. It represents not only an early exploration of British concerns in the early stages of the Cold War but also a crucible for all of Jameson's fears and anxieties about Europe, America and civilization during the preceding two decades. In fact, the previous world wars are referred to by the ageing General Thorburn as 'a sort of rehearsal for this' (1949: 55). As Thorburn remarks, 'In 1945 there was one hope for us and for Europe – a long peace, fifty, a hundred years of peace: we needed at least that to recover from our loss of blood' (1949: 92). The war in the novel represents a sense of exhaustion, of repetition and of resignation which fills its characters. It also demonstrates Jameson's ambivalent attitude to America's growing power at this time, as Britain sought to align itself with this increasingly powerful ally. The novel can be understood not only as a vision of Cold War hostilities and as further testament to Jameson's wartime preoccupations with the demise of European civilization, but also as a crucial link between these concerns and her later interest in ideas around collaboration, resistance and imperialism.

'Brotherhood, peace, a glorious future and the rest of it': The myth of the French Resistance

In the novels discussed previously, resistance features prominently as a part of national myth-making, from the heroics of Czech resistance in *Then We Shall Hear Singing* to the resistance attacks mounted by the Germans in *The Other Side*. Resistance movements, and the promotion of their successes against the Nazis and other occupiers, had been the subject of a propaganda war during the Second World War. Both Beneš's Czechoslovakian government in exile and de Gaulle's *Comité Français de Libération Nationale* (CFLN) did much to support and to publicize the successes of resistance movements, using them to underpin their postwar bids for national government. Following occupation, these organizations went from covert operations to a national presence, with resistance leaders running for government and federal positions, as well as being called upon by other electoral campaigns to support their political credentials. They also became a crucial element in rebuilding formerly occupied nations. For Pieter Lagrou, following the Second World War, 'the liberated societies of Europe were traumatised, and their new fragile national consciousness was in urgent need of the kind of patriotic epic that only resistance could deliver' (2000: 2). The strength, success and widespread participation of citizens in resistance movements were promoted by politicians and the media to counteract feelings of guilt and shame associated with occupation. According to French historian Henry Rousso, during the final years of the war and the early years of peace, France in particular spawned a myth of resistance as part of 'firstly a process that sought to minimise the importance of the Vichy regime and its impact on French society, including its most negative aspects; second the construction of an object of memory, the "Resistance", whose significance transcended the sum of its active parts' (1991: 10). These myths and constructed memories of the Resistance characterize Jameson's novel *The Hidden River* and the narrative actively critiques and undermines these processes.

Jameson's changing feelings towards France during this time are detailed in 'A Note on France', an article published in the *Cornhill Magazine* in 1954. Here, Jameson debates her evolving opinions of the country she still describes as 'something irreplaceable' (1954: 450), but also 'a France of glaring contradictions' (1954: 441). She examines the 'suffering, the despair, the deportations, the summary executions' (1954: 443), which have left what she describes as 'an unhealed wound in the country's instinctive energy' (1954: 447) following the Second World War. For Jameson, the occupation has changed something of the nature of France as this wound 'is not a clean one […] it is poisoned' (1954: 447), and there is 'no doubt that this wound is still suppurating' (1954: 448). She writes that postwar France is both a product of its prewar failings and a shadow of its former self, containing 'the same tricks, the same corruption, the same names' (1954: 441) and describing how 'everywhere you go in France you come on the plaques and single stones carrying the names of men and women shot, hanged or tortured during the Occupation' (1954: 442). France – the country Jameson always credited with a central role in the foundation of European civilization as she understood it – comes to symbolize her disillusionment with Europe during the postwar period. The family drama of *The Hidden River* can also be read as a microcosm for the poison that Jameson saw at work in France at the time. The novel depicts a French family coming to terms with the aftermath of a war in which Jean Monnerie, the eldest son, played a leading role in the Resistance. Monnerie is haunted by his past and particularly by the death of his cousin, Robert, whose mother, Madame Regnier, took in Monnerie and his brother François when they were orphaned as children. Madame Regnier is also haunted by her son's death and idolizes his role in the Resistance and his sacrifice for France. The whole family are preoccupied with the Resistance: the roles their neighbours took in it, their own triumphs and failures as part of it, and with finding those who betrayed Robert to his death. Acting as a metaphor for Jameson's fears for the French nation in the aftermath of war, the novel ends with the family torn apart by the continued power of the myth of the Resistance over their lives.

For Jameson, it was this myth of the Resistance and the postwar obsession with it that was pulling postwar France apart. What 'Notes on France' suggests most strongly is that Jameson's earlier idealized view of France had begun to fracture following the postwar 'purges' of collaborators, in which thousands of people were killed between 1944 and 1948.[7] These purges took place against the backdrop of a glorification of the Resistance, which Rousso calls 'resistancialism' (1991: 10), and was used by political parties and by the French government to help to rebuild and reunite the country following years of occupation and, crucially, division by the Germans.[8] Following the end of the war, Lagrou argues that 'glorification of the contribution of the resistance movement was the only basis available for a true national myth' (2000: 26). This myth is challenged and undermined in the novel, particularly as many of the characters still suffer for their time in the Resistance, which they view as a period not of victory and glory but of suspicion and hardship. Monnerie sees the Resistance as a tremendous sacrifice for all involved, not only for his men who sacrificed their lives to free France, but in terms of his own ethical sacrifice in allowing himself to send them out to execute his plans and often to die at the hands of the Germans, while he remained in safety. In *The Hidden River*, it is largely those who did not serve, such as Regnier's and Monnerie's neighbours, who regard him as a hero, indicating the power of the myth and the discrepancies between it and the realities of life within the Resistance movement. This critique of this myth of the Resistance, its role in the postwar nation, and its negative effects work throughout this novel to indicate Jameson's disillusionment with postwar France and her concerns for postwar Europe as a whole.

For many of the characters – Monnerie's neighbours, his family, and even Captain Adam Hartley, the British soldier who served alongside him – Jean Monnerie is the ultimate patriot. As Ross Poole describes, in terms of early republican statehood of the kind upon which France was founded after the Revolution, 'the object of patriotic commitment was the *patria*, and this was conceived as a political entity, that is, the community organized as a republic' (2008: 129–130). Monnerie's exemplary service in the Resistance shows his commitment to the defence not of this state or of the government, but of this *patria* itself. This marks out the ultimate fulfilment of his patriotic duty to 'put his life on the line in military service in the defence of the republic against external and internal enemies' (Poole, 2008: 129), placing him in a great tradition of patriots beginning with the formation of the first republics of Greece and Ancient Rome.[9] As a result of his embodiment of republican patriotism, and the desire to reunite the republic following the war, Monnerie and his fellow Resistance fighters enjoy high standing in the community. Hartley, an English soldier billeted in the family home to assist Monnerie's group, describes him: 'Bitter-tongued, sometimes brutal, unquestionably honest, incorruptible, unsparing of himself, Monnerie dominated his [Resistance] group as much by his manner as by his greater experience and intelligence' (1955: 20). Even Monnerie's brutality marks him out as the perfect patriot, emphasizing the lengths to which he is willing to go in order to preserve the Republic, which he prizes above all else. Furthermore, he defends the Republic on his own terms, planning his own attacks and engineering his own networks and defences. This emphasizes the absence of hierarchy and Monnerie's actions not as a subordinate but as part of a wider community of citizens. His position is supported by mythic understandings of the Resistance as the ultimate French patriots who continued to defend France even under the dangerous conditions of occupation.

This type of patriotism is irrevocably bound to the masculine. The patriot, defined as the ultimate political participant, has historically been an exclusively male role requiring the right to political representation and the ability to physically defend the nation, both historically denied to women. Monnerie is described from the early pages of the novel in terms of his manly physicality: he has a 'heavy body, still supple, [and a] hard generous mouth' (1955: 22), and he is 'a powerful animal' (1955: 32), dominating the rooms of his house. His capabilities as a landowner, a father figure and a householder are referenced throughout, just as his strength and capability are juxtaposed with the other inhabitants of the Monnerie household – two women and his younger and less overtly masculine brother, François. Just as women were seen as duplicitous and threatening at times of national threat, so François's lack of traditional masculine qualities both supports and suggests his own self-serving disloyalty at a time in which masculinity, through the figure of the patriot, was firmly tied into these myths of the Resistance. Yet there were female members of the Resistance, notably Elizabeth, a distant relative living with the family, whom Monnerie used occasionally to run errands. As Margaret Collins Weitz describes, women's roles in the Resistance have been significantly downplayed and, in fact, 'women's participation in that war-within-a-war was considerably greater than the public roles they played in French society at the time' (1995: 7).[10] In a reflection of this tendency in the novel, Monnerie's patriotism is bound irrevocably to his masculinity, linking the myths of resistance and the rebuilding of France to a masculine tradition of nation-building throughout the novel.[11]

Monnerie is not the only male character to display these patriotic or even heroic attributes – his cousin Robert Regnier is also idolized for his role in the Resistance. Regnier was killed by the Nazis after his activities with the Resistance were revealed. As a result of this, he is a martyr within the family and the wider local community, and his death is viewed as the ultimate patriotic sacrifice. His mother – Mme. Regnier – is the chief protector of Regnier's memory, and she persistently praises 'his good looks, his courage' (1955: 30). She tells Hartley that 'he saved everybody but himself' (1955: 30), implying that Regnier's great sacrifice enabled others such as Hartley himself and even Monnerie to live, undermining their own contribution to the Resistance. Hartley idolizes Regnier: 'What he loved – this word at least was accurate – in Robert Regnier were all the qualities he felt lacking in himself: the spontaneity, the grace and energy of mind and spirit' (1955: 29). This is not an unusual idealization of French (or European) youth compared to Jameson's other novels: Milan in *Then We Shall Hear Singing* and Hana Čarek in *Europe to Let* are similarly romanticized. However, here, this idealized youth signifies the glorification of the dead of the Resistance, rather than the glorious future of the nation. In direct contrast to this, in emphasizing the sacrifice of French youth in this way, the novel places Regnier's death alongside those soldiers of the First World War, whom Jameson has referred to earlier as the 'youngest and the best, who feel keenest, the child-saviours whom no one can save' (1947b: 46). Through this, for the Monnerie/Regnier family, this idea of the sacrifice and bravery of idealized youth becomes synonymous with ideas around the great sacrifice and bravery of the Resistance itself.

The novel not only represents these myths of the Resistance, but also comes to undermine them, displaying the less flattering aspects of this much-lauded national movement. It hints at the level of betrayal and collaboration within France and within the Resistance itself, undermining the myths of solidarity and loyalty propagated during the postwar period. Christopher Lloyd points out that 'betrayal is in fact one of the constant defining features of resistance, whether through dissidence, venality, duplicity or desperation' (2003: ix). During the Occupation, the French people were routinely encouraged to inform on their neighbours who were being actively or passively resistant to the occupiers. While the occupying Nazis tortured members of the Resistance for information, as Peter Davies describes, during the Vichy period, Pétain actively encouraged the betrayal of neighbours and friends to the authorities and many thousands of French citizens obliged, 'with envy and malice masquerading as public-spiritedness' (2001: 50). Much as the French characters in the novel would have Hartley and others believe that all of France resisted its occupiers, even Mme. Regnier admits to the 'people, millions of them, who could have done something, some small thing to resist the Germans and didn't' (1955: 36). In fact, Regnier is betrayed by a Frenchman, a member of the Resistance and a member of his own family. In Jameson's earlier novel *The Green Man*, Andrew Daubney has a similar experience while working with the French Resistance when his unit is compromised. The Resistance is depicted, not as a solid, national effort to gain freedom, as many of the French characters would insist, but as a fractured and fragile organization where loyalty and discretion could not always be relied upon, often with disastrous consequences.

When Hartley first arrives in France he is keen to learn if those who denounced Regnier have been found. As the story progresses it is revealed that it was François, Monnerie's younger brother, who pointed his cousin out to the Gestapo. Monnerie himself is shocked at the discovery but is familiar with his brother's failings and weaknesses, telling him that he is unlucky. Your sort of mildly venal insincerity and self-seeking usually isn't punished. In easier times you would have got away with it. You would never have been pushed on and on, to – to the moment when you pointed out Robert to your German friends... Before that you were trying to please me by involving yourself very gingerly in the Resistance. (1955: 166)

François's membership of the Resistance, like his collaboration, marks out only his desire to be liked and to succeed whatever the circumstances. He was not, as his brother informs him, 'even saving your skin' (1955: 168) – François's 'self-seeking' behaviour arose from a weakness within him, one which his brother believes he does not share. Like many of the other Frenchmen referred to in the novel, from the profiteering peasants to the women who fell in love with Nazi officers, he is attempting to make the best of the Occupation. By foregrounding a character like François to represent the great many French citizens who, like him, were not the heroes of the Resistance Mme. Regnier may wish to remember, *The Hidden River* calls into question the assertion that everyone in France took an active role in resisting the Occupation.

Monnerie determines that his brother must die for his role in Regnier's death and, most importantly, for his unpatriotic betrayal of France. François has hidden his crime for six years, despite his family's obsession with finding the truth about his cousin's death. That the conspirator is a member of the family and a Frenchman is impossible for them to accept, particularly as François had been enjoying significant local acclaim for his role running a clandestine press during the war, which spread Resistance propaganda and news of German defeats and atrocities. François's desire to perpetuate a myth of resistance in his own life only reflected a grim reality in postwar France in which, as Lloyd points out, 'there is no doubt that many profiteers, collaborators and extortionists attempted to masquerade as resisters; the faux "résistant" is a figure of legend' (2003: 36). In order to punish his treachery, Monnerie poisons François, comforting him as he dies but remaining resolute in his conviction that his brother must pay with his life for his betrayal of the family and, most crucially, of France. Mme. Regnier is scandalized by François's actions and supports Monnerie's decision, even though, as Monnerie describes, 'she used to speak of us as my three children' (1955: 26) and François 'never called her anything but Mamma' (1955: 26). When Hartley questions her treatment of François she asks him, 'What is a murderer?' (1955: 158), before declaring, 'My son was a soldier – I believe you were one yourself – he was fighting the invaders of our country' (1955: 158). She tells Hartley that François 'betrayed him to them', demanding 'what does your sentimentality call it?' (1955: 158). For Mme. Regnier, François's death does not even constitute a sacrifice but a purging, ridding the nation of the contamination of treachery, much like the wave of purges which took place immediately after the war across France. What it does signify – in what is a clear critique of these purges and of France's postwar politics – is the country's determination to sacrifice its future in a desperate attempt to reconcile with its past. François is depicted in the early stages of the novel as the future of the Monnerie family, as his brother tells him, 'I think of you as the future. I'm played-out and lame. It's up to you to turn the Monneries into a force again' (1955: 51). Jean Monnerie is willing to sacrifice the future of his family in order to cleanse the French nation of the sins of the past and of occupation, just as he did as a Resistance leader during the war. François's death becomes a symbol of the paradoxical nature of the postwar purges in Jameson's eyes, echoing her anxieties in *The Black Laurel* that the cruelties learned in war might manifest themselves in peacetime calls for justice or even revenge.

Hartley is shocked by the unfeeling way in which Monnerie is able to sacrifice his brother for the nation. For him, this type of patriotism is cold-blooded because 'a simple murder, of the sort which jumps like a knife out of jealousy or hate or some other fault of nature, is innocent by the side of butcheries carried out coldly in the name of brotherhood, peace, a glorious future and the rest of it' (1955: 209). Hartley views François's crime as more forgivable and more acceptable than Monnerie's because it is based on human emotions and human error. He sees Monnerie's dedication to the nation above the family not as patriotic, but as indicative of a coldness or inhumanity he links to Monnerie's time in the Resistance. Monnerie uses the same terms to justify his decision, telling Hartley, 'You weren't occupied. Wait until you've been faced with treachery in your own family' (1955: 184). Hartley voices the opinion of the sympathetic but uncomprehending English, one which is mitigated throughout by charges like this one, that as an Englishman he does not and cannot understand the changes and prejudices brought out in a nation during occupation. Like characters such as David Esk in *Europe to Let* and William Gary and David Renn in *The Black Laurel*, he acts as an observer, a conduit for English incomprehension at the manoeuvrings of nations and populations faced with real experiences of repeated invasion and occupation. Through this murder, Monnerie sacrifices his own life for France in order to save the Republic for others – he leaves France itself immediately afterwards to avoid punishment for his actions. Although this act restores or underlines some of the themes of glory and honour attributed to the Resistance, because in Hartley's (English) eyes it is seen as brave but barbaric, as rational but inhuman, the book ends with the sense, not of the inscrutable honour of the Resistance, but of the damage it did and continues to do to men and families like the Monneries.

Although Monnerie's experiences with the Resistance may be referred to by Mme. Regnier and the local people with a sense of pride and even nostalgia, for Monnerie himself they are a source of conflicting feelings of pride, but also of guilt and regret. Much like Resistance leader Jean Blomart in de Beauvoir's *The Blood of Others* (1945), who watches his wife die after sending her out to complete a mission on behalf of the Resistance, and, overwhelmed by guilt, tells her as she lies dying that it is his fault (1966: 237), Monnerie feels responsible for deaths on missions which he has masterminded and for his own inability to take part in direct action against the occupiers.[12] For Hartley, the Resistance leaves its mark on all of its members, including its leaders like Monnerie himself – he describes how 'mistrust, cruelty, violence, lying, had to become the second nature of a dedicated resistor' (1955: 18). He notes that 'not all resistors had been brave, devoted or even decent men: There was a resistance underworld where private or political accounts were settled brutally, and common neurotics or criminals amused themselves' (1955: 112). By the end of the novel, Monnerie has once again embraced the brutality of this life in the Resistance. Although at the beginning of the novel he is content to leave it behind him, admitting that 'after all – it's over […] past help' (1955: 24), following the revelations about François's involvement in Regnier's death he is aggressively defensive of his actions telling Hartley that he had 'to stop [François] carrying his rottenness about with him everywhere' (1955: 185). The Resistance and its ideals prove too much of an influential force in Monnerie's life. It is not only his patriotism that causes him to kill his brother, but a well-learned reaction which returns him to the unambiguous decision-making of his Resistance days.

Although Lloyd writes that 'the Resistance had little impact on German troops before the closing months of the Occupation' (2003: 35), for the French during this period the victory can belong only to France, to the French Resistance and to the builders of the new nation, the Fourth Republic. *The Hidden River* represents an engagement with these myths of the French nation and their role in defining France in the postwar world, both within the nation itself and elsewhere in Europe. Not only does the novel represent Jameson's view of a France poisoned by the Occupation and by the sacrifices it demanded, it also depicts and undermines popular myths about the Resistance, calling into question the loyalty of its members, as well as claims that it was a nationwide force. The pervasiveness of these myths of the Resistance in the novel – even Hartley is a keen advocate of French bravery and sacrifice, neglecting the more sinister aspects of the Resistance and the collaborators which operated around and sometimes within it – serves not to demonstrate its veracity, but instead to interrogate its power and its pitfalls. Most importantly, this novel represents for Jameson a growing uneasiness about France and about the position she previously accorded it as the epitome of European civilization, as well as cultural and intellectual life. Just as the Monnerie/Regnier family represent a microcosm for the uncivilized and brutal elements growing within the French nation at this time, France itself in the novel represents a microcosm for an Allied Europe obsessed with retribution and with wartime victories, rather than with rebuilding and reconciliation.

Although Jameson's work of the postwar period seems in many ways to be stalled in the themes of the Second World War – of resistance, occupation and nation – it also draws parallels between this earlier conflict and the Cold War itself. As such, these novels represent both a continuation and a break with previous work, moving forwards to engage with issues of the Cold War and the hardships Europe faced in coming to terms with its war experiences, whilst marking clearly the continued decline of Europe, a decline which, in 1938, Jameson and her contemporaries had hoped would be circumvented by the war. Certainly her hope in 1941 that Britain would 'treat us better when it is over' (1941a: 45), a reference to her desire for a more equal postwar Britain in which poverty would be alleviated, seem to have been frustrated. Although many of these were now being enacted, with the election of Attlee's Labour government in 1945 there is a sense that this was too little too late, that something crucial had been lost. Her disappointment is tangible in novels such as *The Moment of Truth*, particularly as she looks towards America but sees little of the old Europe she would like to see restored. Just a short time after the fervour for change which characterized novels written in the final years of the war such as *The Black Laurel* and *Before the Crossing*, these are novels, not of hope, but of disappointment. European civilization, far from being rejuvenated after the war, seems more imperilled than ever, sandwiched between the twin threats of Russian control and Europe's own cyclical desire for revenge.

6

'The same disconcerting shapes': The Cold War, Empire and terrorism in *A Cup of Tea for Mr Thorgill* and *Last Score*

While many of Jameson's novels of the postwar era can seem wholly anachronistic, remaining embedded in the themes and concerns of the interwar and the Second World War period, some do attempt an engagement with more contemporary concerns. Although works such as *The Last Score, or the Private Life of Sir Richard Ormston* (1961) and *A Cup of Tea for Mr Thorgill* (1958) are often inflected with her previous anxieties around Europe, civilization, and justice, their exploration of issues around terrorism, communism and decolonization represents a definitive move on Jameson's part towards interacting with the politics of the 1950s and 1960s. However, she continues to position these issues in her novels in dialogue with the past – her anticolonialism stems from her hatred of occupation, her understandings of treason from her sense of wartime national security. Jameson's instinctual grasp of politics allowed her to envision these changes and to happen upon many issues which are still relevant after her death, from so-called ticking-bomb torture to fifth columnists and political infiltration. Nonetheless, despite their seeming engagement with world politics and postwar Europe, these two novels mark something of a return or a retreat to an examination of Britain and British identity not seen since her fiction of the interwar years.

As Leslie James and Elizabeth Leake point out in the introduction to their 2015 collection *Decolonization and the Cold War: Negotiating Independence*, 'the advent of decolonisation shares more than a chronological partnership with the Cold War' (2). Both constitute 'imaginative projects', they argue, which seek to reimagine and rethink the nature of the state, the nation and ultimately the world order at a time of international political instability. It is the imagined nature of these projects, much like the 'imagined communities' with which

Jameson engages earlier in her career, which characterize these novels. Here the mythological processes she represents relate to a Britain trying to reimagine itself under the new conditions of the postwar world. As such, this novel fits easily within the confines of British Cold War fiction, being, as Andrew Hammond has described, fiction which represent one of several of the following key themes:

> The threat of soviet expansion; the possibility of nuclear annihilation; the growth and influence of the Secret Services; the weakening of British socialist movements; the collapse of the British Empire in the face of superpower and anti-imperialist pressures and the development of US global supremacy. (2013: 1)

Both *Last Score* and *A Cup of Tea for Mr Thorgill* represent clear interactions with Cold War themes, covering between them the collapse of British Empire as well as the anxieties about the strength of the secret services and the fracturing and infiltration of British socialist movements. In fact, *The Moment of Truth* can also be placed firmly within this category, according to Hammond's definition. Jameson's portrayal of these key concerns is unsurprising being that they maintain clear connections with her ongoing interests in nation, power and politics, her position as a Cold War novelist stemming also from her conviction that a writer had no right to 'turn aside' from the pressing conflicts of her time.

In fact Jameson's allegiance to the political left – alongside her anxiety about its future – certainly underpinned her sense of these conflicts. During the postwar period, it was widely felt among the European Left that 'there [wa]s a commitment to oppose the colonialism of one's own nation, […] as a moral duty' (1993: 2). As Lyndsey Stonebridge and Marina MacKay write, 'these cosmopolitan and European-minded intellectuals saw for the first time that their transnational interests could be imperial privilege as enlightened internationalism and that national identification could mean anything from pernicious parochialism to freedom from totalitarian occupation' (MacKay and Stonebridge, 2007: 2). This new-found self-awareness led to a wave of activism. British and French intellectuals set up the League against Imperialism in 1947, which evolved into Congress of People's Against Imperialism (COPAI), in which they worked to support nationalist movements in colonies across the world. Although the majority of the population was not concerned with the fate of the colonies, of whom it had little to no real knowledge, by the 1950s there was 'a new sense of alarm and urgency created by the increasing tempo of crises in colonial territories and by the seemingly repressive response of the Government' (Howe, 1993: 233). As Phyllis Lassner explains in *Colonial Strangers: Women Writing the End of the British Empire* (2004), a great many female novelists also sought to engage with these struggles, seeking to 'construct[s] a new language of resistance – the native interracial, multicultural voice that speaks not only for the colonized self, but for the others, totally silenced and extinguished victims' (2004: 91). Although Jameson's engagement is somewhat undermined by her continued need to see the world through the lens of Europe – her only postcolonial novel is framed by European experience of the Second World War and European experience of anticolonialism, respectively – her novels can be seen as part of this wider interest by the European Left in postcolonial issues.

Just as these depictions can be seen to represent an evolution of Jameson's overarching concerns with the relationship between the citizen and the nation, national identity and civilization, her novels can also be problematic in their representations of a changing modern world in anachronistic terms: *Last Score* maps the experiences of the French Resistance in the Second World War onto those of a colonial resistance campaign in a British colony, creating troubling parallels between these two experiences of conflict and of occupation. Even this outwardly anticolonial novel serves chiefly as a way of examining the aftermath of the war in Europe, grafting myths of European resistance and the weakening of European nations onto a non-European location. Nonetheless, Jameson wrote in the Bombay-based newspaper the *Aryan Path* as early as 1943 that the 'spiritual rebirth of Europe involves a change in the European attitude to other civilisations to take a pressing instance, in the attitude of Great Britain to India' (Maslen, 2014: 308). It was her desire to represent and reform Europe then, rather than a concern for the fate of colonized populations, which informed her engagement with these issues. This continued anxiety about the fate of Europe, and particularly Britain, characterizes many of her novels of the 1950s. While *The Moment of Truth* depicts the international implications of a Cold War world still in the shadow of the Second World War, it is *A Cup of Tea for Mr Thorgill* which critiques most effectively the anxieties and compromised loyalties of British society during the Cold War. Jameson's concern here is with the impact of the political on the personal, overarching ideology on individual relationships and interactions, repeating some of the concerns of novels of the 1930s, such as *Company Parade* and *None Turn Back*. She explores the personal implications of political affiliations, showing the effects on relationships, family and career of dedication to a certain political ideology or dogma. Despite the setting of *Last Score* in an unnamed British colony, both of these novels can be seen to represent a more inward-looking Jameson, pressing upon contemporary anxieties about Britain and Britain's place in the world rather than the more cosmopolitan tendencies of her earlier work.

'Our rotted liberalism': The future of the British Left in *A Cup of Tea for Mr Thorgill*

Jameson's novels of the 1950s and 1960s represent a return to the examinations of Britain and Britishness more characteristic of her work of the 1930s than her more expansive visions of Europe of the 1940s. In this novel this concern with Britishness, as in her examinations of the relations of the individual to the state and crucially to political movements, reappears as a postwar anxiety about British socialism and its infiltration or contamination by communism. Though an avowed socialist for much of her adult life, Jameson is notably unconvinced by communism, an ideology which, in her eyes, is dehumanizing in its contempt for the individual and downright dangerous in its dogmatic tendencies. As Elizabeth Maslen astutely observes, 'dogmatism of any kind worried her' (2014: 106). Jameson's exploration in this novel of the heavy-handed tactics of the British Communist Party – exemplified by the sacrifice of the naive Hetty Smith to its lofty political ideals – underlines her misgivings about a system in which, as she sees it, one set of hierarchical, patriarchal power structures is replaced by another. Here, the shady manipulations of communist agents within an Oxford college demonstrates only that this is a system in which the poor and weak will continue to be oppressed and equality evaded in the face of craven self-interest and personal advancement. The novel's academic setting then offers Jameson not only the atmosphere but also a highly plausible and evocative backdrop in which the shortcomings of communist ideology and the failures of British socialism could be examined. It comes to question not only the future of the left in Britain but also, as Rebecca West did in her 1949 novel, *The Meaning of Treason*, what makes a traitor and how individuals justified their furthering of the cause at the expense of both personal and national loyalties to themselves. This novel shows a significant re-focusing on Britain during this postwar period, but a Britain which is suddenly acutely vulnerable, more so perhaps than even in the interwar years.

The novel also echoes, of course, the case of the famous Cambridge spies, published a year after Burgess and MacLean's Moscow press conference, in which their reasons for defection to the Soviet Union were revealed.[1] It was written in 1956, a year of crisis, in particular for the Communist Party of Great Britain. Whilst the party had expanded and enjoyed a degree of success during the war and in the period immediately following it, by 1956 the British public were growing tired of the CPGB's repeated privileging of Soviet dogma over British values and interests – beginning, though not limited to – its hostility to American financial aid and the European Recovery Programme (Thompson, 2001: 111). In 1956, it lost more than half of its members as a result of Nikita Kruschev's secret speech to the Twentieth Congress of the Communist Party of the Soviet Union, in which he denounced Stalin's methods, and the Soviet invasion of Hungary in which 2,500 Hungarians were killed and 200,000 displaced. Jameson, already raising money for Hungarian refugees through PEN, was also heavily involved with the suspension from PEN of the Hungarian Centre in 1958 for its own deference to Soviet doctrine and neglect of the organization's commitment to defend free expression at all costs. The dogmatic control of the Soviet regime, its refusal to tolerate deviations from or criticism of party policy would certainly have troubled a liberal like Jameson, who would, in the face of her work with and sympathy for Hungarian refugees, have found the CPGB's blind adherence to Soviet control both puzzling and horrifying.

Jameson's misgivings about British Communism, its Soviet influences and its place within British politics are widely articulated in this novel. The narrative changes perspective often, as Birkett discusses, in order to capture a rounded picture of the responses to British political and intellectual society to the nuances of this new Left (2009: 309). There are a multitude of characters in *A Cup of Tea for Mr Thorgill* who are deeply committed to the communist cause and who, as Jameson writes, practise that 'reverence for that fabled Beast, *the proletariat*' (1957: 48 – emphasis in original) intellectually-speaking, but who do not practice this in their daily lives. The book is filled with fury at the hypocrisy of the middle classes who support the theory of working-class empowerment but who shun or actively despise members of the lower classes in practice. This underpins Jameson's distrust of communism, which she sees as an ideology which claims compassion and empathy but is suspiciously dispassionate and indifferent to human suffering in its enactment: 'You swoon over some wretched negro [sic] who is lynched in the United States – you even push bad faith to the point of pretending it is an American custom – but you keep as silent as their graves about the thousands dying of disease and misery in labour camps in Russia' (1957: 51). Jameson seems distrustful of a political mindset that stifles intellectual debate among its followers, promoting instead a creed of blind obedience, without even recourse to basic human empathy.

This new creed, then, has little to distinguish it from the intellectual dishonesty and cultural barbarism that Jameson attributes to the Nazi in the 1930s. The war has failed to stop the rot in Europe, as she had hoped. For her communism is not solely to blame, Europe is once again, to let, and communism represents another way of filling the ideological void. The key problem is that English liberalism is 'rotten in the way a tree can go on standing for years, and suddenly collapse in a high wind, completely gone inside' (1957: 193) and this rot is now represented by communist infiltrators working within the country to undermine the values of European society, just as the fascists had done twenty years before. That it appears that England has survived and even recovered from the war is perhaps the most unsettling element of this metaphor. The tree is still standing but the rot is beneath the surface, undetectable. England is just waiting for that 'high wind' which will lead the whole country to collapse. Most importantly, it has become impossible to tell who the enemy is, without the clear alignments drawn by national boundaries. This integral characteristic of communist witch-hunting in Cold War Britain (and, of course, America) is central to Jameson's portrayal. (1957: 133). The communist threat is also undetectable, insidious – the 'high wind' may come from any direction and at any time.

The opening paragraph of the novel itself shows clearly this return to England, an England characterized as idyllic, soft and safe, much in contrast to the sharp and aggressive political movements of the rest of the novel. As Nevil Rigden is driven through the British countryside he notes a landscape which is 'seemingly empty and so smooth that it gives the impression of being more civilised than a capital city' (1957: 1). The softness of the landscape is ripe for corruption, its uniquely civilized nature compared to that of the busier and more corrupt city, borrowing interwar associations of the countryside with the true nation itself and with purity and a certain vulnerability. The Gloucestershire landscape is 'calm and reassuring', 'groomed and polished' and basking 'in the innocence of sunlight' (1957: 1). There were 'few trees', perhaps a sign that the rot of those trees which are 'gone inside' is not yet all-pervading, that perhaps, at the beginning of the novel, there is hope that some parts of Britain retain this innocence. This return to prewar tropes, albeit ones more akin to the quaint landscapes and cosy villages depicted by more conservative novelists like those that Light discusses, evokes a Britain which is once again vulnerable and yet far more penetrable than the more rugged, dramatic landscapes of Yorkshire familiar from novels such as *The Moon Is Making*. As the eponymous Thorgill says, 'These Southern chaps are as soft as their country' (1957: 37). Through her invocation of this softer Southern landscape, Jameson evokes a Britain more vulnerable than before, this time not to Nazism or modernity but to communism and the demise of the British Left.

Nevil Rigden – one of the novel's cast of central characters – is a working-class man now admired as one of the finest minds in Oxford. His colleagues are sceptical and often cruel about his scholarship and he hides his political allegiances, not even daring to try to influence his students. Like Marriot in *The Moment of Truth*, Rigden is working class. Just as Marriot tells the others that 'you didn't have to scrabble your way up from two rooms in a filthy street' (1957: 120–121), Rigden too frequently returns to his upbringing to explain his decision to become a communist, arguing that to him it 'offers, or seems to offer, a world where the Nevil Rigdens are born free' (1957: 163). Rigden is, crucially, the son of Frank and Sally Rigden who feature in Jameson's novel *None Turn Back* (1936), which deals primarily with the aims and conditions of the General Strike. These earlier Rigdens are stalwarts of the socialist movement, but also responsible, community-minded and hard working. Their socialism is informed by their living conditions and Frank's experiences in the First World War; it is motivated by their feelings of frustration and injustice at a world which takes their work for granted and cares little for their well-being. Nevil marks out both the opportunities available to working-class children available in part through his parents' agitating but also through the advances made by the postwar socialist government. His conversion to communism reveals perhaps that not enough has been achieved, that all of the old inequalities remain and that his parents' particular brand of socialism is dying.

Despite Rigden's academic ability, elements of his working-class upbringing still impede his progress at Oxford. His colleagues are often cruel about him, attributing to him intangible qualities which make them uncomfortable or hostile, all of which quite obviously stem from class-based anxiety and snobbery. Henry Gurney, a fellow of the college, describes his discomfort at Rigden's social climbing, describing him as having 'every fault of the ranker – desperate anxiety to get on, no scruples about the way he does it, no real generosity' (1957: 32). He is disgusted by Rigden's awareness of his own precariousness at Oxford because 'he struggled up from his class, out of his class: in some corner of him he's terribly afraid of tumbling back into it' (1957: 32). For Gurney – who never had to overcome such obstacles – this insecurity and Rigden's awareness of it make him untrustworthy and somehow self-serving. Rigden's very presence at Oxford is a threat to the social order. On discovering Rigden's communist leanings, the Master of his college, outwardly a supporter of his career but always uncomfortable with his background, declares, 'You can't make a decent fellow out of a nobody by educating him' (1957: 133). His ongoing distrust of Rigden is proved right; his working-class background makes him a dishonourable outsider in a system based entirely around lifelong understandings of etiquette and hierarchy, and family and personal connections. For the Master and his class, the undetectability of communists in their midst is troubling, primarily because it hints towards similar anxieties about class. The advances made by Attlee's government, and by men like Rigden, mean that class distinctions are becoming less easy to spot. This leads to anxieties throughout the novel, expressed by men like the Master and Henry Gurney, about a working-class infiltration of previously elitist institutions which is at least as troubling to the British establishment as an influx of communists.

However, not all communists had to shield their affiliation from the world. For many, as Jameson shows, communism can be an intellectual adornment, an idiosyncrasy with just enough of a dangerous edge to boost book sales without damaging reputation. For Miles Hudson, a flirtation with communism showcases his intellectual inquisitiveness and shows off his political commitment. As a political affectation it sits alongside his 'an arrogant mouth' (1957: 15) and his being 'inclined, being blessedly certain of himself, to be mockingly insolent with other people' (1957: 15). His foray into communism is described as 'backhanded exhibitionism' (1957: 11) and not, as in the case of the working-class Nevil Rigden, behaving 'like a pickpocket' (133). Hudson need not disguise his interest because his class background makes his intentions seem rather benign – a man with an independent income has no interest in dismantling the systems which support his privilege. His is intellectual posturing, not motivated by the compassion and sense of injustice which compels Rigden, making him far more dangerous. As James Smith writes, 'The Cambridge spies were instructed by their Soviet handlers to immediately break off any overt left-wing links and sympathies, and instead to patiently use their upper-middle-class connections to work their way into positions of importance in the establishment' (Smith, 2013: 60). The use of class in this way by a system apparently dedicated to its abolition is interesting here and pertinent in this novel, illustrating further the hypocrisies of communist dogma which trouble Jameson and her characters. While Jameson is tolerant and even indulgent of Rigden's communist leanings in light of his personal experiences and frustrations, many of which she shares, she is damning of Hudson's self-serving embrace of a system in which he has no real stake, personal or ideological. Communism is at best a troubling response to the failures of British socialism and at worst a fleeting fad indulged in by publicity-hungry intellectuals.

Hudson, however, rejects communism very publicly by way of his bestselling book, explaining, somewhat ironically, that there was a 'stench of cruelty' (1957: 113) around the movement which made him uncomfortable. In fact this was born out by defectors even from the Communist Party of Great Britain. In the 1940s Douglas Hyde and CH (Bob) Drake had written of their experiences of bullying at the heart of party politics, leaving with 'chilling tales of life inside the Communist Party – of young party members reduced to nervous breakdown by a bullying party "tribunal", of experienced trade union leaders castigated [...] for insufficient devotion to Stalin's person' (Thompson, 2001: 120). The 'stench of cruelty' detected by Hudson is, conversely, also evidenced by the party's revenge for his public disavowal of the communist cause. The CPGB sends the student Hetty Smith to his rooms, charged with recovering a notebook containing a list of names of communist agents. However, the party is aware that her very presence in Hudson's flat may result in a more damaging scandal – Hudson is an infamous womanizer and they surmise that it is likely that he will try to seduce a young woman found in his home alone. This absolute disregard for Smith's safety or her personal feelings demonstrates again the party's indifference to the private suffering of its members. This indifference is combined with a latent misogyny in Smith's case; her disposability to the party is particularly gendered. Although it is Hudson they describe as 'an intellectual tart' for his fickle politics, Smith is unworthy in their eyes of this personal insult being merely a pawn in a wider political game, an object deployed on a chess board in order to affect a series of events to advantage one side.

The party's ploy is effective. However, it is difficult to determine whether, in this instance, it is Smith or Hudson who is the victim of this entrapment. Smith's university career is undermined by this sacrifice and she ends the novel in Rigden's rooms in London, sparse and poor. Blaming herself, despite the manoeuvrings of the men around her who had not warned her that Hudson may return or what her role might be if he did, Smith describes how, on finding her in the flat, Hudson 'laughed at her, made her lie down on the sofa, and began to caress her gently' (1957: 271). She then describes simply being 'afraid of offending him' or of 'making a clumsy vulgar scene' and while Jameson makes little description of the act itself, Smith's allusions to it not being Hudson's fault and her shame and disgust with herself that 'if I'd protested – if I'd made a fuss – he would – he might – have let me go away' (1957: 271) makes it clear that Hudson forced sex on her. Smith asks Rigden 'you don't despise me? I don't disgust you?' (1957: 295) because, despite her manipulation at the hands of both Hudson and the men of the Communist Party in trying to discredit his public criticism, she believes that she is entirely at fault and, like many female victims, that it was her inability to reject his advances which made her complicit in the act itself.

This manipulation of Smith's body can be seen as a metaphor for the British body politic. The idea of a naïve Britain, one unused to this kind of treachery, being penetrated by a highly-masculinized and highly-predatory communism is very much reminiscent of popular rhetoric at the time. In fact, the age-old association of the nation as a woman to be defended, of territory as female and in need of protection from invasion, is highly relevant here, as it was in *Cousin Honoré*. Similarly, Smith's inability to act, her enslavement to convention and to politeness even in the most shocking of circumstances, alludes to the automated compliance which Jameson fears in British society at this time. This is part of the rottenness within liberalism for Jameson, an inability to reject forcibly ideas which are morally wrong. British politeness has become an apathy and inability to confront ethically unsound behaviour, both within the government and within individuals and political groups. Smith 'was expendable, a pinch of human debris joylessly sacrificed to history' (1957: 292). Rigden, who helped to bring about this unhappy incident, is, as he himself realizes at the end of the novel, a man exactly like those Jameson describes in her Foreword to Anne Frank's diary, content 'to sacrifice a generation, two generations to the future they serve' (1954: 10). In fact, as Birkett points out, this Foreword can be seen also to constitute 'her indictment of Communism' (2009: 309), based on the time of its publication in 1954, three years before *A Cup of Tea for Mr Thorgill* was published. This cruelty, the adherence to dogma with no recourse to personal feeling or interpersonal empathy, is central to the critiques of communism throughout the novel. Yet many of these critiques stem from characters with much to gain from the status quo: the idealists for John Spencer-Savage, the Master of the college, do indeed 'keep their idealism clapped over their eyes' (1957: 17). In doing so, they sacrifice Smith's sexual agency, her self-worth and even her university career to the cause, with no remorse.

As much as the threat from communism dominates this novel – which dissects every element of its uses, appeals and shortcomings – this serves also to reflect the shortcomings of the British Left itself. As with so many of Jameson's novels of this period, *A Cup of Tea for Mr Thorgill* marks a look back to the politics of the past as much to the concerns of the present or the future. In its use of Nevil Rigden and his links to the hopeful and just social commitments of his idealistic parents during the 1920s, alongside the figure of Mr Thorgill himself – a Northern WEA lecturer in Oxford – the novel conjures as it dispels the hopes and dreams of Jameson's generation of socialists. When Gurney visits Thorgill on his death bed he observes that Thorgill was 'an old rebel – a socialist of the old innocent simple-hearted sort – his belief that, to be happy, men must be free and wise' (1957: 263). Thorgill has no interest in the creed of communism because he 'had no weakness for the idea of people being happy *in a mass*. He wanted each one of them to be able to see him own happiness, in his own style' (1957: 263). This is Thorgill's outdated socialism, characterized by the decreasing interest in his WEA classes. The next generation is to be enslaved to doctrine, too uninterested in workers' education as a means of emancipation, the freedom of the mind as the means with which to achieve political emancipation, which characterized Rigden's parents' generation, and Jameson's. As Birkett notes, 'with the death of Mr Thorgill, the old Yorkshireman and devoted WEA organizer, who makes two brief appearances and is paid off with his patronising cup of tea, the ambitions of Jameson's socialist generation seem to have gone to sand' (2009: 311).

Fittingly, Rigden heads off at the end of the novel to go to Yorkshire to teach miners as a way of reconnecting with this past and with these ideals. His intellectual development had, after all, failed to allow him to free either himself, his family or his class. He tells Gurney that 'I can't go any further without first going back part of the way' (1957: 298). His return to poverty – or relative poverty – marks a reconnection with his roots, the roots of his political beliefs. Although he maintains that he still 'resents poverty' (1957: 298), he acknowledges following the death of his mother that he must retrace his steps and reaffirm his socialist convictions. At the end of the novel there is both a defeat of Communism, a sense of Rigden uncovering something in his own beliefs that repels him, and a need to re-find a British socialism that might offer hope in this new Britain. While the death of Thorgill marks an ending and a loss of the old guard, it also opens up a hopefulness that new solutions can be found to old problems.

As Rigden describes, 'You start from the idea of freeing the minds and senses of humble people, and end in a vast graveyard where the same quicklime gets rid of the deported, the disobedient, the helpless' (1957: 291). His embrace of communism as a means to empower the poor and improve society has led to nothing more than his own moral decline and his complicity in the exploitation of Smith. Just as Germany's acceptance of the Nazism in its midst and the Allies' acceptance of the dark deeds and mounting cruelty of postwar Berlin marked out a European civilization rotting from the inside, so too *A Cup of Tea for Mr Thorgill* engenders another 'tide of cruelty', one rising once again from beneath the surface to engulf Europe. These novels of the Cold War represent a cruelty and barbarism which remain a threat to Europe. The end of the Second World War did not fill a void or heal any wounds but left Europe, as it had been before, to let. Yet there is a crucial difference: previously for Jameson it was the intellectuals who would save Europe, who would fight Nazism through free speech and free thought. Now she seems to mock intellectuals like herself and the 'incorruptible' Pebsworth – who is 'a liberal of the oldest and most uncompromising school', 'with a sensitive horror of anything he could see as "a threat to the liberty of the mind"' (1957: 189). Jameson sees this apparently old-fashioned conceit of the 'liberty of the mind', as outdated in the postwar world and yet it forms the cornerstone of her love for Europe and of her previous novels. Throughout this novel her approach is wholly ambivalent; it forms both a defence and a heavy critique of all that she admires – Europe, intellectual culture, even the academia which she once aspired to. The novel shows the writer's mind divided between the past and the present, between her desire to see Europe's demise and her desire to preserve it, between her love of intellectual culture and her contempt for its indulgences and its fripperies and between her desire for social justice and her own class prejudices. At this late stage in her career, *A Cup of Tea for Mr Thorgill* still constitutes a crucible for Jameson's personal and intellectual conflicts.

'The same disconcerting shapes': Resistance, recovery and Empire

Just as countries like France and Britain fought for the freedom of Europe in the Second World War, following the war other nations began to seek their own freedom and self-determination, often from French or British imperialist rule. In many cases, the very same fighters who helped to free Europe were employed to prevent the emancipation of European colonies such as Cyprus and Algeria. In *Last Score, or the Private Life of Sir Richard Ormston*, Jameson once more addresses the speed with which occupied can become occupier, or the oppressed can become oppressor, viewing the postwar demise of Empire as the title indicates, through looking at one man's personal crisis as a reflection of wider issues concerning the British imperialism. Between 1960 and 1964, seventeen British colonies had ceremonies of independence. This novel speaks to what Lassner refers to as 'Britain's perceived malaise toward this loss of power and influence abroad' (2004: 10) and as such, it does not necessarily serve an anticolonial purpose but is more concerned with British attitudes to this loss of influence. *Last Score*, again, represents a way of examining the aftermath of the war in Europe, grafting myths of European resistance and anxieties about the waning power of European nations onto a non-European location. Whilst the novel ostensibly concerns a postcolonial nation-building, the myths and nation-building practices which Jameson examines here are the coping mechanisms of a Britain trying to process its own increasing irrelevance in a postwar and postcolonial context.

Jameson's literary agent A.D. Peters wrote to her after receiving a draft of the novel asking whether 'this book ought to be published before the one already delivered to Macmillan [*A Month Soon Goes*] it is, in a sense, topical there aren't many British possessions left in which such circumstances can arise, and the public memory in lamentably short' (18 January 1960). For Peters, the demise of empire represented in the novel made the book timely but also time-sensitive – he anticipates a future in which the total demise of the British Empire would render such a novel irrelevant. *Last Score* centres around Sir Richard Ormston, formerly a high-ranking foreign office official and now governor of an unnamed British colony abroad. In fact, Macmillan's Lovat Dickson wrote to Jameson and Peters that he felt that it was clear that the colony in question was Cyprus (8 February 1960), but this is never made explicit in the novel, and there is little in the text to indicate the partisan nature of Britain's negotiations with Greece over the island in the late 1950s, although there is a mention of an epidemic 'in a town on the coast – Zante', also the name of the most Southern of the Ionian islands (1961: 128).[2] Through this anonymity, Ormston's experiences, though comparable to those of Cyprus, can be universalized to include other British colonies, not to mention colonies of other European powers such as France and Belgium, recently liberated or struggling for independence following the war.[3] The neglect, however, of the viewpoint of the colonized subjects and their experiences of striving for national independence undercut this novel's power as a postcolonial text or examination of postcolonial nationhood.

The novel ties Ormston's professional and familial anxieties, his loss of power as governor, husband and father, to the growing resistance movement in the colony he governs and his increasing inability to protect the people, and even himself, from the violence of this insurgency. This resistance movement is coordinated, rather problematically as I come to discuss, not by an indigenous inhabitant of the colonized country, but by Anthony Boyd, a former schoolfellow of Ormston and a member of the British forces during the Second World War. The resistance struggle turns into a game between Ormston and his childhood playfellow, hence the title 'Last Score'. This childish game serves to emphasize the growing impotence of Europe, and particularly Britain, in international politics during the Cold War, as well as the futility and childishness of its determination to retain the colonies despite significant pressure to withdraw, both at home and abroad.

Whilst it marks a particularly topical foray into the postcolonial politics of the early 1960s, the novel also returns to many of Jameson's wartime concerns around freedom, occupation and the wartime nation. Jameson writes in a brief preface that 'if the reader discovers accidental similarities with events which have taken place anywhere in the world, in Africa, Europe, Asia, that will only be because all revolts against what can be represented as an occupying force follow the same unhappy pattern and take the same disconcerting shapes' (1961: 7). For Jameson, her sympathy with colonized peoples is inspired by her sympathy with occupied peoples – such as the French – during the war because both 'follow the same unhappy pattern'. She draws a troubling parallel here between a European experience of occupation and the victims of European imperialism. Indeed, she was not alone in making this comparison. Jean Paul Sartre wrote in 'The Sleepwalkers' on 19 February 1962 – the day that Algeria gained its independence – that the French 'are no longer ignorant of anything: we know what we have done: In 1945, Parisians shouted for joy because they had been delivered from suffering; today they have this taciturn relief because they are being freed of their crimes' (2001: 72). For him, the experiences of the French during the Nazi Occupation should have made them less ignorant about the suffering of the inhabitants of French colonies overseas. Instead, he argues, their crimes are much greater because, having experienced occupation themselves, they know what they have done in failing to extend the freedom they celebrated in 1945 to their own colonies elsewhere. His words echo the links and ironies which Jameson detects in *Last Score* between the liberation of Europe following the Second World War and continued European colonialism elsewhere in the world.

Last Score can be seen to project ideas about European failure onto a country colonized by Europe, by Britain. Echoing all of the worst Eurocentrism of British imperialist discourse, here even the liberation movements of British colonies are co-opted by British novelists as a backdrop for examinations of the demise of the British Empire itself. The depiction of resistance within the colony explicitly references ideas of European resistance and nation-building familiar in Jameson's other works, such as the idolization of the Resistance and Resistance fighters in *The Hidden River*: both Boyd and Colonel Frent, Ormston's Chief of Police, were engaged in combat in Europe during the war, whilst Ormston spent the war in the Ministry of Defence, and they often refer to his inexperience, each criticizing him for not taking part in active service abroad. It is particularly ironic that Boyd and Frent came from serving on the Allied side in the Second World War to represent opposing sides in this later conflict. Boyd draws upon his experiences in the British Army to lead a guerrilla resistance movement in what he sees as another occupied country, while Frent uses his experiences working with the French Resistance to combat and repel this resistance movement in the colony. Boyd uses his experiences of freedom and occupation gained during the Second World War to try to understand experiences of colonized populations in European colonies elsewhere, whereas Frent has the opposite reaction, taking from the war only a sense of duty and loyalty to Britain and Europe, which overrides any empathy he may feel towards colonized peoples. Where Boyd's experiences in war allow him to transcend national boundaries in his empathy, Frent's wartime experiences have reinforced his nationalistic urges. These two former soldiers display the effects of similar kinds of wartime service and both men's experiences in the Second World War provide a constant frame of reference for their experiences in this new conflict and for Jameson's Eurocentric view of colonialism.

The novel foregrounds Frent's experiences of the Resistance and his experiences of repressing the colonial resistance movement. A clear comparison is created between his desire to free Europe and his unwillingness to apply the same principles elsewhere, marking this out as an inconsistency explained only by his dedication and loyalty to Britain. Frent sees himself solely as a soldier under orders, bound to his duty to defend Britain at all costs and with little regard for the human or political ramifications. It is Frent who tortures Boyd for information when he is captured, bringing up again Ormston's lack of military training and commenting that 'we should have had a soldier in charge here' (1961: 25). He also continually evokes his own experience as a member of a resistance movement, remarking on the landscape as constituting 'splendid guerrilla country, all those hills' (1961: 23). He analyses the organizational strategies of the resistance based on this experience, explaining to Ormston that 'what started, as you say, with scattered groups, has grown into a decently organised force – which is becoming daily more efficient, coordinated, better armed' (1961: 29). Frent is able to place himself in the position of the leader of the resistance: 'for a moment he had an extraordinary sense of intimacy with the unknown guerrilla leader: he felt the parched earth and dry brittle herbs under the skin of the other's hand, and saw the shape of the ground through a pair of sun-reddened eyes [...] It was an intimacy with no trace of kindness' (1961: 24). Still unaware that his new enemy is in fact his old comrade from France, Frent nonetheless feels an affinity or bond with him. The doubling of these two men represents not only the shared experiences of Frent and Boyd, but also their interchangeability – only Frent's training and his national commitment prevent him from leading a resistance movement. This interchangeability marks out not only the Eurocentric focus of the novel, but also the ways in which the last war has laid the foundations of the next, on a personal and a political level.

Boyd's experiences during the Second World War mean that he finds the very existence of this Empire and its powers abroad unconscionable. He explicitly employs Resistance mentality and tactics in his strategies with his guerrilla group. Like the French Resistance, the colonial resistance group is so significantly outnumbered by occupying forces that they are forced to wage an emotive terror campaign rather than a military operation. Boyd tells Ormston that 'we do filthy things – yes', explaining that 'you're so much stronger than we are. You – you force us to fight as we do' (1961: 157). Frent recognizes this, telling Ormston that 'if you have fewer men than your oppressor, a smaller and weaker force, one of the ways you build your side is by spreading horror' (1961: 29). Both men understand these techniques as a result of their previous experiences – Frent uses this understanding to plan defences and Boyd to plan his offensive. Most importantly, that both these men draw such clear parallels between the tactics of resistance movements in occupied countries during the war and colonized countries after it, points again to the evolution of Jameson's empathy with colonized peoples and the modes through which she had come to her anticolonial feeling.

While Frent is representative of a conservative desire to defend a nostalgic ideal of British imperialism, Boyd represents a need for change, fairness and liberation, as rooted in European experiences of the Second World War as in the anticolonial politics of the postwar era. However, Boyd does not express the only anticolonial views in the novel and, tellingly, he is never seen as representing a particularly unreasonable or minority viewpoint on British colonial policy: Charles Cumberland, who runs the local expat newspaper, born in the unnamed country to a settler, 'excused the rebels (they called themselves indifferently rebels, resisters, Partisans, Freedom Fighters) their murders and lesser crimes on the ground that they had a right to what they were seeking through murder – independence' (1961: 17) and 'kept up a nagging and exasperated opposition to the policy of the Colonial Office and the government' (1961: 17) in his newspaper. However, it is his niece Sarah Leng who comes to epitomize the promise and the new ideas of the future. Like her uncle, she is a fervent supporter of the colonial resistance movement, although not an active participant. Leng, as a passive British anticolonialist, is a symbol of the threat to Ormston's office and to the wider imperialist project, but she also threatens ideas of a nostalgic and patriarchal Britishness through her independence, her political commitment and her relationship with Ormston's son. It is her presence which both directly and indirectly begins to establish the cracks within Ormston's family and administration. However, the presence of Leng and her uncle also represents Jameson's desire to express an element of sympathy among British expats with revolutionary struggle and the reasons behind it.

Troublingly this strong narrative of anticolonial opinion among European characters in the novel is entirely undermined by the absence of an indigenous voice. There are no indigenous characters in the main narrative, no speech is given to indigenous characters and, throughout, the colonized population are marked solely by their absence from the novel. This mute population appears almost apparitional where 'the streets were a confusion of dark mouths opening into a silence broken only by [Ormston's] car, and once by the stifled crying of a very young child behind the black rectangle of a window' (1961: 153). Boyd's mistress is the sole characterization of an indigenous woman, but she has no real presence in the narrative save in Boyd's wife's indignation about their affair: she gasps 'how could he? With one of these animals' (1961: 117), which serves only to echo the dehumanization of colonized people evident elsewhere in the text. Certainly this silence can be read as indicative of that of the people themselves, silenced by a European author keen to represent, not their stories, but one filtered through the views and experiences of their colonizers. Even the use of Boyd, a white Englishman, as the leader of the resistance movement, serves more to reflect imperialist attitudes that non-Europeans require European help and organization to overthrow European colonizers than the indigenous population's right to autonomy. All of this demonstrates Jameson's preoccupation in this outwardly anticolonial novel, which lies not in the liberation of British or other European colonies, but in the consequences of this liberation for European characters and for European nations, in the experiences of the colonizers and not of the colonized.

However, this presentation is not unique. Many British writers who wrote or campaigned for anti-imperialist causes or who chose to write about and critique processes of colonialism abroad shied away from the depiction of indigenous populations. Phyllis Bottome's *Under the Skin* (1950) represents several Chinese characters, such as the peculiarly named Whiteleaf, and lots of British expatriates, but very few characters indigenous to the island on which the action takes place. The novel, like Jameson's, is written from the point of view of a European observer, a woman who arrives on the island to take up a position teaching at the local European boarding school. Lucy Armstrong does meet some of the local indigenous people, but the presentation of them is always through her eyes and these portrayals are often prejudiced as in the case of Elvira Loring who was 'very slightly, but unmistakably for the island, a coloured [sic] person' (1950: 22). Anachronistic terminology aside, from this racially-dominated introduction onwards, Elvira is repeatedly invoked as insubordinate and difficult as a teacher, colleague and even friend, both to the school authorities and to the island as a whole. The link between this and the implication that Elvira is mixed race further problematizes her presence, not only as the only teacher at the school who is native to the island, but also as a somewhat disruptive influence among the largely European community presented in the novel. While Lassner has argued that both Bottome and Jameson worked to bring 'the consciousness of racialized Others into the cultural mainstreams that still continued to reflect the whiteness of so many other modernist writers' (2004: 177), these efforts are undermined somewhat by the fact that both writers chose to do so only through the eyes of white or European protagonists and without recourse to the views or the activism of the colonized peoples themselves. Although Bottome can, like Jameson, be seen to look beyond Europe and to attempt empathy with struggles taking place elsewhere in the world, both women's viewpoints are heavily influenced by their overarching attachment to the European.

In fact, Jameson's focus throughout is not on the internal politics of the colonial resistance, of the indigenous population or even of men like Boyd and Frent, but on the private attitudes of Ormston himself and the personal decline, which mirrors the demise of the British Empire taking place at the time. Ormston represents, in his Victorian dedication to duty and nation, Jameson's nostalgic attachment to Britain and its formidable and long-established institutions. While the lessons of the war have taught her the cruel nature of man's desire to conquer and to occupy, she provides a sympathetic account of the colony's governor as he struggles to maintain power both personally and politically. He tells his son that 'it's not easy to govern', continuing that 'if you have to decide between one man, one criminal [...] and all the helpless men, women, children, he is condemning to misery, it becomes an agony of mind' (1961: 224). Yet he is dedicated to the preservation of what Lawrence James refers to in his account of the British Empire as Britain's 'old-style benevolent imperialism' (1994: 527), itself a popular and misleading assumption that British imperialism was somehow softer or better than that of other occupying forces. Ormston epitomizes all of the eccentricities and quirks traditionally associated with Britishness, and he marks their increasing irrelevance in a world of national liberation movements and the Cold War. In many ways, he is the personification of British imperialism at this time. However, this is a loaded association – to depict Ormston as benign and well-meaning is to depict the system he represents as benign and well-meaning, conflating sympathy for the struggle of an elderly man with sympathy for the demise of a long-established and frequently brutal imperial system. This characterization of Ormston hints at Jameson's own ambivalent feelings towards a British Empire which she presents throughout this novel as, by turns, a benign, nostalgic but outdated figure and as an oppressive and brutal force.

Through this characterization, the novel ties Ormston's personal crisis to the political crisis unravelling around him. As the violence escalates in the colony, Ormston increasingly comes to reflect on the failings of his own life, his sacrifices and the price he has paid for his position. He describes how his marriage was wholly strategic, a way of securing the money and prestige of his wife's family to aid him in fulfilling his own ambitions, when she 'counted for so little – nothing – in his life, he knew so little about her and was indifferent to what he knew' (1961: 143). He is troubled by his son's choice of Sarah Leng as his future wife and is devastated by her subsequent anticolonialist views – feeling betrayed, irrelevant and outdated. His struggles come to underline the increasing irrelevance of a way of life, one which symbolized not only a country, but also a generation. As John Gallagher explains, 'In the strenuous conditions of the 1950s and 1960s, Britain lacked the economic power, the military fire power, the expansive thrust for maintaining a world system against the competition of other powers' (1982: 153). Even the US State Department were urging their allies in Whitehall to let the Empire go, seeing the colonies as 'an anachronism' (1982: 142). Through the problematic association of Ormston's personal struggles with the demise of the British Empire, *Last Score* presents increasingly outdated colonial systems and apparatus but maintains a sense of the poignancy of Britain's and his own fall from grace.

It does offer one particularly modern insight into counterterrorism and nation-building: an early account of ticking-bomb torture. Alex Adams in *How to Justify Torture: Inside the Ticking Bomb Scenario* (2019) defines ticking-bomb torture as taking place within an 'urgent time-limited emergency, the guilty captive, and the assumption that perpetrating torture on this captive will produce definite, specific information, that will lead directly to the resolution of the emergency and the rescue of innocent victims' (2019: 10). The brutal torture of Boyd in *Last Score* not only is reminiscent of the Nazi techniques used against Resistance members in Jameson's other novels but is also indicative of the Cold War itself and the increasingly lucrative global trade in information. It is also justified and motivated in its brutality by the 'time-limited emergency', of Frent's conviction that there is a bomb in the city, which may at any moment harm 'innocent [British] victims'. It is under these circumstances that Frent tells Ormston that 'we're not going to break him by normal methods' (1961: 150). When Ormston visits the prisoner after Frent 'breaks' him, 'there [a]re bandages over one eye and across the jaw, and the flesh between them was black and tumefied' (1961: 193), and Ormston notices with horror that Boyd's left eyelid has been singed. For Ormston 'there has been a mistake, a horrible mistake' (1961: 193), yet Frent exclaims jubilantly, 'He broke suddenly [...] we got everything in less than an hour' (1961: 177). Frent seems impressed with Boyd's endurance, commenting that 'I didn't expect him to hold out for so long – fifty-three hours ten minutes is the figure, I think' (1961: 177), offering this as a testament perhaps to Boyd's masculinity or, more likely, to his dedication to his cause. Both Frent and Boyd seem indifferent to this brutality, much like Jean Monnerie in *The Hidden River*, because each is entirely focused on the 'cause' which vindicates all actions, be it nationalism, political ideology or the plight of innocent victims. In fact, the novel may be among the first to represent this type of ticking-bomb torture.[4] In this instance, the deployment of these particularly brutal techniques and the justification of them marks out an increased tolerance for violence, one rooted in the Second World War but which, rather than diminishing in the postwar world, is exacerbated by Cold War politics.

Faced with the loss of his son Andrew to Sarah Leng and the anticolonialists, the failure of his marriage and the possible collapse of the colony in the face of escalating violence, Ormston feels as if 'the whole landscape had been torn up, as by an earthquake, houses reduced to rubble, trees torn down, all known contours effaced' (1961: 201). With 'all known contours effaced', he feels he has lost his way in an unfamiliar world. He interrogates himself constantly, describing that 'his reason was foundering in cold and darkness' (1961: 228) because the world no longer recognizes the privileges – of being male, British and white – upon which he has relied throughout his life and career. When Boyd commits suicide whilst being tried for treason for his role in the colony's armed resistance, Ormston feels solely responsible for his death and, faced with the decline of his career, his family life and the colony itself, kills himself with an overdose of sleeping pills. His death can be read as the end of the Empire, representing its inability to move forwards in the modern world and the need for its swift and painless demise. However, there is no implication that the colony is now free: without Ormston and without Boyd and their paternalistic influences, the independence movement may prove successful, or the colony may simply be handed a new, and younger, governor. This hints at the uncertainty of the end of Empire at this point – there is no guarantee that it will bring peace or war, freedom or further oppression for newly-liberated colonies. This is a concern for both individual anticolonial campaigners and for the Allied powers anxious that liberated colonies may fall under Soviet control. Nonetheless, there remains a sense of inevitability that the resistance will carry on and that the colony will continue until the British government is unable to justify or maintain it. At that point, like Ormston himself, it will be dispensed with.

There is a degree of nostalgia towards Ormston's colonial administration in this novel, just as there is a great deal of sympathy for the anticolonial viewpoint and for the resistance itself. This is indicative of Jameson's habitual inability to decide between a conservative and nostalgic British nationalism and a socially-conscious internationalism. This ambivalence can also be seen in her struggle against prewar isolationist pacifism and her desire to preserve a wider Europe against Nazism at all costs, discussed earlier. She uses characters such as Frent and Boyd, even Ormston himself, to convey the complex emotional responses to the end of the Empire in Britain – of the desire to dispense with Empire, of the nostalgia evoked by the end of an era in British history, and of the private and personal implications of this international problem. Nonetheless, Jameson's portrayal is troubling – she transposes European problems onto colonized countries and avoids any real discussion of the effects and concerns of colonized peoples, preferring to maintain a European perspective on the problems of largely (at this stage, in the case of Cyprus) non-European countries. In many ways, *Last Score*, which represents her most significant engagement with the colonial and with the challenges of the demise of Empire, illustrates not a desire to engage with more contemporary political struggles, but a regression backwards towards a war which took place almost twenty years previously. This is clear in the centrality of former soldiers such as Frent and Boyd, whose experiences in the Second World War litter the narrative. These regressions demonstrate Jameson's continued convictions about the significance of the Second World War in shaping contemporary European ideas and attitudes, but also the central point the war continues to occupy in her own life and in her imagination as a writer.

For all of the rhetoric during the 1930s and 1940s regarding civilization and civilized values, the move towards ideological warfare Jameson depicts in the 1950s and 1960s is shown here to be dangerous and problematic. These ideologies have come to dominate basic human morality, justifying the most heinous acts of treachery and torture and ushering a new era of barbarism. It is this cogent sense of disappointment which characterizes these novels of the 1950s and 1960s. The deaths of Thorgill and Ormston, whilst Jameson does not seem to identify with these characters directly, mark out the demise of her generation and perhaps an increased feeling of irrelevance in this new Cold War world. All but absent from these novels are the idealistic depictions of national myth-making or imaginings of Europe's great or united future. Instead Jameson turns inward to evaluate threats to Britain and Britishness in a postwar world where Britain is marked – like the characters that represent it – by a myopic nostalgia, moral decrepitude and crippling irrelevance. Outdated and outdone, these characters, like the British Empire and the British Left, are quietly euthanized by Jameson, with no fanfare and little sense of loss. Where she had once called for writers 'whose courage is equal to their honesty' (1950: 2), these novels mark her last attempts to be courageous and honest in the terms which characterize her novels of the Second World War. Instead Jameson explores Britain and Britishness, with little nostalgia of her own and comes to register her disappointment in a postwar Europe which has not fulfilled its promise. As such, novels such as *A Cup of Tea for Mr Thorgill* and *Last Score* represent her final engagement with the ideas and the questions which dominated her life and her fiction: war, civilization and Europe.

Conclusion

For Steven Connor, 'the novel promises a view of that fine grain of events and experiences which otherwise tend to shrink to invisibility in the long perspectives of historical explanation' (1). Jameson's novels deal with these minutiae of wartime experience, from conversations about unpopular or marginal political views to the relationship of the individual to the wartime nation, from tiny evolutions in national myth-making to wide-ranging concerns around civilization and Europe itself. As with Connor's account of the postwar novel, I propose a reading of Jameson's war novels which similarly 'sees the novel not just as passively marked with the imprints of history but also as one of the ways in which history is made and re-made' (Connor, 1996: 1). Her novels of the Second World War can be seen to offer insight not only into these 'events and experiences which otherwise tend to shrink to invisibility' in a sense which is evocative of the realist writers of the nineteenth century who inspired her work, but also to offer these details within a more expansive historical and cultural landscape, in which details are underpinned by the overarching manoeuvrings of nation-states and even of Europe itself. It is this larger vision and Jameson's sense of how the 'fine grain' of individual experience operates within it, through which these novels hold out their most potent and illuminating offerings. It is also in this sense in which they offer perspective on the ways in which history is 'made and re-made' both within Jameson's own time and in the years after. Not only do these novels offer perspectives on Jameson's own life and marginalization as a writer, they also offer insight into the national and intra-national processes of myth-making function during wartime.

Recuperating literary reputations is a tricky endeavour. It is tempting to ascribe a central importance or genre-defining characteristic to an author in order to make a case for their future inclusion within certain literary fields or canonical structures. Whilst this book hopes to be a just and reasonable appraisal of Jameson's writing, of her productivity, her insight and her contribution to the literary landscape of the growing field of midcentury studies, it is also mindful of her limitations in terms of her representations of an elitist European culture, her ambivalent descriptions of women, and her often uncomfortable and racially-specific depictions of Jewish characters. Yet each of these idiosyncrasies adds to our understandings of her as an author and to a wider understanding of the prejudices and preoccupations which operated within the period in which she wrote, even among the most liberal thinkers. Offering an analysis of Jameson's marginalization, alongside readings of her novels which concentrate specifically on their unique characteristics, the elements which set her apart from her contemporaries rather than arguing for her membership of certain groups or schools, this study opens up new ways of understanding Jameson's work and gestures towards ways of reading other marginalized female writers which concentrate not on the factors of their marginalization – although these too are important from a feminist perspective – but on the reasons for their continued study and consideration.

Adam Piette describes his analysis of the literature of the Cold War as an attempt to isolate or explain 'activist and/or reactionary temptations. Specific and detailed historicist occasions, and deep rhetorical tropes' (2009: 7). Placing Jameson's ambivalences and her prejudices alongside their historical and cultural contexts sheds a great deal of light on the intricacies and preoccupations of her work, underpinned by her activist and reactionary tendencies. Using archival and bibliographical material, this study traces her political evolution – from pacifist to supporter of the war, from isolationist to European and from optimist to pessimist about Britain's and Europe's future – re-establishing each change of heart within its own social and historical context to unearth the reasoning behind her 'activist and/or reactionary temptations'. Through exploring the rhetorical evidence of these changes and the sense of history carried throughout each of these novels alongside the ambivalences and inconsistencies caused by her evolving ideas, it is possible to detect the shifting political circumstances in which they unfold. Her writing is rarely a straightforward polemic – often it is the ambivalences and inconsistencies that betray her deepest prejudices and preoccupations and those she perceives around her. In *The Moon Is Making* and *Cousin Honoré*, it is her inability to reconcile her desire to avoid another war with her desire to rid Europe and the world of Nazism, which comes to the surface through her depictions of England and France. In *The Other Side* and *The Black Laurel* (1947), she moves from earlier associations of the inhumanity and savagery of Nazism with Germanness to depict sympathetic Germans and Germans as Europeans, often mixing good Germans with bad and problematizing her portrayals through the observations of British or French characters, such as Captain Aubrac and William Gary. In *Last Score, A Cup of Tea for Mr Thorgill* and *The Moment of Truth*, Jameson moves between her national pride and her desire to see colonies freed, between her hope for Europe and her acknowledgement of its continued shortcomings. This is indicative of her continued inability to reconcile her nostalgic conservatism with her socialism and internationalism. It can be seen elsewhere in the novels, underpinning her distrust of social climbers such as de Freppel in *Cloudless May* or her suspicion of penny-pinching peasants such as Honoré Burckheim in *Cousin Honoré*, and points to the disparities between the prejudices of her upbringing in the provincial lower middle class and her education and experiences in later life. It is the resurfacing of these feelings, the occasional glimmer of indiscrepancy in her narratives, which creates her most fraught but fruitful work, in which the author is stretched to depict a range of viewpoints in order to create a rich and interwoven narrative of ideas.

Perhaps most valuable in (re-)situating Jameson within the literary landscape of the mid-century is the establishment of an alternative narrative to that which posits British writing as 'Anglocentric' (Esty, 2004: 5) or as a climate in which writers functioned primarily to 'scrutinise the political and moral claims of insular nationality' (MacKay, 2007: 2). Jameson's sustained concentration on Europe, to the exclusion of renderings of British life, experience or responses to the war, offers an important nuance to the prevalent literary trends of the period. There were, as Bluemel and Lassner assert, a number of writers who focused their literary lenses on the continent at this time, but Jameson's sustained analysis, across at least twelve novels, sets her apart from her peers. In this she offers a way of nuancing the ways in which the writing of the midcentury might be read and understood, and gestures toward a new way of seeing and grouping writing which strayed away from the 'insular nationality' which MacKay notes. Jameson's engagement with European nation-building, with European perspectives and with the idea of Europe during this period certainly offers a new way of regarding the work of her peers and of tracing the ways in which other writers engage with these processes, to a greater or lesser extent. How might we now read the work of other little-known writers such as Phyllis Bottome or Naomi Jacobs within the context of a wider look outwards? How might this reading help us to understand the lesser but significant engagements with Europe in the work of more well-known figures such as Wells, Christopher Isherwood, Forster, Woolf, Doris Lessing, Jean Rhys, Aldous Huxley or Graham Greene? How indeed might these readings help us to think about ways in which

British writing engaged not only with European perspectives or ideas but with other British writing of this period? To begin to pry into this look outwards, prevalent though it is in Jameson's writing, offers a way of opening up questions about the ways in which other British writers and British writing might also be seen to look beyond itself and to explore ideas beyond the British nation during this time. In our own times, as the British nation seeks once again to turn inwards on itself, Jameson's expansive vision might offer us crucial insight into what we might discover about ourselves if we attempt to see the world from a perspective beyond that of our own small island nation.

Notes

Introduction

1. The PEN Club was established in 1921, the first worldwide association of writers. At first it was largely a forum for international networking but, particularly during the 1930s, it became increasingly politicized and involved in issues such as human rights, protecting writers from persecution, and using literature to promote understanding between different cultures and nationalities. For further discussion of the organisation and its significance in the early twentieth century see Rachel Potter's work on PEN.
2. For example, her novel *The Green Man* (1952) sold 14,000 copies in the first year of its release, including 3,000 copies in Italy (Sales 1 July 1952–30 June 1953). Many of her novels, particularly the war novels, sold very well in Europe and America.
3. Any recuperation of Jameson's work is inherently problematic as it runs against the writer's own wishes. As Catherine Clay attests, there is an 'emotional and ethical dilemma' (2006) inherent in examining particularly the private papers of someone who expressed a wish not to be remembered or scrutinized in this way. However, it is my contention that Jameson's attitudes in this respect were extremely ambivalent – a writer wishing to sink without a trace, for example, does not go on to write a two-volume autobiography.
4. Jameson, when she first went to London after leaving university in the 1920s, did attempt to enter the life of the literary salon, attending parties at literary hostess Naomi Royde-Smith's flat with Rose Macaulay, Siegfried Sassoon, Arnold Bennett and Eddie Marsh. She was horrified at the artificiality of these salons, describing after one such event that 'I had agreed eagerly with comments that aroused only hostility or derision in me, and had made promises it would destroy me to keep. I was trembling with disgust' (*Journey from the North I*, 162). Even at this early stage in her career, she did not like compromising her personal integrity in order to integrate herself into literary groups or fashions.
5. Virago republished novels such as *Company Parade* (1934 – reissued in 1982), *Love in Winter* (1935 – reissued in 1984), *None Turn Back* (1936 – reissued in 1983) and the short story collection *Women against Men* (1933 – reissued in 1982), which examine women's lives in the 1920s with particular reference to the General Strike and the aftermath of the First World War. It also republished both volumes of her autobiography *Journey from the North* (1969) in 1984.

6   See William Lamb, *Loving Memory* (1937), *The World Ends* (1937) and *No Victory for the Soldier* (1938).
7   Of course, other women writers also sought to explore war or public affairs in their work, particularly during this period. See, for example, Margery Allingham's *Traitor's Purse* (1941) in which Albert Campion uncovers a treacherous fifth-column plot, and Naomi Jacob's *Private Gollancz* (1943), which is set in Italy and foregrounds the experiences of a Jewish soldier, Emmanuel Gollancz.
8   Contemporary reviewers were sceptical about a woman writing war novels, commenting that 'Miss Jameson does not quite bring off the idea' and pointing to 'a nervous feminine intensity' which implied that her gender stood as a direct barrier to her ability to write convincing war novels ('Review of *Then You Shall Hear Singing*', *TLS*, 31 October 1942).
9   The *Triumph of Time* trilogy is a series of historical novels based around a ship-owning family in Whitby, consisting of *The Lovely Ship* (1928), *The Voyage Home* (1930) and *A Richer Dust* (1931).
10 Her brother Harold, a pilot, was shot down and killed over No Man's Land in 1917, and a number of her close university friends were also lost or never fully recovered from their wartime experiences.
11 Hart wrote a number of books, including the army's official *Infantry Training Manual* (1920) and later more academic texts such as *The Real War, 1914–1918* (1930), *A History of the World War* (1934) and *The Other Side of the Hill* (1948), for which he interviewed a number of German generals.
12 She had good access to military information through her husband Guy Chapman, himself a veteran of the First World War and a tutor at a military training college in Britain in the Second World War. She also enlisted the help of Colonel J.F.W. Rathbone (a relative of her friend Irene Rathbone) of the Legal Division Control Commission for Germany, who wrote to her detailing the full procedure faced in military courts in occupied Berlin based on his time there. He explains to her in a letter that the German civilians in her novel 'would not be tried by German courts but by special military government courts, which were set up by us when we entered Germany' (Letter from Colonel J.F.W. Rathbone to Storm Jameson, 27 March 1946).
13 The PEN Club was founded in 1921 by the writer, playwright and poet Catherine Amy Dawson-Scott, whose objective was 'to bring writers of the world together for the purposes of friendliness and hospitality' ('PEN Pledge').
14 Birkett describes this process ('Mobilising Commitment', 81–89).
15 The Awakeners used Czech literature, most notably the plays of writers such as Václav Thám and Prokop Šedivý, which were written in the Czech language, as a basis for the idea of a Czech nation. Pelcl produced the first Czech history in the Czech language, and Dubrovský developed Czech language studies. Alongside the established Czech literature, which also represented ideas about Czech identity

and identification, these were integral to later campaigns for recognition of the Czech nation and its rights to national territory. For more information, see Arnošt Klíma, *The National Question in Europe in Historical Context* (1993: 228–247).
16 See Homi Bhabha, *The Location of Culture* (1994).
17 See George Orwell, 'Toward European Unity', *The Partisan Review* (July–August 1947).
18 The idea of Europe as a supranational entity grew alongside that of the nation, often forming an integral part of burgeoning national identities, such as in Italy where Giuseppe Mazzini founded *La Giovine Italia* (Young Italy) party in 1831 and went on to found the Young Europe party three years later, viewing the two as mutually constitutive. Mazzini was the leader of the Italian *Risorgimento*, the unification movement of the nineteenth century. However, as Stefano Recchia and Nadia Urbanati point out in the Introduction to their edited collection of Mazzini's writings, *A Cosmopolitanism of Nations: Mazzini's Writings on Democracy, Nation-Building and International Relations* (2009), he was also a key thinker in terms of the evolution of wider thought on Europe itself, which he viewed as synonymous with his ideas about Italian nationalism. They write that Mazzini 'argued for a reshaping of the European political order on the basis of two seminal principles: democracy and national self-determination' (1), yet he also wrote in 'Nationalism and Nationality' (1871) that 'our final goal is the establishment of a united states of Europe' (63).
19 See correspondence with A.D. Peters '1 July 1952–30 June 1953'.

Chapter 1

1 Certainly her understanding of 'Yorkshireness' is evidenced in many of her novels which are either set in that area, such as *The Pitiful Wife* (1924) or *The Lovely Ship* (1928), or whose protagonists hail from Whitby or a fictional equivalent such as Wik or Danesacre, such as Mary Hervey in *Love in Winter*, David Esk in *Europe to Let* or Gregory Mott in *The Road to the Monument* (1962). Her passion for Yorkshire and its traditions was always undermined in her writing by her frustration at the parochialism and backwardness which came, like the qualities she admired, from its isolation and sense of independence.
2 Following the publication of *The End of This War*, Vera Brittain, still a keen proponent of the pacifist cause and a former close friend of Jameson, had the latter removed from her will and as legal guardian of her children, as well as attempting to have the book itself blackballed for its decimation of the pacifist viewpoint. Jameson was relieved to be free of Brittain, whom she describes as 'a monument to self-pity, vanity, unconscious malice' (Birkett, *A Life*, 197).

3 Raymond Williams's examination of this in *The Country and the City* (1973) highlights the need to move away from the romanticization of this countryside to a deeper understanding of it as a site for production and innovation as influential as the city itself. Building on this and the work of later geographers and cultural theorists, Neal's more recent work argues that, even in contemporary discourses about national strength, decline or precariousness, the rural idyll continues to stand as both metaphor and microcosm for the nation. Neal's work specifically demands a more rigorous appraisal of the countryside not as an idyll but as a place of conflict and disruption particularly in terms of ethnicity and multiculturalism. See, Sarah Neal, *Rural Identities: Ethnicity and Community in the English Countryside* (2009), and Neal and Julian Aygeman, The *New Countryside? Ethnicity, Nation and Exclusion in Contemporary Rural Britain* (2006).

4 See, for example, Luce Irigaray, *Elemental Passions* (1992) and *An Ethics of Sexual Difference* (1993), Elizabeth Grosz, *Volatile Bodies* (1994) and Moira Gatens, *Imaginary Bodies: Ethics, Power and Corporeality* (1996).

5 See Katherine Cooper, '"His Dearest Property": Women, Nation and Displacement in Storm Jameson's *Cloudless May*' in Angela K. Smith and Sandra Barkhof (eds) *War and Displacement in the Twentieth Century* (2013) or Miranda Pollard's *Reign of Virtue: Mobilising Gender in Vichy France* (1998).

6 For more discussion of ethnonationalism, see Antony D. Smith, *The Ethnic Revival* (1981) and *National Identity* (1991), especially chapters 5 and 6; for an account of contemporary nation theory relating to ethnonationalism, see Walker Connor, *Ethnonationalism: The Quest for Understanding* (1994), especially Part I.

7 Several of Jameson's more independent or emancipated female characters display a similar inability to conceive: from Evelyn Lamb in *None Turn Back* (1936) to the scheming adulteress Georgina Swan in *Before the Crossing* (1947). This sterile modern woman is repeatedly made reference to in literature throughout this period, from the symbolism of the sterile ground and the promiscuous typist in Eliot's *The Waste Land* (1922) to Miss Kilman in Woolf's *Mrs Dalloway* (1925) and Julia Flyte in Waugh's *Brideshead Revisited* (1945) to name but a few.

Chapter 2

1 Jameson was interested in W.H. Auden's work, and in particular, in the ways he articulated feelings of despair and fears about the destruction of Europe during the 1930s. She wrote an essay entitled 'W.H. Auden: The Poet of Angst' in *The Writer's Situation* (1950), in which she interrogates Auden's role as a war poet, his attitudes to Communism and his departure from Europe, and 'his vision of a confused and destructive future' (1950: 84).

2 Tower is based on Jameson's husband Guy Chapman's close friend and colleague, the economic historian R.H. Tawney.
3 See *Journey from the North Vol. I*: 373–378.
4 *Europe to Let* is dedicated to that 'great country, the country of Masaryk and Beneš Czechoslovakia', as is *Then We Shall Hear Singing* (1942).
5 Overy's study, *The Morbid Age: Britain between the Wars* (2009), examines the prevalence of these narratives of disease, decay and the decline of civilization across a range of disciplines and media during the interwar period.
6 An earlier form of this chapter was first published as '"Something Must Be Done to Stop the Rot": The City, Civilisation and the Threat to Europe in Storm Jameson's *Europe to Let*', Journal of War and Culture Studies, 7.2 (May 2014): 147–161.
7 Jameson as a keen observer of European literary culture would certainly have heard of the German author and poet Herman Hesse and be familiar with some of his works during this period, linking him into a German tradition which included her great love of Goethe and Schiller.
8 For further discussion of German industrialism under Nazism, see Stackelberg (1998), especially pp. 121–125, and Ian Kershaw and Moshé Lewin, *Stalinism and Nazism: Dictatorships in Comparison* (1997). For a discussion of attitudes to modernization and technology in Germany during the interwar years more generally, especially the links between debates between modern technology and the romantic traditions of German nationalism, see Jeffrey Herf, *Reactionary Modernism: Technology, Culture and Politics in Weimar and the Third Reich* (1986).
9 As Taylor notes in *The Course of German History*, this arose from a break-in policy between National Socialism as an ideology and the Third Reich as a state (257). Although National Socialism predicated itself on a commitment to agrarianism, the Third Reich's expansionist policies demanded advanced industrialization.
10 In promoting a particular brand of 'social realism' the Communist Party sought in the 1920s and 1930s to control artists, insisting that all art was valueless if it did not help to promote the ideologies of the Russian Communist state. This, inevitably, led to censorship, exile and even the torture of writers who refused to produce work in accordance with these rules.
11 See, for example, Nietzsche, *On the Advantage and Disadvantage of History for Life* (1874), Le Bon, *The Crowd: A Study of the Popular Mind* (1896) or Canetti, *Crowds and Power* (1960), or for an overview of the idea of the crowd, see Jeffrey T. Schnapp and Matthew Tiews, *Crowds* (2006).

Chapter 3

1 Although the Germans annexed certain areas of the Sudetenland as a result of the Munich Pact in 1938, effectively ending the period known as the First Republic,

it was not until 15 March 1939 that the President of the Second Czechoslovakian Republic, Emil Hàcha, signed a treaty creating the Czech Protectorate. It is this Protectorate which, I argue, is depicted in the novel.

2   For more information on domesticity and nation-building and, in particular, on the strength of state propaganda in enforcing these images of the German Häusfrau, see Nancy Ruth Reagin, *Sweeping the German Nation: Domesticity and National Identity in Germany* (2007).

3   However, once again, language can serve as a divisive object both within the nation-state and within the national community itself, often isolating and ostracizing minorities and constructing and defining the hegemony of the dominant groups. See Judith Butler and Gayatri Chakravorty Spivak, *Who Sings the Nation State?* (2007) for a discussion of the meaning of nation for immigrant communities and other minority groups. In terms of Czechoslovakia during this period, this is a problematic way of attributing nationality, as the Czechoslovakia nation included German and Hungarian speakers, many of whom were increasingly disadvantaged in the Czechoslovakian nation through the privileging of Czech and Slavic dialects within the state, as Heimann, Feinberg and Orkzoff acknowledge.

4   This has been observed by theorists of nation throughout the twentieth century, from Hans Kohn (1944), whose study began to explore and expose the constructedness of nation, particularly through cultural artefacts, through to Anderson's work on both artworks and specifically print languages as building in *Imagined Communities* (1983), to Bhabha's explicit analysis of the role of the novel in nation-building in *Nation and Narration* (1994).

5   When Jameson was living in London with her young son, she worked as an advertising copywriter for the Carlton Agency (Birkett, 2009: 59).

6   I make a distinction here between the Czech nation and Czechoslovakia because it was the Czech sections of the community which chiefly drove this move towards nation and which evolved and articulated this national identity, primarily on their own terms.

7   J.T. is PEN member Jiřina Tůmová with whom Jameson was indeed reunited after the war, as she describes in *Journey from the North Volume II* (1984: 174–176). Tůmová was the secretary of the Czech Centre of PEN.

8   The Pact remains somewhat controversial. While Feinberg (*Elusive Equality*, 169–170), Heimann (80–90) and Orzoff (179–180) regard it as testament to their theses of the self-serving nature of President Beneš and others among the Czech government, other scholars have historically regarded it as a betrayal of Czechoslovakian interests and have seen Beneš as the martyr to the Allied cause – Jameson wrote twenty years later that 'what happened at Munich in 1938 is spoken of as a respite for France and England. In effect it was more like a syncope, a failure of the heart which might have ended in the death of both countries' (*Journey from the North I*, 406). This demonstrates the political importance which she continued

to attach to Czechoslovakia during this period. For many Czechs, it marked a betrayal by the founders of the First Republic, which undermined the promises and achievements of the preceding twenty years (see Heimann, 95–96).

9   Having divided the Czechoslovakian state by encouraging Slovakia to establish a (Fascist-led) state on 14 March 1939, Hitler had Beneš's replacement Emil Hácha flown to Berlin where he presented him with a document and an ultimatum: Prague could be signed over peacefully or taken by brute force. Hácha, shocked by the Führer's demands, opted for the former (Bryant, 28–29).

10 For a selection of Masaryk's writings in English, including extracts from *Our Present Crisis* (1908) or *Palacký's Idea of the Czech Nation* (1898), see Masaryk, *The Meaning of Czech History* (1974).

11 For more details on their activities at this time, see, for example, T.G. Masaryk, *The Making of a State: Memories and Observations 1914–18* (1927) or, for a more contemporary viewpoint, Mary Heimann's *Czechoslovakia: The State That Failed* (2009).

12 These Awakeners were the Nationalist writers, artists and historians of the nineteenth century such as the historian František *Palacký* and the composer Bedrich Smetana, whose most famous work is the rousing *Má Vlast* or *My Country* (1867).

13 Franz Kafka's novel, *The Castle* (1926), may well be similarly seen to draw upon the shadowy and mythical nature of this Castle.

14 Landsberg's book, *Prosthetic Memory: The Transformation of American Remembrance in the Age of Mass Culture* (2004), looks at the way in which popular culture, in particular cinema, can create memories of events which an individual has never experienced.

15 This performance of *Romeo and Juliet* takes place during the visit of a group of English writers to Prague before the German occupation. This is an event based upon Jameson's personal experience – her visit in 1938 to Prague as President of English PEN described in her autobiography (*Journey from the North I*, 373–381). It was a visit which became a definitive experience for Jameson and one which is indicative of her social as well as political affiliations with the Castle and to Czechoslovakia itself. It was through this visit that she came into contact with a host of Czechoslovakian intellectuals who were either knowingly or simply through their own nationalist convictions propagators of this Castle Myth to a wider European intellectual community. She even organized an event in London in 1940 to commemorate the death of the Czech playwright Karel Čapek, who organized the PEN visit, and to promote the Czech cause ('Čapek's Death from a Broken Heart', *The Times*, 3 January 1940).

16 Yet this self-same president fled to America and later London following the occupation, where he established a government in exile. Orzoff writes that 'even the Czech people hated Beneš after Munich but his popularity reached an all-time

height with resistance rallying around the President-in-exile once it looked like the Allies were heading toward victory' (Orzoff, 206).

Chapter 4

1. Thank you to Petra Rau for her comments on this section and her advice about the literary depictions – or lack thereof – of Germany during this period.
2. It is possible that the character of Paul von Galen is a reference to Bishop Clemens August Graf von Galen, a member of the German Catholic Church and a Count. Like von Galen, he was a fervent German nationalist but also a critic of Nazi policies around euthanasia and racial politics (though noticeably not vocal on the issues of the concentration camps and the treatment of the Jews).
3. See also Emil Wolf, the Jewish surgeon destined for death in *Europe to Let* and Rachel Earlham in *Love In Winter* who has 'fires in her thin body' (1984d: 214), demonstrating her hard work and political commitment.
4. Jameson also meant to depict his 'extreme appealingness [*sic*] and goodness' (*The Black Laurel MS*, 20), annotating the manuscript to this effect.
5. Ibid., p. 11.
6. The legal theorist Carl Schmidt famously worked with Hitler to explore ways of facilitating and legally justifying the false prosecution and, eventually, the denationalization of millions of Jews and other minorities. The idea of the 'state of emergency' was in wide circulation in intellectual circles during the 1920s, and Schmitt combined it with historical precedents to make the case that parliamentary democracy would always fail in the face of exceptional circumstances. As Hans Kelsen described at the time, Schmitt's approach to law allowed him to reduce the whole German legal system to Article 48, which allowed the President (or the Führer) complete sovereign power in a state of emergency (McCormick, 233). He used this to support Hitler's government from a legal standpoint and to allow the Führer and the Nazi Party to overturn elements of the German constitution, enabling Hitler to usurp parliament as the ultimate sovereign authority in Germany. For further discussion of Schmitt's political thought, see Gopal Balakrishnan, *The Enemy: An Intellectual Portrait of Carl Schmitt* (2002), D. Dyzenhaus, *Law as Politics: Carl Schmitt's Critique of Liberalism* (1998) and Michael Salter, *Carl Schmitt: Law as Politics, Ideology and Strategic Myth* (2010).
7. For more information on women as victims of war in Jameson's novels see Katherine Cooper, '"His Dearest Property"': Women, Nation and Displacement in Storm Jameson's *Cloudless May*' in Angela K. Smith and Sandra Barkof, (eds) *War and Displacement in the Twentieth Century* (Abingdon: Routledge, 2014), pp. 168–182.

Chapter 5

1. In the case of Britain, for example, the nation needed thousands of immigrants to help to rebuild the country economically and physically following the war. Immigrants were encouraged primarily from Europe, but thousands of people from colonies in India, Pakistan and Africa were also encouraged to come to Britain. In particular, large numbers of immigrants arrived from the West Indies and the Caribbean as a result of the British Nationality Act of 1948, which gave Commonwealth citizens free entry into Britain.
2. Elizabeth Maslen asserts that women's writing during the postwar period tends to look both to the past and to the future to appraise the changes, particularly in gender roles, in the postwar world (2003: 17–28).
3. Novels such as *The Early Life of Stephen Hind* (1966), *A Month Soon Goes* (1962) and *The Road from the Monument* (1962) examine Englishness, private lives and, most significantly, creative talent and the figure of the writer herself.
4. The Yalta Conference took place from 4 to 11 February 1945 and was attended by Franklin D. Roosevelt, then in his fourth term as President of the United States, Winston Churchill and Josef Stalin. For Roosevelt, the conference was an opportunity to encourage cooperation after the war and to consolidate these countries' support for his United Nations project. The conference is more often viewed, however, as a key trigger for the increase of hostilities between the United States and Russia and tends to be regarded as the catalyst of the Cold War. For a recent analysis of the historical and political significance of Yalta for Britain and America, see Fraser J. Harbutt, *Yalta 1945: Europe and America at the Crossroads* (2010).
5. This is a problematic way of evaluating refugees, and one which is also relevant to some of PEN's work in saving worthy writers and intellectuals from the continent. It suggests that refugees should qualify in some way for rescue and for asylum by demonstrating an ability to contribute intellectually to the survival of European civilization. This approach inherently deems those who cannot be seen to contribute in this way as being unworthy of saving, creating an inhuman system which favours the lives of some over others.
6. Jameson's effort joined that of other writers and the British Ministry of Information and the British council, all attempting to promote the role of America in the Second World War in order to secure their help in winning the war. This promotional campaign on Britain's part bears remarkable similarities to the Castle campaign in Czechoslovakia in the early years of the war. See Nicholas John Tull, *Selling War: The British Propaganda Campaign against American 'Neutrality' in World War Two* (1995).
7. See Henry Rousso, *The Haunting Past: History Memory and Justice in Contemporary France* (2002), Peter Davies, *France and the Second World War: Occupation,*

Collaboration and Resistance (2001), Christopher Lloyd, *Collaboration and Resistance in Occupied France: Representing Treason and Sacrifice* (2003) and Herbert Lottman, *The People's Anger: Justice and Revenge in Post-Liberation France* (1986).

8. The 'resistancialism' to which Rousso refers in his definitive book was integral to the rebuilding of the country and the regaining of national pride following years of humiliation and capitulation. Although he refers to this as taking place predominantly between 1958 and 1974, Jameson's novel points to an awareness of this myth-making slightly earlier.
9. Patriotism is a contentious issue in both philosophy and politics, marking out deep divisions between republicans and liberals and calling into question the moral implications of privileging the needs of one group of people over another. For further discussion of these issues across a range of topics, see Igor Primoratz and Aleksander Pavcović's edited collection *Patriotism: Philosophical and Political Perspectives* (2008).
10. For more information on the role of women in the resistance, see Margaret Collins Weitz's *Sisters in the Resistance: How Women Fought to Free France 1940–45* (1995), or for an account of a group of women involved in the Resistance, their activities and their capture by the Nazis, see Charlotte Delbo's *Convoy to Auschwitz: Women of the French Resistance* (1997).
11. If, in *The Hidden River*, French men are celebrated by their communities for their wartime activities, then in many ways French women are vilified. Women are frequently the subjects of stories of collaboration or cowardice in the novel, usually related by angry French villagers deemed unreasonable or unreliable by the narrative voice of Hartley.
12. Resistance leaders did not take part in operations because they were usually the sole points of contact for the organization, holding details and contacts for operatives as well as plans for future operations, which could be extracted under torture or which would be lost in the event of death.

Chapter 6

1. Guy Burgess and Donald MacLean were former members of the British Foreign Office who disappeared from Britain in 1951, only to resurface in Moscow on 11 February 1956. Here, they met with journalists and gave out a joint statement detailing the reasons for their defection to the Soviet Union but denying serving as Soviet spies in Britain.
2. Lawrence James points out that this policy was carried out with 'wherever possible the retention of strategic bases, behind-the-scenes political influence

and commercial advantages' (1994: 544), such as in Cyprus where, according to William Mallinson, 'more than half' of the Treaty of Establishment (1960) between Cyprus and Britain, on which the Republic of Cyprus was founded, 'was devoted to Britain's rights vis-á-vis the Sovereign Base Areas, other sites on the island, rights of access and over-flying rights' (2001: 6). In India and Pakistan, in Palestine and in Egypt, the British government's attempts to withdraw and whilst maintaining a level of political control led to a great deal of bloodshed and territorial disputes, many of which remain unresolved to this day.

3   It should be noted that, although Cyprus is now a central point of the European community, both geographically and politically, at this time it was still sufficiently Eastern, geographically and culturally, to stand as a non-European country for the purposes of Jameson's narrative.

4   The novel's depiction of torture also picks up on popular debates of the time, particularly in light of the popularity in France of Jean Lartéguy's novel *The Centurions* (1960). David O'Connell writes in *The French Review* in 1972 that 'there can be no doubt that during the sixties he [Lartéguy] was among the most widely read novelists in France' and that 'with the publication in 1960 of *Les Centurions* Jean Lartéguy's name became almost overnight something of a household word in France' (1087). Lartéguy's novel is widely accepted as the first to contain a representation of ticking-bomb torture in fiction, as a French General and his men battle to save civilians from a series of bombs planted by resistance movements in Algeria. This makes Jameson's novel important in terms of its representations of this type of torture, particularly in a similar circumstances – *The Centurions* also represents the psychological impact of maintaining a colony in the face of resistance and of the impact of torture on both instigator and victim. Although there is no literal 'ticking bomb' in Jameson's novel, Frent defends his techniques on the basis of extracting information from Boyd about future and potentially imminent attacks on civilians.

Bibliography

Articles, monographs and edited collections

Adams, Alex. (2019), *How to Justify Torture: Inside the Ticking Bomb Scenario*, London: Repeater.
Adolph, Andrea. (2009), *Food and Femininity in Twentieth Century Women's Fiction*, Farnham: Ashgate.
Agamben, Giorgio. (1998), *Homo Sacer: Sovereign Power and Bare Life*, Stanford: Stanford University Press.
Allingham, Margery. ([1941]1973), *Traitor's Purse*, Harmondsworth: Heinemann.
Allingham, Margery. ([1941]1987), *The Oaken Heart*, Ingatestone: Sarsen.
Anderson, Benedict. (1991), *Imagined Communities: Reflections on the Origin and Spread of Nationalism*, London: Verso.
Andreski, Stanislav. (1983), 'Introduction', in Stanislav Andreski (ed), *Max Weber on Capitalism, Bureaucracy and Religion: A Selection of Texts*, London: George Allen & Unwin, 1–12.
Anthias, Nira and Floya Yuval-Davis. (1994), 'Women and the Nation-State', in John Hutchinson and Anthony D. Smith (eds), *Nationalism*, Oxford: Oxford University Press, 312–316.
Auden, W.H. ([1930]1940), 'The Wanderer', *Some Poems*, London: Faber, 19–20.
Beauman, Nicola. (1983), *A Very Great Profession: The Woman's Novel, 1914–1939*, London: Virago.
Benjamin, Walter. ([1921]2004a), 'Critique of Violence', in trans. Rodney Livingstone, Marcus Bullock and Michael W. Jennings (eds), *Selected Writings: Volume 1, 1913–1926*, Cambridge: Harvard University Press, 236–252.
Benjamin, Walter. ([1921]2004b), 'Capitalism as Religion', trans. Rodney Livingstone, Marcus Bullock and Michael W. Jennings (eds), *Selected Writings: Volume 1, 1913–1926*, Cambridge: Harvard University Press, 288–296.
Bergonzi, Bernard. (1978), *Reading the Thirties*, London: Macmillan.
Bergonzi, Bernard. (1993), *Wartime and Its Aftermath: English Literature and Its Background, 1939–1960*, Oxford: Oxford University Press.
Berman, Jessica. (2012), *Modernist Commitments: Ethics, Politics and Transnational Modernism*, New York: Columbia University Press.
Betts, Paul and Greg Eghigian. (2003), *Pain and Prosperity: Reconsidering Twentieth-Century German History*, Stanford, CA: Stanford University Press.

Bhabha, Homi. (1990), 'Introduction: Narrating the Nation', in Homi K. Bhabha (ed), *Nation and Narration*, London: Routledge, 1–7.

Bhabha, Homi. (1994), *The Location of Culture*, Abingdon: Routledge.

Birkett, Jennifer. (1998), 'Beginning Again: Storm Jameson's Debt to France', *Critical Survey*, 10 (3): 3–12.

Birkett, Jennifer. (2006), 'Margaret Storm Jameson and the London PEN Centre: Mobilising Commitment', *EREA*, 4 (2): 81–89.

Birkett, Jennifer. (2009), *Margaret Storm Jameson: A Life*, Oxford: Oxford University Press.

Birkett, Jennifer and Chiara Briganti. (2007), *Margaret Storm Jameson: Writing in Dialogue*, Newcastle upon Tyne: Cambridge Scholars Press.

Bluemel, Kristin. (2009), *Intermodernism: Literary Culture in Mid-Twentieth-Century Britain*, Edinburgh: Edinburgh University Press.

Bluemel, Kristin and Phyllis Lassner. (2018), 'Feminist Inter/Modernist Studies', *Feminist Modernist Studies*, 1 (1–2): 22–35.

Boehmer, Elleke. (2005), *Stories of Women: Gender and Narrative in the Postcolonial Nation*, Manchester: Manchester University Press.

Bottome, Phyllis. ([1938]1944), *The Mortal Storm*. London: Faber&Faber.

Bowen, Elizabeth. (1949), *The Heat of the Day*. London: Jonathan Cape.

Bradbury, Malcolm. (1976), 'The Cities of Modernism', in Malcolm Bradbury and James McFarlane (eds), *Modernism: A Guide to European Literature, 1890–1930*, London: Penguin, 96–104.

Braudel, Fernand. (1994), *A History of Civilisations*, trans. Richard Mayne, London: Penguin.

Breiully, John. (1993), *Nationalism and the State*, Manchester: Manchester University Press.

Brinkler-Gabler, Gisela and Sidonie Smith. (1997), 'Gender, Nation and Immigrants in Contemporary Europe', in Gisela Brinker-Gabler and Sidonie Smith (eds), *Writing New Identities: Gender, Nation and Immigration in Contemporary Europe*, Minneapolis: University of Minnesota Press, 1–30.

Brittain, Vera. ([1941]1982), *England's Hour*, London: Futura Macdonald.

Bryant, Chad Carl. (2007), *Prague in Black: Nazi Rule and Czech Nationalism*, Cambridge: Harvard University Press.

Burleigh, Michael. (2001), *The Third Reich: A New History*, London: Pan Macmillan.

Butler, Judith and Gayatri Chakravorty Spivak. (2007), *Who Sings the Nation State? Language, Politics, Belonging*, Oxford: Seagull Books.

Canetti, Elias. ([1960]2000), *Crowds and Power*, trans. Carol Stewart, London: Phoenix Press.

Čapek, Karel. ([1938]1971), *Masaryk: On Thought and Life Conversations with Karel Čapek*, trans. M.R. Weatherall, New York: Books for Libraries Press.

Chapman, Guy. (1975), *A Kind of Survivor: The Autobiography of Guy Chapman*, Storm Jameson (ed), London: Victor Gollancz.

Clay, Catherine. (2006), *British Women Writers 1914–1945: Professional Work and Friendship*, Aldershot: Ashgate.
Connor, Steven. (1996), *The English Novel in History, 1950–1990*, London: Routledge.
Connor, Walker. (1994), *Ethnonationalism: The Quest for Understanding*, Princeton: Princeton University Press.
Cooke, Miriam and Angela Woollacott. (1993), 'Introduction', in Miriam Cooke and Angela Woollacott (eds), *Gendering War Talk*, Princeton: Princeton University Press, ix–xiv.
Cooper, Helen M., Adrienne Auslander Munich and Susan Merrill Squier. (1989), 'Arms and the Woman: The Con[tra]caption of the War Text', in Helen M. Cooper, Adrienne Auslander Munich and Susan Merrill Squier (eds), *Arms and the Woman: War, Gender and Literary Representation*, Chapel Hill: University of North Carolina Press, 9–24.
Cooper, Katherine. (2014), '"His Dearest Property": Women, Nation and Displacement in Storm Jameson's *Cloudless May*', in Sandra Barkhof and Angela K. Smith (eds), *War and Displacement in the Twentieth Century*, Abington: Routledge, 168–182.
Cooper, Katherine. (2020), 'British Women Writing War: The Case for Storm Jameson', in Sue Kennedy and Jane Thomas (eds), *British Women's Writing 1930–1960*, Liverpool: Liverpool University Press.
Cunningham, Valentine. (1988), *British Writers of the Thirties*, Oxford: Oxford University Press.
Dante. (1990), *The Divine Comedy I: Inferno Vol. 1*, trans. Charles S. Singleton, Princeton: Princeton University Press.
Davies, Peter. (2001), *France and the Second World War: Occupation, Collaboration and Resistance*, Basingstoke: Routledge.
De Beauvoir, Simone. ([1945]1964), *The Blood of Others*, London: Penguin.
Deák, István. (2000), 'Introduction', in Jan T. Gross István Deák and Tony Judt (eds), *The Politics of Retribution in Europe: World War Two and Its Aftermath*, Princeton: Princeton University Press, 3–15.
Dedman, Martin. (2008), *The Origins and Development of the European Union 1945–2008*, Basingstoke: Routledge.
Delanty, Gerard. (1995), *Inventing Europe: Idea, Identity, Reality*, New York: St Martin's Press.
Den Boer, Pim. (1993), 'Europe to 1914: The Making of an Idea', in Kevin Wilson and Jan Van Der Dussen (eds), *What Is Europe? The History of the Idea of Europe*, London: Routledge, 13–78.
Dowson, Jane. (2002), *Women, Modernism and British Poetry: 1910–1939*, London: Routledge.
Doyle, Laura and Winkiel, Laura (Eds) (2005), *Geomodernisms: Race, Modernism, Modernity*, Bloomington: Indiana University Press.
Earl, Hilary. (2009), *The Nuremberg SS-Einsatzgruppen Trial, 1945–1958: Atrocity, Law and History*, Cambridge: Cambridge University Press.

Eghigian, Greg. (2003), 'Pain, Entitlement and Social Citizenship in Modern Germany', in Paul Betts and Greg Eghigian (eds), *Pain and Prosperity: Reconsidering Twentieth-Century German History*, Stanford: Stanford University Press, 16–34.
Eliot, T.S. (1953), 'Virgil and the Christian World', *The Sewanee Review*, 61 (1): 1–14.
Eliot, T.S. ([1922]1954), 'The Waste Land', in *Selected Poems*, London: Faber, 40–57.
Esty, Jed. (2004), *A Shrinking Island: Modernism and National Culture in England*, Princeton: Princeton University Press.
Fanon, Frantz. (1963), *The Wretched of the Earth*, trans. Constance Farrington, New York: Grove Weidenfeld.
Farmer, Sarah. (2000), 'Postwar Justice: Bordeaux 1953', in Jan T. Gross István Deák and Tony Judt (eds), *The Politics of Retribution in Europe: World War Two and Its Aftermath*, Princeton, NJ: Princeton University Press, 194–211.
Feinberg, Melissa. (2006a), 'Dumplings and Domesticity: Women, Collaboration and Resistance in the Protectorate of Bohemia and Moravia', in Nancy M. Wingfield and Maria Bucur (eds), *Gender and War in Twentieth Century Eastern Europe in Gender and War in Twentieth Century Eastern Europe*, Bloomington: Indiana University Press, 95–111.
Feinberg, Melissa. (2006b), *Elusive Equality: Gender, Citizenship and the Limits of Democracy in Czechoslovakia, 1918–1950*, Pittsburgh: University of Pittsburgh Press.
Fritszche, Peter. (2003), 'Cities Forget, Nations Remember: Berlin and Germany and the Shock of Modernity', in Paul Betts and Greg Eghigian (eds), *Pain and Prosperity: Reconsidering Twentieth-Century German History*, Stanford: Stanford University Press, 35–60.
Gallagher, John. (1982), *The Decline, Revival and Fall of the British Empire*, in Anil Seal (ed), Cambridge: Cambridge University Press.
Garrity, Jane. (2003), *Step-Daughters of England: British Women Modernists and the National Imaginary*, Manchester: Manchester University Press.
Gatens, Moira. (1996), *Imaginary Bodies: Ethics, Power and Corporeality*, London: Routledge.
Gellhorn, Martha. ([1940]1986), *A Stricken Field*, London: Virago.
Gellner, Ernest. (1983), *Nations and Nationalism*, Ithaca: Cornell University Press.
Gerrard, Deborah. (2011), 'In Dialogue with English Modernism: Storm Jameson's Early Formation as a Writer, 1919–1931', PhD Thesis, De Montfort University, Leicester.
Grant-Duff, Sheila. ([1942]1970), *A German Protectorate: The Czechs under Nazi Rule*, London: Frank Cass & Co.
Greenfeld, Liah. (1992), *Nationalism: Five Roads to Modernity*, Cambridge: Harvard University Press.
Grosz, Elizabeth. (1994), *Volatile Bodies*, Bloomington: Indiana University Press.
Hammond, Andrew. (2013), *British Fiction and the Cold War*, Basingstoke: Palgrave Macmillan.
Harbutt, Fraser J. (2010), *Yalta 1945: Europe and America at the Crossroads*, Cambridge: Cambridge University Press.

Harding, Desmond. (2004), *Writing the City: Urban Visions and Literary Modernism*, New York: Routledge.

Hartley, Jenny. (1997), *Millions Like Us: British Women's Fiction of the Second World War*, London: Virago.

Heimann, Mary. (2009), *Czechoslovakia: The State the Failed*, New Haven: Yale.

Hepburn, Allan. (2016), 'Introduction', in Allan Hepburn (ed), *After 1945: Literature, Citizenship, Rights*, Montreal: McGill-Queen's University Press, 1–28.

Herf, Jeffrey. (1986), *Reactionary Modernism: Technology, Culture and Politics in Weimar and the Third Reich*, Cambridge: Cambridge University Press.

Higonnet, Margaret Randolph, Jane Jenson, Sonya Michel, Margaret Collins Weitz. (1987), 'Introduction', in Higonnet et al. (eds), *Behind the Lines: Gender and the Two World Wars*, New Haven: Yale University Press, 1–17.

Hobsbawm, Eric. (1983), 'Mass-Producing Traditions: Europe 1870–1914', in Eric Hobsbawm and Terence Ranger (eds), *The Invention of Tradition*, Cambridge: Cambridge University Press, 263–307.

Holtby, Winifred. (1935), 'Apology for Armourers', in Storm Jameson (ed), *Challenge to Death*, New York: E.P. Dutton & Co., 113–138.

Holton, R.J. (1986), *Cities, Capitalism and Civilization*, London: Allen and Unwin.

Howe, Stephen. (1993), *Anticolonialism in British Politics: The Left and the End of Empire, 1918–1964*, Oxford: Clarendon.

Humble, Nicola. (2004), *The Feminine Middlebrow Novel, 1920s to 1950s: Class, Domesticity, and Bohemianism*, Oxford: Oxford University Press.

Hutchinson, John. (1994), 'Cultural Nationalism and Moral Regeneration', in Anthony D. Smith and John Hutchinson (eds), *Nationalism*, Oxford: Oxford University Press, 122–131.

Huxley, Aldous. (1934), *Brave New World*, London: Chatto & Windus.

Hynes, Samuel. (1972), *The Auden Generation: Literature and Politics in England in the 1930s*, Princeton: Princeton University Press.

Irigaray, Luce. (1992), *Elemental Passions*, trans. Joanne Collie and Judith Still, London: Athlone.

Irigaray, Luce. (1993), *An Ethics of Sexual Difference*, trans. Carolyn Burke and Gillian C. Gill, London: Athlone.

Jackson, Julien. (2003), *The Fall of France: The Nazi Invasion of 1940*, Oxford: Oxford University Press.

Jacobs, Naomi. (1943), *Private Gollancz*. London: Hutchinson.

Jaillant, Lise. (2014), *Modernism, Middlebrow and the Literary Canon: The Modern Library Series, 1917–1955*, London: Routledge.

James, Lawrence. (1994), *The Rise and Fall of the British Empire*, London: Little, Brown and Company.

James, Leslie and Elizabeth Leake. (2015), 'Introduction', in Leslie James and Elizabeth Leake (eds), *Decolonization and the Cold War: Negotiating Independence*, London: Bloomsbury, 1–18.

Jameson, Storm. (1919), *The Pot Boils*, London: Constable and Co.
Jameson, Storm. (1920), *Modern Drama in Europe*, London: W. Collins and Sons.
Jameson, Storm. (1924), *The Pitiful Wife*, New York: Alfred A. Knopf.
Jameson, Storm. (1928), *Farewell to Youth*, New York: Alfred A. Knopf.
Jameson, Storm. (1928), *The Lovely Ship*, London: Heinemann.
Jameson, Storm. (1930), *The Voyage Home*, London: Heinemann.
Jameson, Storm. (1931), *A Richer Dust*, London: Heinemann.
Jameson, Storm. (1933), *No Time Like the Present*, London: Cassell.
Jameson, Storm. (1935a), 'In the End', in Storm Jameson (ed), *Challenge to Death*, New York: E.P. Dutton & Co., 322–332.
Jameson, Storm. (1935b), 'The Twilight of Reason', in Storm Jameson (ed), *Challenge to Death*, New York: E.P. Dutton & Co., 1–20.
Jameson, Storm. (1937a), 'Documents', *FACT*, 4 (13): 11–16.
Jameson, Storm. (1937b), *In Loving Memory* (as James Hill), London: Collins.
Jameson, Storm. (1937c), *The Moon Is Making*, London: Cassell.
Jameson, Storm. (1937d), *The World Ends* (as William Lamb), London: J.M. Dent & Sons.
Jameson, Storm. (1938), *No Victory gor the Soldier* (as James Hill), London: Collins.
Jameson, Storm. (1939a), 'Apology for My Life', in *Civil Journey*, London: Cassell, 7–24.
Jameson, Storm. (1939b), 'City to Let – Berlin 1932', in *Civil Journey*, London: Cassell, 7–24.
Jameson, Storm. (1939c), 'The Defence of Freedom', in *Civil Journey*, London: Cassell, 152–180.
Jameson, Storm. (1939d), 'Fighting the Foes of Civilisation: The Writer's Place in the Defence Line', *TLS*, 7 October: 571.
Jameson, Storm. (1939e), 'On Patriotism', in *Civil Journey*, London: Cassell, 248–260.
Jameson, Storm. (1939f), *Here Comes a Candle*, London: Cassell.
Jameson, Storm. (1940a), *Cousin Honoré*, London: Cassell.
Jameson, Storm. (1940b), *Europe to Let*, London: Cassell.
Jameson, Storm. (1941a), *The End of This War*, London: George Allen & Unwin.
Jameson, Storm. (1941b), *The Fort*, London: Cassell.
Jameson, Storm. (1942a), 'Introduction', in Storm Jameson (ed), *London Calling: A Salute to America*, New York: Harper and Brothers, 1–17.
Jameson, Storm. (1942b), *Then We Shall Hear Singing: A Fantasy in C Major*, London: Cassell.
Jameson, Storm. ([1941]1945a), *Cloudless May*, London: The Reprint Society.
Jameson, Storm. (1945b), *The Diary of Mary Hervey Russell*, London, Macmillan.
Jameson, Storm. (1946), *The Other Side*, London: Macmillan.
Jameson, Storm. (1947a), *The Black Laurel*, London: Macmillan.
Jameson, Storm. (1947b), *Before the Crossing*, London: Macmillan.
Jameson, Storm. (1949), *The Moment of Truth*, London: Macmillan.
Jameson, Storm. ([1949]1950a), 'The Form of the Novel', in *The Writer's Situation and Other Essays*, London: Macmillan, 37–61.
Jameson, Storm. (1950b), 'The Novel Today – 1949', in *The Writer's Situation and Other Essays*, London: Macmillan, 62–82.

Jameson, Storm. (1950c), 'The Writers Situation', in *The Writer's Situation and Other Essays*, London: Macmillan, 1–36.
Jameson, Storm. (1952), *The Green Man*, London: Macmillan.
Jameson, Storm. (1953/55), 'A Note on France', *The Cornhill Magazine*, Autumn 1953/54–Winter 1954/55: 167: 997–1002.
Jameson, Storm. (1954), 'Foreword', in *The Diary of Anne Frank*, London: Pan Books, 5–11.
Jameson, Storm. (1955), *The Hidden River*, London: The Reprint Society.
Jameson, Storm. (1958), *One Ulysses Too Many*, London: Harper Brothers.
Jameson, Storm. (1961), *Last Score, or, the Private Life of Sir Richard Ormston*, London: Macmillan.
Jameson, Storm. (1962a), *A Month Soon Goes*, London: Macmillan.
Jameson, Storm. (1962b), *The Road from the Monument*, London: Macmillan.
Jameson, Storm. (1966), *Early Life of Stephen Hind*, London: Macmillan.
Jameson, Storm. (1973), *There Will Be a Short Interval*, London: Harvill.
Jameson, Storm. ([1934]1984a), *Company Parade*, London: Virago, 1984.
Jameson, Storm. ([1969–70]1984b), *Journey from the North Volume I*, London: Virago.
Jameson, Storm. ([1969–70]1984c), *Journey from the North Volume II*, London: Virago.
Jameson, Storm. ([1935]1984d), *Love in Winter*, London: Virago.
Jameson, Storm. ([1936]1984), *None Turn Back*, London: Virago.
Jameson, Storm. ([1936]2004), *In the Second Year*, Nottingham: Trent Editions.
Joannou, Maroula. (1995), *Please Ladies, Please Don't Smash These Windows: Women's Writing, Feminist Consciousness and Social Change, 1918–1938*, London: Bloomsbury.
Judt, Tony. (2010), *Postwar: A History of Europe since 1945*, London: Vintage.
Kafka, Franz. ([1926]1963), *The Castle*, Harmondworth: Penguin.
Kalliney, Peter. (2015), *Modernism in a Global Context*, London: Bloomsbury.
Kedward, H.R. (1995), *In Search of the Maquis: Rural Resistance in Southern France, 1942–1944*, Oxford: Oxford University Press.
Kershaw, Ian and Moshé Lewin. (1997), 'Afterthoughts', in Ian Kershaw and Moshe Lewin (eds), *Stalinism and Nazism: Dictatorships in Comparison*, Cambridge: Cambridge University Press, 343–358.
Kime Scott, Bonnie. (1990), *The Gender of Modernism: A Critical Anthology*, Bonnie Kime Scott (ed), Bloomington: Indiana.
Kime-Scott, Bonnie (Ed) (2007), *Gender and Modernism: New Geographies, Complex Intersections*, Champaign: University of Illinois Press.
Klíma, Arnošt. (1993), 'The Czechs', in Mikulas Teich and Roy Porter (eds), *The National Question in Europe in Historical Context*, Cambridge: Cambridge University Press, 228–247.
Kohn, Hans. (1945), *The Origins of Nationalism: A Study in Its Origins and Background*, New York: Macmillan.
Lagrou, Pieter. (2000), *The Legacy of Nazi Occupation: Patriotic Memory and National Recovery in Western Europe, 1945–1965*, Cambridge: Cambridge University Press.
Landsberg, Alison. (2004), *Prosthetic Memory: The Transformation of American Remembrance in the Age of Mass Culture*, New York: Columbia University Press.

Lassner, Phyllis. (1997), *British Women Writers of World War Two: Battlegrounds of Their Own*, Basingstoke: Macmillan.

Lassner, Phyllis. (2004), *Colonial Strangers: Women Writing the End of the British Empire*, Piscataway: Rutgers University Press.

Le Bon, Gustave. ([1895]2009), *The Crowd: A Study of the Popular Mind*, New York: Classic Books.

Lehan, Richard. (1998), *The City in Literature: An Intellectual and Cultural History*, Berkeley: University of California Press.

Light, Alison. (1991), *Forever England: Femininity, Literature and Conservatism between the Wars*, London: Routledge.

Lipgens, Walter. (1982), *A History of European Integration 1945–1947: The Formation of the European Unity Movement*, Oxford: Clarendon.

Lister, Ruth. (1997), *Citizenship: Feminist Perspectives*, 2nd edn, New York: New York University Press.

Lloyd, Christopher. (2003), *Collaboration and Resistance in Occupied France: Representing Treason and Sacrifice*, Basingstoke: Palgrave Macmillan.

Loth, Wilfried. (1985), 'General Introduction', in Walter Lipgens and Wilfried Loth (eds), *Documents on the History of European Integration: The Struggle for European Union by Political Parties and Pressure Groups in Western European Countries, 1945–1950*, trans. Paul D. Falla, Berlin: Walter de Gruyter, 1–16.

Lottman, Herbert. (1986), *The People's Anger: Justice and Revenge in Post-Liberation France*, London: Hutchinson.

Lukács, Georg. (1970), 'Art and Objective Truth', in Arthur D. Kahn (ed), *'Writer and Critic' and Other Essays*, London: Merlin, 25–60.

Macaulay, Rose. (1950), *The World My Wilderness*, London: Collins.

MacKay, Jane and Pat Thane. (1986), 'The Englishwoman', in Robert Colls and Philip Dodd (eds), *Englishness: Politics and Culture, 1880–1920*, London: Routledge, 191–289.

MacKay, Marina. (2007), *Modernism and World War Two*, Cambridge: Cambridge University Press, 1–16.

MacKay, Marina. (2009), 'Introduction', in Marina MacKay (ed), *The Cambridge Companion to the Literature of World War Two*, Cambridge: Cambridge University Press, 1–12.

MacKay, Marina. (2016), 'Citizenship and the English Novel in 1945', in Allan Hepburn (ed), *After 1945: Literature, Citizenship, Rights*, Montreal: McGill-Queen's University Press, 29–47.

MacKay, Marina and Lyndsey Stonebridge. (2007), 'Introduction', in Marina MacKay and Lyndsey Stonebridge (eds), *British Fiction after Modernism: The Novel at Mid-Century*, Basingstoke: Palgrave Macmillan, 1–16.

Mallinson, William. (2011), *Britain and Cyprus: Key Themes and Documents since World War Two*, London: I.B. Tauris.

Mankowitz, Zeev W. (2002), *Life between Despair and Hope: The Survivors of the Holocaust in Occupied Germany*, Cambridge: Cambridge University Press.

Mann, Michael. (1997), 'The Contradictions of Continuous Revolution', in Ian Kershaw and Moshe Lewin (eds), *Stalinism and Nazism: Dictatorships in Comparison*, Cambridge: Cambridge University Press, 135–157.

Marsh, Jan. (1982), *Back to the Land: The Pastoral Impulse in England, from 1880 to 1914*, London: Quartet Books.

Masaryk, T.G. ([1938]1971), *Masaryk: On Thought and Life Conversations with Karel Čapek*, trans. M.R. Weatherall, New York: Books for Libraries Press.

Masaryk, T.G. (1974), *The Meaning of Czech History*, Chapel Hill: University of North Carolina Press.

Maslen, Elizabeth. (2003), 'Legacies of the Past: Postwar Women Looking Forward and Back', in Jane Dowson (ed), *Women's Writing, 1945–1960*, Basingstoke: Palgrave Macmillan, 17–28.

Maslen, Elizabeth. (2009), 'A Cassandra with Clout: Storm Jameson, Little Englander and Good European', in Kristin Bluemel (ed), *Intermodernism: Literary Culture in Mid-Twentieth Century Britain*, Edinburgh: Edinburgh University Press, 21–34.

Maslen, Elizabeth. (2014), *Life in the Writings of Margaret Storm Jameson*, Evanston: Northwestern University Press.

Mazzini, Guiseppe. (2009), 'Nationalism and Nationality', in Stefano Recchia and Nadia Urbinati (eds), *A Cosmopolitanism of Nations: Mazzini's Writings on Democracy, Nation-Building and International Relations*, Princeton: Princeton University Press, 62–65.

McLintock, Anne. (1993), 'Family Feuds: Gender, Nationalism and the Family', *Feminist Review*, 44: 61–80.

McLoughlin, Kate. (2007), 'Voices and Values: Storm Jameson's *Europe to Let* and the Munich Pact', in Chiara Briganti and Jennifer Birkett (eds), *Margaret Storm Jameson: Writing in Dialogue*, Newcastle upon Tyne: Cambridge Scholars, 109–125.

McLoughlin, Kate. (2011), *Authoring War: The Literary Representation of War from the Iliad to Iraq*, Cambridge: Cambridge University Press.

Mellor, Leo. (2011), 'London and Modern Prose, 1900–1950', in Lawrence Manley (ed), *The Cambridge Companion to the Literature of London*, Cambridge: Cambridge University Press, 201–221.

Messina. Anthony M. (2007), *The Logics and Politics of Post-World War Two Migration to Western Europe*, Cambridge: Cambridge University Press.

Miller, Tyrus. (1999), *Late Modernism: Politics, Fiction and the Arts between the World Wars*, Berkeley: University of California Press.

Montefiore, Janet. (1996), *Men and Women Writers of the 1930s: The Dangerous Flood of History*, London: Routledge.

Moyn, Samuel. (2010), *The Last Utopia: Human Rights in History*, Cambridge: Harvard University Press.

Mumford, Lewis. (1961), *The City in History: Its Origins, Its Transformations, and Its Prospects*, New York: Harcourt, Brace and World.

Neal, Sarah. (2009), *Rural Identities: Ethnicity and Community in the English Countryside*, Farnham: Ashgate.

Neal, Sarah and Julian Aygeman. (2006), *The New Countryside? Ethnicity, Nation and Exclusion in Contemporary Rural Britain*, Bristol: Policy Press.
Nietzsche, Friedrich. (1980), *On the Advantage and Disadvantage of History for Life*, Indianapolis: Hackett.
Nora, Pierre. (1996), *Realms of Memory*, New York: Columbia University Press.
Orwell, George. ([1947]1961), 'Toward European Unity', in Sonia Orwell and Ian Angus (eds), *The Collected Essays, Journalism and Letters of George Orwell Volume IV: In Front of Your Nose 1945-1950*, London: Secker and Warburg, 370-375.
Orwell, George. ([1937]2001a), *The Road to Wigan Pier*, Harmondsworth: Penguin.
Orwell, George. ([1939]2001b), *Coming Up for Air*, Harmondsworth: Penguin.
Orzoff, Andrea. (2009), *Battle for the Castle: The Myth of Czechoslovakia in Europe 1914-18*, Oxford: Oxford University Press.
Otis, Laura. (1994), *Organic Memory: History and the Body in the Late Nineteenth and Early Twentieth Centuries*, Omaha: University of Nebraska Press.
Overy, Richard. (2009), *The Morbid Age: Britain between the Wars*, London: Penguin.
Paxton, Robert O. (1982), *Vichy France: Old Guard and New Order 1940-1944*, New York: Columbia University Press.
Phillips, Ann L. (2000), *Power and Influence after the Cold War: Germany in East Central Europe*, Lanham: Rowman and Littlefield.
Pick, Daniel. (1989), *Faces of Degeneration: A European Disorder 1848-1918*, Cambridge: Cambridge University Press.
Piette, Adam. (2009), *The Literary Cold War, 1945 to Vietnam*, Edinburgh: Edinburgh University Press.
Plain, Gill. (1996), *Women's Fiction of the Second World War: Gender, Power and Resistance*, Edinburgh: Edinburgh University Press.
Plain, Gill. (2013), 'Women's Writing in the Second World War', in Maroula Joannou (ed), *The History of Women's Writing, 1920-1945*, Basingstoke: Palgrave Macmillan, 233-249.
Plain, Gill. (2014), *Literature of the 1940s: War, Postwar and 'Peace'*, Edinburgh: Edinburgh University Press.
Pollard, Miranda. (1998), *Reign of Virtue: Mobilizing Gender in Vichy France*, Chicago and London: University of Chicago Press.
Poole, Ross. (2008), 'Patriotism and Nationalism', in Igor Primoratz and Aleksander Pavcović (eds), *Patriotism: Philosophical and Political Perspectives*, Farnham: Ashgate, 129-145.
Potter, Rachel. (2013a), 'Modernist Rights: International PEN, 1921-1936', *Critical Quarterly*, 55 (2): 66-80.
Potter, Rachel. (2013b), *Obscene Modernism: Literary Censorship and Experimentation, 1900-1940*, Oxford: Oxford University Press.
Rau, Petra. (2009), *English Modernism, National Identity and the Germans, 1890-1950*, Farnham: Ashgate.
Reagin, Nancy Ruth. (2007), *Sweeping the Nation: Domesticity and National Identity in Germany*, Cambridge: Cambridge University Press.

Recchia, Stefano and Nadia Urbinati. (2009), 'Introduction', in Stefano Recchia and Nadia Urbinati (eds), *A Cosmopolitanism of Nations: Mazzini's Writings on Democracy, Nation-Building and International Relations*, Princeton: Princeton University Press, 1–30.

Renan, Ernest. (1994), 'Qu'est-ce qu'une nation?', in John Hutchinson and Anthony D. Smith (eds), *Nationalism*, New York: Oxford University Press, 17–18.

Roberts, Geoffrey. (2006), *Stalin's Wars: From World War to Cold War, 1939–1953*, New Haven: Yale University Press.

Rose, Sonia O. (2004), *Which People's War? National Identity and Citizenship in Wartime Britain 1939–1945*, Oxford: Oxford University Press.

Rossi, Ugo. (2014), *Cities in Global Capitalism*, Hoboken, John Wiley and Sons.

Rousso, Henry. (1991), *The Vichy Syndrome: History and Memory in France since 1944*, trans. Arthur Goldhammer, Cambridge: Harvard University Press.

Rousso, Henry. (2002), *The Haunting Past: History Memory and Justice in Contemporary France*, Philadelphia: University of Pennsylvania Press.

Saint Amour, Paul K. (2015), *Tense Future: Modernism, Total War, Encyclopedic Forms*, New York: Oxford University Press.

Sartre, Jean Paul. ([1962]2001), 'The Sleepwalkers', in *Colonialism and Neocolonialism*, trans. Azzedine Haddour, Steve Brewer and Terry McWilliams, Abingdon: Routledge, 72–74.

Schivelbusch, Wolfgang. (2004), *The Culture of Defeat: On National Trauma, Mourning and Recovery*, London: Granta.

Schmitz, Helmut. (2007), *A Nation of Victims? Representations of German Wartime Suffering, 1945 to the Present*, Amsterdam: Rodophi.

Schnapp, Jeffrey T. and Matthew Tiews. (2006), *Crowds*, Stanford: Stanford University Press.

Smith, Anthony D. (1981), *The Ethnic Revival*, Cambridge: Cambridge University Press.

Smith, Anthony D. (1991), *National Identity*, London: Penguin.

Smith, Anthony D. (1998), *Nationalism and Modernism*, London: Routledge.

Smith, Anthony D. (1999), *Myths and Memory*, New York: Open University Press.

Smith, Anthony D. and John Hutchinson. (1994), 'Introduction', in Anthony D. Smith and John Hutchinson (eds), *Nationalism*, Oxford: Oxford University Press, 3–16.

Smith, David M. and Wistrich, Enid. (2007), 'Introduction', in David M. Smith and Enid Wistrich (eds), *Regional Identity and Diversity in Europe: Experience in Wales*, Silesia and Flanders, London: Federal Trust for Education and Research, 1–20.

Smith, James. (2013), *British Writers and MI5 Surveillance, 1930–1960*, Cambridge: Cambridge University Press.

Smith, Stevie. ([1936]1980), *Novel on Yellow Paper*, London: Virago.

Spengler, Oswald. (1991), *The Decline of the West*, Oxford: Oxford University Press.

Spicer, Andrew. (2002), *Film Noir*. Abingdon: Routledge.

Stackelberg, Roderick. (1998), *Hitler's Germany: Origins. Interpretations, Legacies*. London: Routledge.

Stonebridge, Lyndsey. (2011), *The Judicial Imagination: Writing after Nuremberg*, Oxford: Oxford University Press.
Tawney, R.H. (1920), *The Acquisitive Society*, New York: Harcourt, Brace and Company.
Tawney, R.H. (1978), 'The Study of Economic History', in J.M. Winter (ed), *Essays on History and Society*, London: Routledge and Kegan Paul Ltd, 47–65.
Taylor, A.J.P. (1961/2001), *The Course of German History*, Chris Wrigley (ed), London: Routledge.
Thody, Philip. (2000), *Europe since 1945*, Abingdon: Routledge.
Thompson Willie. (2001), 'British Communists in the Cold War, 1947–1952', *Contemporary British History*, 15 (3): 105–132.
Todorova, Maria. (1997), *Imagining the Balkans*, Oxford: Oxford University Press.
Toynbee, Arnold. (1987), *A Study of History*, Oxford: Oxford University Press.
Tull, Nicholas John. (1995), *Selling War: The British Propaganda Campaign against American 'Neutrality' in World War Two*, Oxford: Oxford University Press.
Victor, George. (2000), *Hitler: The Pathology of Evil*, Dulles: Brasseys.
Voltaire. ([1756]1963), *The Age of Louis XIV and other selected writings*, J.H. Brumfitt (ed), New York: Washington Square Press.
Von Hindenberg, Hannfried. (2007), *Demonstrating Reconciliation: State and Society in West German Foreign Policy towards Israel, 1952–1965*, Oxford: Berghahn.
Wallace, Diana. (2004), *The Woman's Historical Novel: British Women Writers, 1900–2000*, Basingstoke: Palgrave Macmillan.
Warner, Geoffrey. (1986), 'Britain and Europe in 1948: The View from the Cabinet', in Josef Becker and Franz Knipping (eds), *Power in Europe? Great Britain, France, Italy and Germany in a Postwar World, 1945–1950*, Berlin: Walter de Gruyter, 27–46.
Watts, Philip. (1998), *Allegories of the Purge: How Literature Responded to the Postwar Trials of Writers and Intellectuals in France*, Stanford: Stanford University Press.
Waugh, Evelyn. ([1930]2000a), *Vile Bodies*, Harmondsworth: Penguin.
Waugh, Evelyn. ([1945]2000b), *Brideshead Revisited*, Harmondsworth: Penguin.
Weber, Max. (1983), 'The Uniqueness of Western Civilisation', in Stanislav Andreski (ed), *Max Weber on Capitalism, Bureaucracy and Religion: A Selection of Texts*, London: George Allen & Unwin, 21–29.
Weinberg, Gerhard L. (2002), 'The Allies and the Holocaust', in Michael Berenbaum and Abraham J. Peck (eds), *The Holocaust and History: The Known, the Unknown, the Disputed and the Re-Examined*, Bloomington: Indiana University Press, 480–491.
Weitz, Margaret Collins. (1995), *Sisters in the Resistance: How Women Fought to Free France, 1940–45*, Hoboken: Wiley.
Welch, David. (2002), *The Third Reich: Politics and Propaganda*, London: Routledge.
Wells, H.G. (1921), *The Salvaging of Civilization*, London: Cassell.
Wells, H.G. (1939), *The Fate of Homo Sapiens*, London: Secker and Warburg.
Wells, H.G. ([1940]2015), *Rights of Man*, London: Penguin.
West, Rebecca. ([1947]1982), *The Meaning of Treason*, London: Virago.

Wevill, Richard. (2011), *Britain and American after World War Two: Bilateral Relations and the Beginnings of the Cold War*, London: I.B. Tauris.
Whitworth, Michael H. (2007), 'Introduction', in Michael H. Whitworth (ed), *Modernism*, Chichester: Wiley-Blackwell, 3–60.
Williams, Raymond. (1975), *The Country and the City*, St Albans: Granada Publishing.
Winter, J.M. (1978), 'Introduction', in J.M. Winter (ed), *Essays on History and Society*, London: Routledge and Kegan Paul, 1–40.
Woolf, Leonard. (1939), *Barbarians at the Gate*, London: Victor Gollancz.
Woolf, Virginia. ([1941]1998), *Between the Acts*, Oxford: Oxford University Press.
Woolf, Virginia. ([1925]2000), *Mrs Dalloway*, London: Penguin.
Yuval-Davis, Nira, Floya Anthias and Jo Campling. (1989), *Women-Nation-State*, Basingstoke: Macmillan.
Yuval-Davis, Nira, Floya Anthias and Jo Campling. (1997), 'Women, Citizenship and Difference', *Feminist Review*, 57: 4–27.
Yuval-Davis, Nira, Floya Anthias and Jo Campling and Pnina Werbner. (1999), 'Introduction: Women and the New Discourse of Citizenship', in Nira Yuval-Davis and Pnina Werbner (eds), *Women, Citizenship and Difference*, London: Zed Books, 1–38.
Zamyatin, Yvegeny. ([1924]2007), *We*, London: Vintage.

Letters and archive material

Anon., 'PEN Pledge'. Nd. Date unknown. [Misc.], PEN Archive, Harry Ransom Center, University of Texas at Austin.
'The Black Laurel', *Ms. Works*, Storm Jameson Papers, Harry Ransom Center, University of Texas at Austin.
Dickson, Lovat. 'Letter to Storm Jameson and A.D. Peters', 8 February 1960. *Peters, A.D., Literary Agent* [Correspondent files May 1959–1960]. Storm Jameson Papers, Harry Ransom Center, University of Texas at Austin.
Jameson, Storm. 'The Future of the Novel' [Notebook 1, ams. 1930], *Letters/Works*. Margaret Storm Jameson Papers, Harry Ransom Center, University of Texas at Austin.
Jameson, Storm. 'Letter to A.D. Peters, 5 January 1932', *Letters/Works*, Margaret Storm Jameson Papers, Harry Ransom Center, University of Texas at Austin.
Jameson, Storm. 'Letter to Basil Liddell Hart, 14 September 1939', Correspondents [J]. Basil Liddell Hart Archive. King's College, London.
Jameson, Storm. Letter to Basil Liddell Hart. 6 April 1940. Correspondents [J]. Basil Liddell Hart Archive. King's College, London.
Jameson, Storm. Letter to Basil Liddell Hart. 26 June 1940. Correspondents [J]. Basil Liddell Hart Archive. King's College, London.
Jameson, Storm. Letter to Basil Liddell Hart. 3 April 1941. Correspondents [J]. Basil Liddell Hart Archive. King's College, London.

Jameson, Storm. Letter to Basil Liddell Hart. 21 December 1941. Correspondents [J]. Basil Liddell Hart Archive. King's College, London.

Jameson, Storm. 'Speech to the PEN Coming of Age Conference 1942', PEN Misc., Group 1, PEN Archive, Harry Ransom Center, University of Texas at Austin.

Jameson, Storm. 'Letter from Colonel J.F.W. Rathbone to Storm Jameson, 27 March 1946', *Letters/Works*, Margaret Storm Jameson Papers, Harry Ransom Center, University of Texas at Austin.

Jameson, Storm, 'Letter to John Montgomery, 6 December 1951', *Peters, A.D., Literary Agent* [Correspondent files 1938–July 1954], Margaret Storm Jameson Papers, Harry Ransom Center, University of Texas at Austin.

Jameson, Storm. 'Letter to A.D. Peters, 9 November 1951', *Peters, A.D., Literary Agent* [Correspondent files 1938–July 1954], Margaret Storm Jameson Papers, Harry Ransom Center, University of Texas at Austin.

Jameson, Storm. 'Letter to Nancy Cunard, 3 November 1953', Series II Correspondence: Subseries B: Incoming Correspondence [Jameson, Storm 1933–1959], *Nancy Cunard Collection 1895–1965*, Harry Ransom Center, University of Texas at Austin.

Jameson, Storm. Letter to John Montgomery. 16 June 1954. *Peters, A.D., Literary Agent* [Correspondent files 1938–July 1954]. Storm Jameson Papers. Harry Ransom Center, Austin, Texas.

Jameson, Storm. 'Letter to Margaret Stevens, 22 January 1955', *Peters, A.D., Literary Agent* [Correspondence files 1955], Margaret Storm Jameson Papers, Harry Ransom Center, University of Texas at Austin.

Jameson, Storm. 'Letter to A.D. Peters. 30 December 1955', *Peters, A.D., Literary Agent* [Correspondence files 1956]. Margaret Storm Jameson Papers, Harry Ransom Center, University of Texas at Austin.

Jameson, Storm. 'Letter to A.D. Peters, 3 January 1957', *Peters, A.D., Literary Agent* [Correspondence files 1957], Margaret Storm Jameson Papers, Harry Ransom Center, University of Texas at Austin.

Jameson, Storm. 'Letter to Francis Henry King, 20 February 1975', Francis Henry King Papers [Correspondence files G–J 1956–1991], Harry Ransom Center, University of Texas at Austin.

Jameson, Storm. 'Letter to Josephine Pullein-Thompson, 27 March 1982', Correspondence [Jameson, Storm], Group 1, PEN Archive, Harry Ransom Center, University of Texas at Austin.

Liddell-Hart, Kathleen. 'Letter to Downing Street, copied to David Carver', 5 June 1973', [Correspondence: J] Group 1, PEN Archive, Harry Ransom Center, University of Texas at Austin.

Mannin, Ethel. 'Postcard to Storm Jameson, 18 May 1936', *Letters/Works*, Margaret Storm Jameson Papers, Harry Ransom Center, University of Texas at Austin.

Peters, A.D. 'Letter to Storm Jameson, 18 January 1960', *Peters, A.D., Literary Agent* [Correspondence files May 1959–1960], Margaret Storm Jameson Papers, Harry Ransom Center, University of Texas at Austin.

Peters, A.D. 'Sales 1 July 1952–30 June 1953', *Peters, A.D., Literary Agent* [Correspondent files 1938–July 1954], Margaret Storm Jameson Papers, Harry Ransom Center, University of Texas at Austin.

Newspapers

'Čapek's Death from A Broken Heart', *The Times*, 3 January 1940: 9.

'TLS Novel of the Week: Review of *Then You Shall Hear Singing*', *TLS*, 31 October 1942. Correspondents [J]. Basil Liddell Hart Archive. King's College, London.

Jameson, Storm and Hermon Ould. 'Letter to the Editor', *The Times*, Saturday 13 July 1940, Issue 2006: 339.

Index

Note: Locators with letter 'n' refer to notes.

acceptance 12, 39, 46–7, 141
Acquisitive Society, The (Tawney) 57
aftermath, of war 13, 91–2, 111–29, 133, 142–3, 157 n.5
Algeria 142, 144, 167 n.4
alienation 52, 65, 67, 68
Allingham, Margery 12, 13, 30–1, 158 n.7
ambivalence 5, 11, 22, 30, 32, 34, 39, 44, 49, 50, 55, 61, 62, 68, 71, 91, 95, 105, 118, 120, 142, 149, 151, 154, 157 n.3
America 3, 16, 44–8, 56, 83, 89, 111, 113, 114–20, 129, 135, 136, 157 n.2, 163 n.16, 165 n.4, 165 n.6
Anderson, Benedict 19, 23, 71, 79, 81, 86, 162 n.4
anonymity 61–2, 67, 83, 104, 143
Anthias, Flora 74, 81
anticipatory syndrome 32, 52
anti-fascism 2
anxiety 11, 12, 26, 31, 32, 34, 40, 43, 45, 46, 52, 54, 62, 64, 66, 69, 83, 91, 92, 103, 113, 117, 118, 120, 127, 131–4, 137–8, 142–3, 151
Arendt, Hannah 107
Atheneum, The (magazine) 56
Attlee, Clement 116, 129, 138
Auden, W. H. 6, 13, 53, 160 n.1
Austria 16, 17, 29, 50, 51, 58, 84, 98, 115

Balzac, Honoré de 3, 10, 20
barbarism 25, 26–7, 56, 57, 60, 62, 87, 94, 96, 115–16, 118, 127–8, 135, 141, 152
Beauman, Nicola 8
Behind the Lines: Gender and the Two World Wars (Higonnet) 10
belonging 11, 20, 21, 33, 41, 44, 47, 73, 86, 111

Beneš, Edouard 82, 83, 88, 89, 121, 161 n.4, 162–3 nn.8–9, 163 n.16
Benjamin, Walter 56, 106
Bennett, Arnold 157 n.4
Between the Acts (Woolf, Virginia) 31
Bhabha, Homi 19, 20, 72, 162 n.4
Birkett, Jennifer 2, 3, 5, 6, 10, 18, 21, 30, 33, 53, 93, 102, 135, 140, 141, 158 n.15
Blood of Others, The (de Beauvoir) 128
Bluemel, Kristin 2, 7, 155
Blunden, Edmund 34
Bonnet, Georges 59
Bottome, Phyllis 3, 95–6, 147, 148, 155
Bowen, Elizabeth 12, 13
Bradbury, Malcolm 6
Bratislava 17
Braudel, Fernand 25, 54
Brave New World (Huxley) 64
Brecht, Bertolt 2
Brideshead Revisited (Waugh) 160 n.7
Briganti, Chiara 6, 10
British Empire 132, 142–52
Brittain, Vera 3, 5, 10, 13, 26, 34, 35, 159 n.2
Burdekin, Katherine 53, 64, 65
Burgess, Guy 134, 166 n.1
Burnett, Ivy Compton 30
Butler, Judith 79, 162 n.3

Canetti, Elias 65
Čapek, Karel 84, 163 n.15
capitalism 53–65, 69–70, 75, 84, 115, 118
Castle, The (Kafka) 163 n.13
censorship 9–10, 15, 161 n.10
Centurions, The (Lartéguy) 167 n.4
Chapman, Guy 4, 5, 158 n.12, 161 n.2
chiaroscuro effect 66–7
Christie, Agatha 30

Churchill, Winston 26, 165 n.4
Cities, Capitalism and Civilisation (Holton) 61–2
citizenship 27, 42, 50–2, 78, 84, 111
city 32, 51–2, 54, 60, 61–70
City in History: Its Origins, Its Transformations, and Its Prospects, The (Mumford) 70
civilization, conceptions of 25, 51–70, 80, 83, 98, 105–6, 112, 114–20, 122, 129, 131, 133, 141, 151–3, 161 n.5, 165 n.5
Clay, Catherine 5, 10, 157 n.3
Cold War 11, 12, 24, 27, 32, 70, 111–15, 118, 120, 129, 131–52, 154, 165 n.4
colonialism 5, 8, 19–20, 27, 71–3, 111, 131–3, 142–51
Coming Up for Air (Orwell) 55
Comité Français de Libération Nationale (CFLN) 121
Communism 13, 63, 111–29, 131, 134–41, 160 n.1, 161 n.10
conservatism 12, 30–1, 35, 39, 41, 44, 46, 49, 81, 155
Constructivism 87
Cosmopolitanism of Nations, A (Recchia and Urbanati) 159 n.19
Country and the City, The (Williams) 160 n.3
country house novel 8
Course of German History, The (Taylor) 48, 161 n.9
criminality 61–2, 67, 108, 128, 148
'Crisis of the Mind, The' (Valéry) 56
cruelty 14, 34, 38, 51–70, 88, 96, 105, 107, 109, 127, 128, 138–41
Cubism 87
culture 2, 11, 13, 18, 20, 21–8, 33–40, 50–2, 55–8, 62, 65, 68–70, 71–109, 112, 116, 117, 119, 142, 154, 157 n.1
Cyprus 2, 50, 142, 143, 151, 167 nn.2–3
Czech Awakeners 20, 84, 158 n.15, 163 n.12
Czechoslovakia 2, 3, 8, 12, 13, 16, 19–20, 22, 23, 29, 50, 51, 58, 70, 71–90, 91, 92, 97–8, 100, 116, 121, 158–9 n.16, 161 n.4, 162–3 nn.6–9, 162 n.1, 162 n.3, 163 nn.15–16, 165 n.6

Dante 62
Davies, Peter 124
Dawson-Scott, Catherine Amy 158 n.13
de Gaulle, Charles 121
de la Mare, Walter 3
Decline of the West, The (Spengler) 56
dehumanization 59, 63–6, 68, 70, 75, 91, 107, 134, 147
Delafield, E.M. 118
democracy 14, 17, 19, 21, 27, 52–60, 64, 70, 73, 83–9, 159 n.19, 164 n.7
Depression 7
despair 46, 52–3, 62, 70, 113, 116, 121, 160 n.1
Dickson, Lovat 143
disease 52, 59–60, 66, 68, 69, 117, 135, 161 n.5
Divine Comedy (Dante) 62
domesticity 5–9, 13, 46, 71–82, 89, 98, 162 n.2
Dostoyevsky, Fyodor 14
Dubrovský, Josef 20, 158 n.15
dystopia 12, 56, 64, 112, 114

Elemental Passions (Irigaray) 42
Eliot, T.S. 6, 26, 160 n.7
empathy 17, 32, 36, 49, 66, 78, 83, 89, 92, 100–1, 109, 117, 135, 140, 145, 146, 148
empowerment 8, 135, 141
Englishness 4, 28, 33–9, 50, 53, 92, 96, 165 n.3
Enlightenment 53, 55, 57, 58, 62, 63, 64
Erasmus 23
Esty, Jed 2, 53
Ethics of Sexual Difference, An (Irigaray) 47
ethnicity 17, 81, 160 n.3
ethnonationalism 45, 160 n.6
Eurocentrism 144, 145, 146
Europe
  decline of, postwar 114–20
  idea of 21–8, 159 n.19
European civilization. *See* civilization
European community 22, 148, 167 n.3
European community of letters 23–4
European literature 23, 25

FACT (journal) 14
Fall of France: The Nazi Invasion of 1940, The (Jackson) 59

Fanon, Frantz 72
fascism 9, 12, 14, 34, 51, 52, 54–5, 57, 60–4, 67, 70, 86, 108, 111, 136, 163 n.9
Fate of Homo Sapiens, The (Wells) 25
Feinberg, Melissa 74, 77, 85, 86, 162 n.3, 162 n.8
feminism 8, 10–11, 41–2, 79, 81, 154
Fichte, Johann Gottlieb 18, 95
First World War 9–12, 22, 29, 32, 34, 37–8, 40, 43, 48, 52, 54, 56, 72, 80, 83, 91–2, 95, 98, 100, 120, 125, 137, 157 n.5, 158 n.12
Forster, E.M. 3, 10, 25, 118
France 2, 3, 6, 12, 18, 22–5, 31–50, 51, 52, 54, 56–9, 63–4, 71, 84, 91, 92, 95, 97–100, 111–14, 121–9, 132–3, 142–6, 154–5, 162 n.8, 166 n.11, 167 n.4
freedom 8, 14, 23, 30, 43, 47, 57, 64, 73, 79, 83–5, 88–9, 112, 125, 132, 141–6, 151
Functionalism 87

Gellhorn, Martha 84, 93
gender 3–11, 13, 15, 17, 29–30, 42, 74–5, 98, 158 n.8, 165 n.2
General Strike 137, 157 n.5
Germany 3, 12, 13, 15, 18, 20–1, 23, 25, 29, 31, 36, 38, 40, 43–50, 51–70, 75, 77–80, 83, 86–7, 91–109, 114–15, 121–8, 141, 154, 158 nn.11–12, 161 nn.7–9, 162 nn.2–3, 163 n.15, 164 n.6, 164 nn.1–3
Goethe, Johann Wolfgang von 2, 3, 24, 94, 95, 161 n.7
Grant-Duff, Sheila 79–80, 84, 87, 96
Graves, Robert 13, 108, 135
Greece 123, 143
greed 31, 38, 57, 59
Greene, Graham 155

Hàcha, Emil 162 n.1, 163 n.9
Hart, Basil Liddell 13, 34, 56, 60, 92, 118, 158 n.11
Hartley, Jenny 9, 10
Heat of the Day, The (Bowen) 13
Hegel, Georg William Friedrich 63, 95
Heine, Heinrich 24
Hesse, Herman 161 n.7

hierarchy 31, 57, 98, 114, 123, 134, 138
historical novel 11–12, 158 n.9
History of the World War, A (Hart) 158 n.11
Hitler, Adolf 35, 48–9, 58, 64, 83, 96, 105, 163 n.9, 164 n.6
Hobsbawm, Eric 19
Holocaust 27, 93, 100–9
Holtby, Winifred 7, 36
hope 11, 14, 19, 21, 24–5, 29, 32, 52–3, 58, 60–2, 62, 70, 72, 75, 78, 79, 82–3, 85–6, 89, 92, 95, 98, 99, 108, 113, 115–20, 129, 136, 140, 141, 155
House of Commons 26
How to Justify Torture: Inside the Ticking Bomb Scenario (Adams) 149
Humble, Nicola 8
Hungary 2, 17, 22, 23, 49, 51, 85, 135, 162 n.3
Huxley, Aldous 53, 64, 65, 155
Huxley, Julian 34
hybridity 6, 11

ideologies 17, 19, 20, 30, 47, 54–8, 63, 80, 81, 89, 98, 103, 116, 133–5, 138, 150–2, 161 nn.9–10
idylls 30, 36, 38, 39, 136, 160 n.3
imagery 20, 50, 64
Imagined Communities (Anderson) 81, 162 n.4
imagined community 20, 131–2
immigrants 83, 162 n.3, 165 n.1
individualism 57
industrialization 46, 48, 49, 59, 60, 64, 66, 161 nn.8–9
inequality 14, 39, 58, 69–70, 78, 137
Infantry Training Manual (Hart) 158 n.11
Inferno (Dante) 62
Intermodernism (Bluemel) 7
interwar period 10–12, 24, 30–2, 35, 43, 46, 52–3, 56, 64, 91, 131, 134, 136, 161 n.5, 161 n.8
Irigaray, Luce 42, 43, 47
irony 38, 57, 64, 73, 76, 77, 95, 98, 118, 138–9, 145
Isherwood, Christopher 155
isolationism 28–9, 38, 39, 49–50, 52, 104, 109, 151, 154, 159 n.1

Jacobs, Naomi 155
Jameson, Margaret Storm
  critical reception 3–4, 6, 15, 31, 158 n.8
  decline 4–5
  'Future of the Novel, The' 1
  life and career 1–11, 13–14, 33, 39, 157 n.4, 162 n.5
  multiple identities, national and regional 33–50
  pseudonyms: William Lamb and James Hill 9
  role at PEN 2, 3, 4, 11, 13, 14, 15–16, 24–5, 54, 88, 94, 117, 135, 157 n.1, 158 n.13, 162 n.7, 163 n.15, 165 n.5
  socialist convictions 14–15, 16, 21–2, 30, 31, 32, 41, 49, 134, 141
  styles and themes 6–14
Jameson, Margaret Storm (works)
  Before the Crossing 6, 9, 26, 67, 114, 129, 160 n.7
  Black Laurel, The 9, 12, 15, 16–17, 18, 20, 26, 77, 91–4, 100, 101–9, 112–13, 114, 117, 118, 127, 129, 154, 164 n.2, 164 n.5
  Challenge to Death 12, 34, 46, 55
  'City to Let – Berlin 1932' 17
  Civil Journey 12, 34
  Cloudless May 155
  Company Parade 9, 12, 66, 91, 133, 157 n.5
  Cousin Honoré 11, 12, 16, 20–1, 29–50, 51, 60, 63–4, 68, 81, 91, 92, 95, 97, 99, 112, 115–18, 140, 154–5
  Cup of Tea for Mr Thorgill, A 12, 16, 114, 131–42, 152, 155
  Early Life of Stephen Hind, The 165 n.3
  End of This War, The 56–7, 86, 159 n.2
  Europe to Let 8, 11, 12, 16, 19, 20, 24, 51–70, 71, 80, 82, 84, 85, 87, 88, 89, 90, 95, 103, 104, 108–9, 112, 115, 117, 120, 124, 127, 159 n.1, 161 n.4, 161 n.6, 164 n.4
  Farewell to Youth 11
  Fort, The 41, 117
  'Future of the Novel, The' 1, 6
  Green Man, The 12, 112, 114, 117, 125
  Here Comes a Candle 51, 61, 66, 69
  Hidden River, The 3, 12, 16, 102, 111–29, 144, 150, 166 n.11
  Journey from the North 54, 71, 101, 157 nn.4–5, 162 n.7, 162 n.8, 163 n.15
  Last Score, or the Private Life of Sir Richard Ormston 8, 11, 12, 16, 27, 132, 133, 142–52, 155
  London Calling: A Salute to America 118
  Love in Winter 55, 157 n.5, 159 n.1
  Lovely Ship, The 158 n.9, 159 n.1
  Mirror in Darkness trilogy 9
  Modern Drama in Europe 94
  Moment of Truth, The 9, 12, 16, 111–29, 132, 133, 137, 155
  Month Soon Goes, A 8, 13, 117, 143, 165 n.3
  Moon Is Making, The 12, 16, 29–50, 55, 60, 68, 136, 154
  No Time Like the Present 12, 33
  None Turn Back 6, 66, 133, 137, 157 n.5, 160 n.7
  'Novel Today – 1949, The' 16
  One Ulysses Too Many 112
  Other Side, The 16, 18, 20, 21, 24, 41, 92, 94–101, 102, 108, 121, 154, 158 n.11
  Pitiful Wife, The 3, 6, 8, 11, 159 n.1
  Pot Boils, The 11
  Richer Dust, A 158 n.9
  Road from the Monument, The 13, 117, 159 n.1, 165 n.3
  In The Second Year 12, 56, 69
  Then We Shall Hear Singing 9, 12, 16, 18, 19, 71–90, 92, 97, 121, 124, 158 n.8, 161 n.4
  Triumph of Time trilogy 11, 158 n.9
  Voyage Home, The 158 n.9
  Women against Men 8, 157 n.5
  Writer's Situation, The 160 n.1
Joannou, Mary 10
journalism 1, 8, 11, 13, 29, 34, 35, 59, 69, 84, 166 n.1
Judicial Imagination: Writing after Nuremberg, The (Stonebridge) 93
justice 7, 13, 14, 23, 27, 38, 52, 54, 55, 57, 58, 62, 70, 73, 91–4, 100, 101–9, 112–13, 117, 127, 131, 137, 138, 142
Justice after Nuremburg (Stonebridge) 27

Kafka, Franz 163 n.13
Kant, Immanuel 95
King, Francis Henry 4
Kleist, Heinrich 94
Knopf, Alfred J. 4
Kohn, Hans 84, 162 n.4

Lamarckism 86
Lamb, Evelyn 6
Lartéguy, Jean 167 n.4
Lassner, Phyllis 2, 7, 10, 75, 132, 142, 148, 155
League of Nations 25
Lenin, Vladimir 114
Lessing, Doris 155
Lessing, Gotthold Ephraim 94
Liddell-Hart, B. H. 13, 34, 56, 60, 92, 118
Light, Alison 10, 30–1, 39, 136
literary culture 7, 161 n.7
Lloyd, Christopher 125, 126, 128
London blitz 13
loss 8, 9, 12, 29, 44, 52–3, 69, 70, 71, 116, 120, 141, 142, 143, 150, 152
Lukács, Georg 10

Macaulay, Rose 13, 118, 157 n.4
MacLean, Donald 134, 166 n.1
Malraux, André 24
Mannin, Ethel 4
Mansfield, Katherine 5
Margaret Storm Jameson: Writing in Dialogue (Birkett and Briganti) 6, 10
marginalization 3–11, 28, 153, 154
Marsh, Eddie 157 n.4
Marx, Karl 56
Masaryk, Tomáš 83–4, 87, 89, 161 n.4, 163 n.10
Maslen, Elizabeth 7, 10, 21, 23, 30, 93, 133, 134, 165 n.2
Mazzini, Guiseppe 18, 159 n.18
McLintock, Anne 42
McLoughlin, Kate 15
memory 33, 34, 69, 73, 75, 76, 77, 78, 80–2, 84–6, 92, 97, 98, 109, 121, 124, 143
metaphors 31, 38, 42, 59–60, 69, 115, 122, 136, 140, 160 n.3
middlebrow 7, 8, 10
Miller, Betty 12, 13

Millions Like Us (Hartley) 10
Milton, John 20
misogyny 31, 139
modernism 2, 3–11, 48, 65, 92, 148
modernity 6, 26, 30, 31, 46–50, 51, 53–4, 56, 61–70, 92, 118, 136, 160 n.7
Montefiore, Janet 10, 14
morality 2, 11, 13, 14, 25, 27, 49, 54, 57, 58, 62, 65–6, 70, 93–4, 100, 101, 106, 107, 117, 132, 140, 141, 151–2, 155, 166 n.9
Morbid Age: Britain between the Wars, The (Overy) 26, 161 n.5
Mortal Storm, The (Bottome) 95–6
motherhood 8, 46
Moyn, Samuel 27, 93
Mrs Dalloway (Woolf) 12, 160 n.7
multiculturalism 133, 160 n.3
Mumford, Lewis 51–2, 70
Munich Pact 34–5, 54, 58, 85, 161 n.1
myth/myth-making 1, 16–21, 35, 36, 48, 49, 71–90, 86, 91–109, 112–16, 120, 121–9, 132, 133, 142–3, 152, 153, 163 n.13, 166 n.8

Nation and Narration (Bhabha) 162 n.4
nation/nationalism/nation-building (European)
  concept/idea 16–21, 31, 45, 81
  cultural identities 18–19, 71–90
  gendered identity 17, 41–8, 71–90
  ideological stages 17–21
  Jameson's themes 20–1
  myth and myth-making 19–20, 49, 71–2, 83–4
  neoclassical conception 17–18
National Socialism 55, 161 n.9
Nazism 3, 13, 18, 19, 22, 31, 32–3, 35, 38, 47–9, 51–70, 71–80, 83–90, 91–109, 111, 114–17, 121, 124–6, 135, 136, 141–2, 144, 149, 151, 154, 161 n.8, 166 n.10
Neal, Sarah 35, 160 n.3
neo-classicism 17–18
Nietzsche, Friedrich 63, 65
Nineteen Eighty-Four (Orwell) 64
noir 67–8
Nordic Twilight (Forster) 25
nostalgia 5, 12, 30–2, 48, 128, 146–52, 155

Oaken Heart, The (Allingham) 30
On the Side of Angels (Miller) 13
oppression 24, 27, 58, 85, 151
Organic Memory (Otis) 86
Orwell, George 14, 21, 53, 55, 64, 65
Other Side of the Hill, The (Hart) 158 n.11
otherness/Others 36, 72, 96, 100, 147–8
Ould, Hermon 16, 94
Overy, Richard 25, 26, 59, 161 n.5

pacifism 12, 26, 29–50, 151, 154, 159 n.2
Palacký, František 163 n.12
Passionate Prodigality, A (Chapman) 4
pastoral 29–32, 50
patriotism 17, 38, 121, 123–4, 124, 126–8, 166 n.9
peasants 37, 38, 39, 42, 43, 45, 88, 126, 155
PEN (Poets, Essayists and Novelists Club) 2, 3, 4, 10, 11, 13, 14, 15–16, 24–5, 54, 88, 94, 117, 135, 157 n.1, 158 n.13, 162 n.7, 163 n.15, 165 n.5
    Coming of Age Conference 14
PEN Fund 94
Peters, A.D. 4, 5, 24, 143
Piette, Adam 10, 106, 154
placelessness 4, 5, 9, 21, 103
Plain, Gill 10, 13, 41–2
politics 8, 9, 12–13, 17, 20, 24, 45, 47, 61, 68, 70, 78, 87, 89, 98, 107, 113, 127, 131–2, 135, 139–40, 144, 146, 148, 150, 164 n.3
popular culture 37, 163 n.14
postcolonialism 19–20, 27, 71–3, 111, 133, 143–5
Potter, Rachel 15, 24
poverty 51, 54, 61–2, 66, 69–70, 79, 129, 141
power/power struggle 38, 42, 44, 56–8, 72–3, 75–6, 80, 82, 88, 98, 107, 114, 116–17, 120, 122–3, 129, 132, 134, 142–3, 148–9, 164 n.7
PPU (Peace Pledge Union) 13, 29
Prague 17, 24, 51, 54, 57, 58, 66, 68, 69, 71, 77, 80, 82, 83, 85, 87, 109, 163 n.9, 163 n.15
Priestley, J.B. 3, 36, 118
primitivism 25, 47, 60
Private Gollancz (Jacobs) 158 n.7

progress 26, 32, 47, 50–4, 56–8, 60, 61–70, 76, 80, 87, 105, 113, 125, 137
'Protestant Ethic and the Spirit of Capitalism' (Weber) 56

Racine 19
Rathbone, J.F.W. 158 n.12
rationalism 54, 55, 95
Real War, 1914–1918, The (Hart) 158 n.11
realism 6, 9, 12, 14, 108, 153, 161 n.10
Recchia, Stefano 159 n.18
reconciliation 27, 90, 91, 102, 108, 111–29
Renaissance 23, 57
Renan, Ernest 18
resistance/resistance movements 8, 22, 74–82, 94–101, 111–29, 142–52
'resistancialism' 122, 166 n.8
'Respublica Litteraria' 23–4
retribution 27, 93, 100, 101–9, 111–13, 129
Return of the Soldier (West) 11
Rhys, Jean 155
Road to Wigan Pier, The (Orwell) 14
Romeo and Juliet 57, 87, 163 n.15
Ronsard, Pierre 24, 99
Roosevelt, Franklin D. 165 n.4
Rousseau, Jean-Jacques 18
Royde-Smith, Naomi 157 n.4
rural landscape 13, 30–50, 51

Sartre, Jean Paul 144
Sassoon, Siegfried 157 n.4
savagery 25, 44, 64, 91, 92, 95, 100, 154
Schiller, Friedrich 94, 95, 161 n.7
Schmitt, Carl 164 n.6
Shakespeare, William 20, 24, 87
shared culture 24, 35, 50, 69, 70, 84, 87, 89, 101
On the Side of Angels (Miller) 13
signifier/signified 20
Simmel, Georges 65
Sinclair, May 12
Slaughter, Joseph 93
'Sleepwalkers, The' (Sartre) 144
Smetana, Bedrich 163 n.12
Smith, Stevie 96
socialism 2, 14, 15, 16, 21, 30, 31, 32, 41, 49, 55, 83, 85, 132, 134, 137, 138, 140–1, 155
solidarity 17, 24, 76, 80, 88, 102, 125

Soviet Union 114–20, 132, 134–5, 138, 151, 166 n.1
Spengler, Oswald 56
Stalin, Josef 114, 135, 139, 165 n.4
Stendhal 3, 6, 10
sterility 45, 46, 160 n.7
Streathfeild, Noel 3
Stricken Field, A (Gellhorn) 84
Study of History, A (Toynbee) 56
suffering 79, 82, 89, 90, 93, 98, 100, 101–5, 107, 117, 121–2, 135, 139, 144
Swastika Night (Burdekin) 64
symbolism 6, 35, 105
Symbolistes 6
sympathy 50, 63, 72, 89, 97, 104–5, 117, 127, 135, 138, 144, 147–9, 151, 154

Tawney, R.H. 53, 54, 56–7
Taylor, A.J.P. 48, 53, 161 n.9
Taylor, Elizabeth 12
terrorism 131–52
threat 3, 13, 16, 17, 26, 30–2, 37, 39, 40–50, 51–70, 74, 88, 96, 111–17, 124, 129, 132, 136–7, 140–2, 147, 152
Times magazine 94
Tolstoy, Leo 20
torture 58–60, 70, 105, 108, 122, 125, 131, 145, 149–50, 152, 161 n.10, 166 n.12, 167 n.4
Tower, R.B. 56
Toynbee, Arnold 56
Traitor's Purse (Allingham) 158 n.7
trauma 12, 34, 52, 121
Tree of Heaven, The (Sinclair) 12
tropes 29, 30, 41, 46, 50, 65, 97, 136, 154
Tůmová, Jiřina 162 n.7
Twilight of Reason, The (Forster) 25

uncivilized, the 25, 58, 129
Under the Skin (Bottome) 147–8
United Nations 165 n.4
Universal Declaration of Human Rights 113
urban 30, 47, 51, 52, 55, 62–3, 65, 69
urbanization 30, 48, 69

Valéry, Paul 56
values 17, 18, 21–3, 31, 49, 51–5, 57–8, 61, 63–4, 71, 78, 86, 88–90, 109, 134, 136, 151
Very Great Profession: The Woman's Novel 1914–1939, A (Beauman) 7
Vichy France 43, 48, 121, 125
Virago Press 7–8, 157 n.5
Volkisch movement 49, 64
Voltaire 2, 23–4

Wall Street crash 56
Wallace, Diana 9
war studies 10
war themes 8–21
Warner, Sylvia Townsend 7
Waste Land, The (Eliot) 160 n.7
Waugh, Evelyn 55, 160 n.7
We (Zamyatin) 64
Weber, Max 54, 56
Weitz, Margaret Collins 124, 166 n.10
Wells, H.G. 3, 10, 25, 155
West, Rebecca 11, 134
'What Is a Nation?' (Renan) 18
Whitby 1–2, 5, 12, 25, 29–31, 33, 35, 41, 159 n.1
White, Antonia 7
women
  bodies 41–6
  and domesticity 5–9, 13, 46, 71–82, 89, 98, 162 n.2
  resistance 77–9, 124
  role in the resistance 166 nn.10–11
  as victims of war 107, 164 n.7
  war experiences 8, 13, 82
Woolf, Leonard 6, 13, 54, 56, 62
Woolf, Virginia 6, 30–1, 36, 155, 160 n.7
Wordsworth, William 19
Writing and Revolt (FACT) 14

Yalta Conference 165 n.4
Yorkshire 1, 17, 31, 33–4, 36, 38, 39, 50, 136, 141, 159 n.1

Zamyatin, Yvegeny 64, 65

www.ingramcontent.com/pod-product-compliance
Lightning Source LLC
Chambersburg PA
CBHW050327020526
44117CB00031B/1981